Careers in
Sports & Fitness

Careers in
Sports & Fitness

SALEM PRESS
A Division of EBSCO Information Services, Inc.
Ipswich, Massachusetts

GREY HOUSE PUBLISHING

Publisher's Cataloging-In-Publication Data
(Prepared by The Donohue Group, Inc.)

Title: Careers in sports & fitness.
Other Titles: Careers in sports and fitness | Careers in--
Description: [First edition]. | Ipswich, Massachusetts : Salem Press, a division of EBSCO
        Information Services, Inc. ; [Amenia, New York] : Grey House Publishing,
        [2017] | Includes bibliographical references and index.
Identifiers: ISBN 978-1-68217-322-0 (hardcover)
Subjects: LCSH: Sports--Vocational guidance--United States. | Physical fitness--
        Vocational guidance--United States.
Classification: LCC GV734.3 .C37 2017 | DDC 796.023--dc23

First Printing

CONTENTS

PUBLISHER'S NOTE

Careers in Sports & Fitness contains twenty-one alphabetically arranged chapters describing specific fields of interest in this industry. Merging scholarship with occupational development, this single comprehensive guidebook provides students planning to pursue a career in sports and fitness with the necessary insight into potential opportunities, and provides instruction on what job seekers can expect in terms of training, advancement, earnings, job prospects, working conditions, relevant associations, and more. *Careers in Sports & Fitness* is specifically designed for a high school and undergraduate audience and is edited to align with secondary or high school curriculum standards.

Scope of Coverage

Understanding the wide net of jobs in sports, fitness, and recreation industry is important for anyone preparing for a career within it. *Careers in Sports & Fitness* comprises twenty-one lengthy chapters on a broad range of occupations including traditional and long-established jobs such as Coach, Scout, and Referee, as well as in-demand jobs: Personal Trainer, Physical Therapist, and Professional Athlete. This excellent reference also presents possible career paths and occupations within high-growth and emerging fields in this industry.

Careers in Sports & Fitness is enhanced with numerous charts and tables, including projections from the US Bureau of Labor Statistics, and median annual salaries or wages for those occupations profiled. Each chapter also notes those skills that can be applied across broad occupation categories. Interesting enhancements, like **Fun Facts**, **Famous Firsts**, and dozens of photos, add depth to the discussion. A highlight of each chapter is **Conversation With** – a two-page interview with a professional working in a related job. The respondents share their personal career paths, detail potential for career advancement, offer advice for students, and include a "try this" for those interested in embarking on a career in their profession.

Essay Length and Format

Each chapter ranges in length from 3,500 to 4,500 words and begins with a Snapshot of the occupation that includes career clusters, interests, earnings and employment outlook. This is followed by these major categories:

- **Overview** includes detailed discussions on: Sphere of Work; Work Environment; Occupation Interest; A Day in the Life. Also included here is a Profile that outlines working conditions, educational needs, and physical abilities. You will also find the occupation's Holland Interest Score, which matches up character and personality traits with specific jobs.

- **Occupational Specialties** lists specific jobs that are related in some way, like Sports Attorney, Bodyguard, and Director of Physical Therapy. Duties and Responsibilities are also included.

- **Work Environment** details the physical, human, and technological environment of the occupation profiled.

- **Education, Training, and Advancement** outlines how to prepare for this field while in high school, and what college courses to take, including licenses and certifications needed. A section is devoted to the Adult Job Seeker, and there is a list of skills and abilities needed to succeed in the job profiled.

- **Earnings and Advancements** offers specific salary ranges, and includes a chart of metropolitan areas that have the highest concentration of the profession.

- **Employment and Outlook** discusses employment trends, and projects growth to 2020. This section also lists related occupations.

- **Selected Schools** list those prominent learning institutions that offer specific courses in the profiles occupations.

- **More Information** includes associations that the reader can contact for more information.

Special Features

Several features continue to distinguish this reference series from other career-oriented reference works. The back matter includes:
- Appendix A: Guide to Holland Code. This discusses John Holland's theory that people and work environments can be classified into six different groups: Realistic; Investigative; Artistic; Social; Enterprising; and Conventional. See if the job you want is right for you!
- Appendix B: General Bibliography. This is a collection of suggested readings, organized into major categories.
- Subject Index: Includes people, concepts, technologies, terms, principles, and all specific occupations discussed in the occupational profile chapters.

Acknowledgments

Thanks are due to Allison Blake, who took the lead in developing "Conversations With" and to the professionals who communicated their work experience through interview questionnaires. Their frank and honest responses provide immeasurable value to *Careers in Sports & Fitness*. The contributions of all are gratefully acknowledged.

EDITOR'S INTRODUCTION

An Overview

You don't have to be an athlete to have a job in the field of sports and fitness, and you don't have to have your eyes on a multi-million dollar contract as a professional player on a national team to make a living. In fact, the range of job types and sectors in the sports and athletics fields are open to all kinds of skills, attributes and abilities. You don't even have to be a fanatic about participating in sports. You might want to be in this field as an entrepreneur with your own fitness club, or as someone catering to personal clients as a nutritionists or trainer, or even as a manufacturer producing cutting edge sports and fitness equipment. There are many areas where someone with a love of fitness and sports to find a satisfying, rewarding career.

You may find jobs in this field as the member of an athletic department at a public or private school, in colleges and universities as an athletic director, athletic trainer, a coach or assistant coach, an instructor, a program developer or coordinator, or as an information director. Other careers in the health and fitness sector might fall into the general area of fitness training and therapy. You might consider sports massage, nutrition, physiologist, or physical therapist.

Recreational sports and fitness is yet another aspect of the industry. There are openings for as directors and instructors working in programs sponsored by local communities, camps, and, increasingly, on cruise lines.

Referees and Sports Officials

Umpires, referees, and other sports officials are expected to seean increase in job availability of 5 percent from 2014 to 2024. The demand for umpires, referees, and other sports officials is projected to grow as population growth increases the overall number of people participating in organized sports. As high school enrollment is projected to increase over the next decade, the result is that there will be a greater number of student-athletes participating in sports. College sports programs are also projected to increase in number and size, as many small, Division III colleges expand their sports programs and add new teams to help promote the school and recruit students. While these are positive trends for those looking for work as umpires or referees, there are some other considerations.Funding for athletic programs in high schools is often cut first when budgets become tight. New rules allowing an increase in the scholarship payments to student-athletes may result in funding cuts to smaller collegiate sports programs. Still, the overall outlook is expected to be good at the youth and high school levels. Those with prior officiating experience will have the best job opportunities.

For those interested in working at the college and professional levels, however, competition is always very strong since jobs as a referee or umpire at the collegiate and professional levels have low turnover.

Coaches and Scouts

As high school and college programs continue to grow, so will the demand for coaches and scouts. Colleges want to attract the best athletes to remain competitive. There is an increasing reliance on successful teams tohelp colleges enhance their reputation, recruit future students, and raise donations from alumni. Colleges, therefore, will increasingly rely on scouts to recruit the best possible high school athletes. In addition, as college tuition increases and scholarships become more competitive, high school athletes will hire scouts directly, in an effort to increase their chances of receiving a college scholarship. Coaches in girls' and women's sports may have better job opportunities due to a growing number of participants and leagues

Coaching jobs at the high school level jobs typically go to those already teaching in the school, so having a degree or certification to teach academic subjects enhances your chances of securing coaching and instructor jobs at high schools.Competition is likely to continue to be strong for jobs as scouts, particularly for professional teams.

Professional Athletes

Growth and geographic shifts in population may lead to an increase in the number of professional sports teams, and some professional sports leagues may expand to new cities in the United States. All of this could mean that there will be new teams and new job opportunities for professional athletes. However, creating new teams is very costly and risky, and when leagues do expand, they typically only create one or two teams at a time. it is even possible that leagues may contract, instead of expand, as some teams and sports leagues disband altogether due to a lack of interest in the sport or relocate to another city with greater interest in the sport and a larger fan base.

Competition for positions as a professional athlete has always been extremely intense and will undoubtedly remain so. Very few high school or college athletes become professional athletes. In a major sport, such as basketball, only about 1 in 3,000 high school athletes make it to the professional level. There are other challenges for those seeking work as a professional athlete: Most professional athletes can deliver peak performances for only a short time, and it is often the case that a career can be cut short because of debilitating injuries or retirements.

Physical Therapists

A growing demand for physical therapy services is likely to comes in large part from the large number of aging baby boomers. These individuals are driving that trend in two ways. First, they are staying more active later in life. Second, as boomers age, they are more likely to experience heart attacks, strokes, and mobility-related injuries that require physical therapy for rehabilitation.

Another factor that appears to be driving job opportunities in this area is the growing number of chronic conditions, such as diabetes and obesity, that have become more prevalent in recent years. More physical therapists will be needed to help these patients maintain their mobility and manage the effects of chronic conditions.

Advances in medical technology means that outpatient surgery can be used to treat a variety of injuries and illnesses as well as to achieve successful outcomes for a growing number of trauma victims and newborns with birth defects to survive. This is also driving an increase jobs available in the areas of fitness and rehabilitation care.

Licensed physical therapists will find job prospects to be particularly good in acute-care hospitals, skilled-nursing facilities, and orthopedic settings, where the elderly are most often treated. Those who are willing to live and work in rural areas will have lighter competition than those in highly populated urban and suburban areas.

Trainers and Instructors

As businesses, government, and insurance organizations continue to recognize the benefits of health and fitness programs for their employees, incentives to join gyms or other types of health clubs are expected to increase the need for fitness trainers and instructors. For example, some organizations may open their own exercise facilities onsite to promote employee wellness.

Obesity is also driving the trend toward exercise to encourage healthier lifestyles for people of all ages. Aging baby-boom generation, likewise, are encouraged to remain active to help prevent injuries and illnesses associated with aging. These factors have led to increased participation in all types of fitness programs; yoga and Pilates are especially likely to increase, as older adults look for low-impact forms of exercise and relief from arthritis and other ailments.

Nutritionists and Dieticians

According to the Centers for Disease Control, more than one-third of U.S. adults are obese. Many diseases, such as diabetes and kidney disease, are associated with obesity. The importance of diet in preventing and treating illnesses is now well known. More dietitians and nutritionists are required to provide care for people with these conditions. They can find work in hospitals and nursing homes, schools, and even in grocery stores to help consumers make healthy food choices.Dietitians and nutritionists who have earned advanced degrees or certification in a specialty area may enjoy better job prospects.

Choosing a career in the field of sport, exercise, and fitness is more complicated today than ever. Never have so many career options been available in so many exciting areas. You can choose from coaching, sport marketing, sport promotion, athletic administration, sport officiating, sports medicine, sport psychology, and more. A career in the exercise and fitness arena can be very rewarding, whether as a personal trainer, exercise rehabilitation specialist, conditioning coach, fitness center manager, or a geriatric exercise specialist.Or, you might have decided that a career in teaching sport and exercise or coaching is the best path for you, teaching physical education, high-level sport instruction, exercise instruction, or specialized instruction for those with disabilities. No matter which path you intend to travel, the first step toward fulfilling your career aspirations is to learn more about your chose occupation and then seek out the training and experiences that will equip you with the knowledge and skills you need to succeed.

—Editors of Grey House

Activities Therapist

Snapshot

Career Cluster: Health Care; Human Services

Interests: Patient rehabilitation, therapeutic programs and services, special needs services, teaching/leading activities, social work

Earnings (Yearly Average): $41,775

Employment & Outlook: Average Growth Expected

OVERVIEW

Sphere of Work

Activities therapists provide creative therapeutic services and treatments aimed at helping their patients improve their emotional and mental well-being, gain independence, improve self-expression, build new skills, and develop self-confidence. They develop and implement medically approved therapies and programs to meet the needs, abilities, and interests of patients with mental and physical illnesses or disabilities. The range of therapies used by activities therapists during rehabilitation or treatment is wide and includes art therapy, music therapy, dance therapy, recreational therapy, horticultural

or nature therapy, sports therapy, religious therapy, social therapy, and manual arts therapy.

Work Environment

Activities therapists work in medical settings that include psychiatric facilities, hospitals, and substance abuse facilities, as well as community and institutional settings, such as schools, prisons, and retirement facilities. In medical environments, activities therapists generally partner with medical and social service professionals, such as doctors and social workers, to increase a patient's confidence, skill set, and mood or outlook. In community and institutional settings, activities therapists partner with educational and therapeutic professionals, such as teachers, special education coordinators, and recreational therapists, to meet students' or patients' therapeutic needs.

Profile

Working Conditions: Work Indoors
Physical Strength: Light to Medium Work
Education Needs: Bachelor's Degree, Master's Degree
Licensure/Certification: Recommended
Physical Abilities Not Required: No Heavy Labor
Opportunities For Experience: Internship, Volunteer Work, Part-Time Work
Holland Interest Score*: SEI

* See Appendix A

Occupation Interest

Individuals attracted to the field of activities therapy tend to be physically strong and energetic people who people who have the ability to teach and lead a variety of activities. They exhibit traits such as imagination, problem solving, desire to help, patience, sense of humor, and caring. Activities therapists must be able to work as part of a team of therapy professionals to meet patient needs.

A Day in the Life—Duties and Responsibilities

The daily occupational duties and responsibilities of activities therapists will be determined by the individual's area of job specialization and work environment. Areas of activities therapy job specialization include art therapy, music therapy, dance therapy, recreational therapy, sports therapy, religious therapy, social therapy, horticultural or nature therapy, and manual arts therapy. Activities therapists encourage their patients to make more frequent use of available resources, build on existing but overlooked skills, and try new activities.

In general, activities therapists should be prepared to greet patients as they arrive for therapeutic activities. Activities therapists interact with patients throughout the day in a friendly and supportive manner and conduct patient assessments so that they can record the needs, interests, and abilities of patients. As they monitor patients' symptoms, reactions, and progress through the assessments, activities therapists constantly revise patient treatment plans and implement treatment through activities, therapy sessions, and workshops. Examples of group activities include arts and crafts, nature-oriented activities such as gardening, and performing arts activities, as well as personal hygiene and self-care instruction and individual and small group community integration exercises such as bus riding practice and restaurant ordering.

In addition to patient interaction, activities therapists are often required to meet with patient treatment teams, physicians, or patient families and describe patient progress in therapeutic activities. This occupation includes supervising and scheduling tasks such as supervising therapeutic staff and volunteers, preparing therapeutic materials and equipment, and overseeing the safety, upkeep, and maintenance of therapeutic equipment and facilities. Activities therapists schedule therapeutic program events such as nature studies, recreational sports leagues, dances, adapted team sports, and classes.

Duties and Responsibilities

- Conferring with a patient's physician and rehabilitation team
- Planning the rehabilitation program and instructing the patient in the performance of specific activities
- Revising activity programs based on an evaluation of patient's progress
- Preparing reports describing patient's reactions and symptoms

OCCUPATION SPECIALTIES

Horticultural Therapists

Horticultural Therapists plan, coordinate and conduct therapeutic gardening programs to facilitate the rehabilitation of physically and mentally handicapped patients. They conduct gardening sessions and revise the programs to conform and grow with the progress of the patients.

Art Therapists

Art Therapists plan and direct activities that help mentally ill and physically disabled patients use art for nonverbal expression and communication.

Music Therapists

Music Therapists plan, organize and direct instrumental and vocal music activities and experiences to help patients with communication, social, daily living or problem solving skills.

Dance Therapists

Dance Therapists plan, organize and lead dance and body movement activities to improve patients' mental outlook and physical well-being.

Manual-Arts Therapists

Manual-Arts Therapists plan and organize woodworking, photography, metalworking, agriculture, electricity and graphic arts activities in collaboration with a rehabilitation team and prepare reports that show development of patient work tolerance, emotional and social development and ability to meet physical and mental demands of employment.

WORK ENVIRONMENT

Physical Environment

Activities therapists work in rehabilitation facilities, hospitals, nursing homes, therapy clinics, and schools. Therapeutic office settings used by activities therapists may be shared with other therapeutic professionals, including recreational, physical, occupational, or speech and language therapists.

Relevant Skills and Abilities

Communication Skills
- Persuading others
- Speaking effectively
- Writing concisely

Interpersonal/Social Skills
- Being patient
- Being sensitive to others
- Cooperating with others
- Providing support to others
- Working as a member of a team

Organization & Management Skills
- Coordinating tasks
- Making decisions
- Managing people/groups
- Performing duties that change frequently

Research & Planning Skills
- Creating ideas
- Developing evaluation strategies
- Using logical reasoning

Human Environment

Activities therapists interact with a wide variety of people and should be comfortable providing therapeutic services to those with physical, mental, and emotional illnesses and special needs. Activities therapists usually work as part of a patient treatment team, which includes patient families, social workers, teachers, doctors, and additional therapists. As a member of a treatment team, activities therapists participate in frequent team meetings and are responsible for communicating patient progress to fellow team members.

Technological Environment

Activities therapists use a wide range of technology and equipment in their work, including telecommunication tools, word processing software, and computer applications such as spreadsheets. Equipment used by activities therapists during therapy sessions may include musical instruments, sports equipment, art supplies, and adaptive technology such as wheelchairs and pool lifts.

EDUCATION, TRAINING, AND ADVANCEMENT

High School/Secondary

High school students interested in pursuing the profession of activities therapist should develop good study habits. High school courses in the arts, physical education, psychology, anatomy, and sociology will prepare students for collegiate studies. Students interested in the activities therapy field will benefit from seeking internships or part-time work in therapeutic programs or with people with mental and physical special needs.

Suggested High School Subjects
- Arts
- Child Growth & Development
- College Preparatory
- Crafts
- English
- Health Science Technology
- Instrumental & Vocal Music
- Metals Technology
- Ornamental Horticulture
- Photography
- Physical Education
- Physiology
- Pottery
- Psychology
- Social Studies
- Sociology
- Theatre & Drama
- Woodshop

Famous First

Susan E. Tracy, considered the first occupational therapist, served as the director of the Training School for Nurses at the Adams Nervine Asylum in Boston, pictured here. In 1906 Tracy set up the first training course in activities therapy to prepare students for teaching patient activities. She advised that variety in activity choices was key in order to match individual patient interests and therapeutic goals.

College/Postsecondary

Postsecondary students interested in pursuing training in activities therapy should complete coursework in their preferred specialization (i.e. art therapy, music therapy, dance therapy, recreational therapy, horticultural or nature therapy, or manual arts therapy), as well as courses on counseling, physical education and therapy, special education, abnormal psychology, ethics, anatomy, physiology, and assistive technology. Postsecondary students interested in attending graduate school will benefit from seeking internships or work in therapeutic programs or with people with mental or physical special needs. Membership in the American Therapeutic Recreation Association (ATRA) may provide networking opportunities and connections. Prior to graduating, college students interested in joining the activities therapy profession should apply to graduate school in their preferred therapeutic specialization or secure related work such as therapy assistant or special education assistant.

Related College Majors
- Art Therapy
- Dance Therapy
- Music Therapy
- Occupational Therapy

Adult Job Seekers

Adult job seekers in the activities therapy field have generally completed bachelor's- or master's-level training in art therapy, music therapy, dance therapy, recreational therapy, or occupational

therapy from an accredited university, as well as earned necessary
professional certification. Activities therapists seeking employment
will benefit from the networking opportunities, career workshops,
and job lists offered by professional therapy associations such as the
ATRA.

Professional Certification and Licensure

Some states regulate activities therapists by requiring specified
education and experience for certification to practice. Those who meet
the requirements can qualify for certification by the professional
association representing their area of specialization. Requirements
usually entail either a bachelor's or a master's degree in the area of
specialization, a written examination and an internship of at least 480
hours. Attendance and participation in professional conferences and
workshops is common in order to enhance efficiency and knowledge in
the field.

Additional Requirements

 Individuals who find satisfaction, success, and job
security as activities therapists will be knowledgeable
about the profession's requirements, responsibilities,
and opportunities. Successful activities therapists
engage in ongoing professional development
and find satisfaction from working as collaborative members of
interdisciplinary teams devoted to improving the health and well-
being of patients. Because individuals in this profession work with
emotionally or physically vulnerable people and have access to
personal patient information, they must strive to maintain high
ethical and professional standards. Membership in professional
therapy associations is encouraged among all types of activities
therapists as a means of building status within the professional
community and networking.

Fun Fact

Participating in art projects or music practice often helps physically or
developmentally disabled people develop fine motor skills – as well as enhance
self-expression.
Source: wisegeek.net

EARNINGS AND ADVANCEMENT

Salaries of activities therapists vary according to the type and size of employer, educational background, work experience, professional registration and region of the country. Median annual earnings of activities therapists were $41,775 in 2013. The lowest ten percent earned less than $26,118, and the highest ten percent earned more than $66,430.

Activities therapists may receive paid vacations, holidays and sick days; life and health insurance; and retirement benefits. These are usually paid by the employer.

Metropolitan Areas with the Highest Employment Level in this Occupation

Metropolitan area	Employment [1]	Employment per thousand jobs	Hourly mean wage
New York-White Plains-Wayne, NY-NJ	980	0.19	$25.67
Philadelphia, PA	580	0.32	$21.61
Chicago-Joliet-Naperville, IL	560	0.15	$21.94
Boston-Cambridge-Quincy, MA	510	0.29	$18.60
Nassau-Suffolk, NY	380	0.31	$23.94
Los Angeles-Long Beach-Glendale, CA	340	0.09	$30.24
Atlanta-Sandy Springs-Marietta, GA	320	0.14	$19.87
Washington-Arlington-Alexandria, DC-VA-MD-WV	300	0.13	$23.55
Warren-Troy-Farmington Hills, MI	260	0.23	$24.54
St. Louis, MO-IL	230	0.18	$20.05

[1]Does not include self-employ ed. Source: Bureau of Labor Statistics

EMPLOYMENT AND OUTLOOK

There were about 20,000 recreational therapists, of which activities therapists are a part, employed nationally in 2012. About two-thirds worked in nursing care facilities and hospitals. The remainder worked in residential facilities, community mental health centers, adult day care programs, correctional facilities, community programs for people with disabilities, and substance abuse centers.

Employment of activities therapists is expected to grow about as fast as the average for all occupations through the year 2022, which means employment is projected to increase 10 percent to 15 percent. In nursing care facilities, employment will grow slightly faster than the occupation as a whole as the number of older adults continues to grow. Employment is expected to slow, however, in hospitals as services shift to outpatient settings and employers try to contain costs.

Employment Trend, Projected 2010–20

Health Diagnosing and Treating Practitioners: 20%

Activities Therapists: 13%

Total, All Occupations: 11%

Note: "All Occupations" includes all occupations in the U.S. Economy. Source: U.S. Bureau of Labor Statistics, Employment Projections Program

Related Occupations
- Art Therapist
- Music Therapist
- Occupational Therapist
- Physical Therapist
- Recreational Therapist

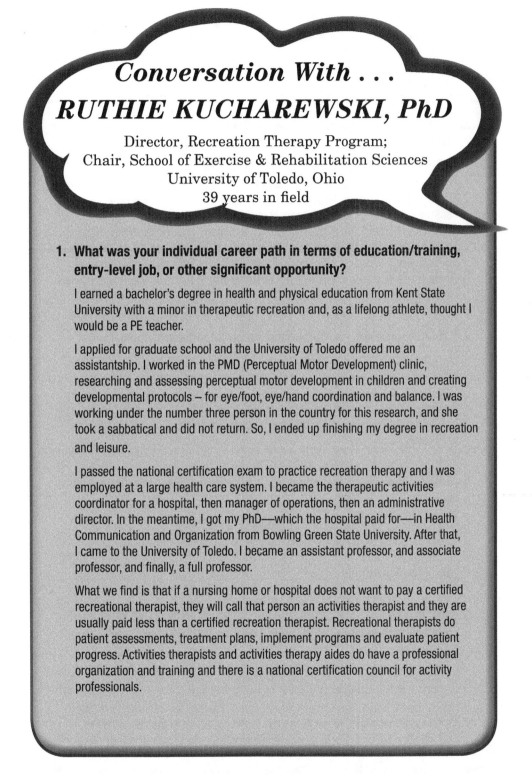

Conversation With . . .
RUTHIE KUCHAREWSKI, PhD

Director, Recreation Therapy Program;
Chair, School of Exercise & Rehabilitation Sciences
University of Toledo, Ohio
39 years in field

1. What was your individual career path in terms of education/training, entry-level job, or other significant opportunity?

I earned a bachelor's degree in health and physical education from Kent State University with a minor in therapeutic recreation and, as a lifelong athlete, thought I would be a PE teacher.

I applied for graduate school and the University of Toledo offered me an assistantship. I worked in the PMD (Perceptual Motor Development) clinic, researching and assessing perceptual motor development in children and creating developmental protocols – for eye/foot, eye/hand coordination and balance. I was working under the number three person in the country for this research, and she took a sabbatical and did not return. So, I ended up finishing my degree in recreation and leisure.

I passed the national certification exam to practice recreation therapy and I was employed at a large health care system. I became the therapeutic activities coordinator for a hospital, then manager of operations, then an administrative director. In the meantime, I got my PhD—which the hospital paid for—in Health Communication and Organization from Bowling Green State University. After that, I came to the University of Toledo. I became an assistant professor, and associate professor, and finally, a full professor.

What we find is that if a nursing home or hospital does not want to pay a certified recreational therapist, they will call that person an activities therapist and they are usually paid less than a certified recreation therapist. Recreational therapists do patient assessments, treatment plans, implement programs and evaluate patient progress. Activities therapists and activities therapy aides do have a professional organization and training and there is a national certification council for activity professionals.

As a junior faculty member the focus of my research was an assessment tool called the clock test. It's used in nursing homes, with people with possible dementias and memory problems. Teaching is still a big part of my job; I enjoy teaching and developing and mentoring prospective professionals.

2. What are the most important skills and/or qualities for someone in your profession?

Good assessment skills and organizational skills, because you are developing a treatment plan based on need. You need to be an advocate. You need good follow-through, good listening skills, the ability to create good rapport. You need to be trustworthy because if your patients or clients don't trust you, they're not going to do what you want them to do. Think about somebody who has become a recent amputee. His whole life is changing, he's scared or insecure, and is looking to trust someone who is non-threatening and compassionate. I always look at being a therapist as being a good leader with empathy and compassion who helps a person improve the quality of his life.

3. What do you wish you had known going into this profession?

I tell my students this is a discovery profession. Often, if students don't get into a competitive major like nursing or pharmacy, they go shopping for a new major. Since they've had the sciences and anatomy, we often try to steer them into something related, and this is one of those most popular majors. It's a springboard to doctoral programs like occupational or physical therapy or a master's in speech-language pathology.

4. Are there many job opportunities in your profession? In what specific areas?

A fair amount; three came across my desk in the past three days. Opportunities are in hospitals, including VA hospitals, long-term care, camps, schools, prisons, group homes, and therapeutic riding centers. There's also opportunity in municipal recreation departments.

5. How do you see your profession changing in the next five years, what role will technology play in those changes, and what skills will be required?

The kids I'm educating now are tech dependent. The upcoming Generation Z, born in 2000 and later, were introduced to technology at age 3 or 4. A lot of software is being used in simulation games that are part of therapy, for veterans, for example. Software is being used to teach children meditation and mindfulness. They're learning to calm themselves down while they're playing a game and they don't even know it. You can chart on a person with an iPad while you're talking to them. It's more tolerable and quicker for patients who don't feel well.

6. **What do you enjoy most about your job? What do you enjoy least about your job?**

I love teaching and when I was a therapist I loved practicing. As an educator I love imparting my practical knowledge on the students and my enthusiasm for a great profession. I love helping someone improve the quality of his or her life through recreation therapy.

If I were an entry-level therapist, I would say the biggest challenge is the short length of stay for acute care. When I was practicing, it averaged 19 days on the psychiatric unit. Now it's three days, maybe longer if the patient is suicidal. Activities therapists or recreation therapists today don't have time to build rapport, see the etiology of the disease, or see the healing that takes place.

7. **Can you suggest a valuable "try this" for students considering a career in your profession?**

Shadow a therapist in various settings with various populations, so that you can see all aspects of what they do. I would encourage students to practice in a clinical setting and a non-clinical setting so they can experience the different types of therapy that take place. We aim to restore, remediate and rehabilitate functional abilities so that a person can improve the quality of their life through leisure pursuits.

SELECTED SCHOOLS

Many colleges and universities have bachelor's degree programs in recreational therapy or related subjects. The student may also gain an initial grounding at a technical or community college. Consult with your school guidance counselor or research post-secondary programs in your area. The online Therapeutic Recreation Directory (see below) contains a listing of accredited schools and programs.

MORE INFORMATION

American Art Therapy Association
225 North Fairfax Street
Alexandria, VA 22314-1574
888.290.0878
www.arttherapy.org

American Dance Therapy Association
10632 Little Patuxent Parkway
Suite 108
Columbia, MD 21044-3263
410.997.4040
www.adta.org

American Music Therapy Association
8455 Colesville Road, Suite 1000
Silver Spring, MD 20910
301.589.3300
www.musictherapy.org

National Center on Physical Activity and Disability
1640 W. Roosevelt Road
Chicago, IL 60608-6904
800.900.8086
www.ncpad.org

National Council for Therapeutic Recreation Certification
7 Elmwood Drive
New City, NY 10956
845.639.1439
www.nctrc.org

Therapeutic Recreation Directory
www.recreationtherapy.com

Simone Isadora Flynn/Editor

Dietitian & Nutritionist

Snapshot

Career Cluster: Health Science, Food Science, Human Services

Interests: Science, Health & Wellness, Food

Earnings (Yearly Average): $56,445

Employment & Outlook: Faster Than Average Growth Expected

OVERVIEW

Sphere of Work

Dietitians and nutritionists are responsible for assessing patients' nutritional needs and planning healthy food regimens that help prevent and treat medical conditions. They manage institutional food programs, oversee meal preparation, recommend dietary modifications, and provide education to individuals and groups of all ages. Increased interest in public nutrition means that there is a growing demand for dietitians and nutritionists who analyze food products and report information on nutritional content and vitamin supplements, among other issues of concern, to the public. The primary difference

between a dietitian and a nutritionist is education: a dietitian must have academic credentials and clinical experience, while a nutritionist typically does not.

Work Environment

Dietitians and nutritionists work in medical clinics, nursing homes, sports centers, hospitals, correctional facilities, schools, and corporations such as food manufacturing companies. Many travel to see patients who need at-home care. Some dietitians and nutritionists are consultants. This profession offers flexible hours in a variety of work settings, including kitchens, laboratories, and bright, organized offices. Kitchens can often be hot, crowded, fast-paced environments.

Profile

Working Conditions: Work Indoors
Physical Strength: Light Work
Education Needs: Bachelor's Degree, Master's Degree
Licensure/Certification: Required
Physical Abilities Not Required: No Heavy Labor
Opportunities Or Experience: Military Service, Volunteer Work, Part-Time Work
Holland Interest Score*: ISR, SEI, SIE

* See Appendix A

Occupation Interest

Individuals who wish to be dietitians and nutritionists should find satisfaction in working with people, educating patients, and making a positive impact on the nutritional status of individuals and communities. Those who excel in science and math may be well suited to the work. Dietitians and nutritionists tend to be patient, well organized, and detail oriented. They can listen attentively, express themselves clearly and articulately, analyze data to solve problems, and make sound decisions. Other valuable qualities include teamwork, initiative, and compassion for others.

A Day in the Life—Duties and Responsibilities

During a typical workday, dietitians and nutritionists visit patients, assess patients' or clients' nutritional needs, design and coordinate nutrition programs, evaluate and report results, and confer with other health professionals to balance patients' food needs with their medical needs. Dietitians and nutritionists encourage patient compliance with nutrition plans by teaching them how foods interact with specific medications or clinical treatments. In schools, hospitals, and other institutional settings, they may also meet with the clinical manager and dietetic technician for updates, provide medical nutrition therapy, or oversee food preparation. Those who are employed as consultants often suggest specific diet modifications for their clients.

Dietitians and nutritionists frequently work in a public health capacity by regulating food serving sizes, giving presentations on nutrition, or teaching the aging population how to shop for food. They may prepare and distribute a variety of educational materials on subjects related to health and nutrition. Many are involved in conducting nutrition research and enacting public policies that relate to food processing, consumer information about food, and national dietary guidelines and recommendations.

Duties and Responsibilities

- Selecting, training, and directing food-service workers
- Providing diet counseling services
- Coordinating dietary services with those of other departments
- Acting as a consultant to management
- Preparing records and reports
- Promoting sound eating habits through education and research
- Supervising the planning, preparation, and service of meals

OCCUPATION SPECIALTIES

Clinical Dietitians

Clinical Dietitians plan and direct the preparation and service of diets in consultation with physicians. They create both individualized and group nutritional programs based on the health needs of patients or residents.

Management Dietitians

Management Dietitians plan general meal programs. They work
in food service settings such as cafeterias, hospitals, and food
corporations. They may be responsible for buying food and for carrying
out other business-related tasks.

Community Dietitians

Community Dietitians plan, develop, administer and coordinate
nutrition programs and services as part of the health care services for
an organization.

Research Dietitians

Research Dietitians conduct, evaluate and interpret research to
improve the nutrition of healthy and sick people.

WORK ENVIRONMENT

Physical Environment

Dietitians and nutritionists tend to work in facilities that are clean, bright, and well ventilated. In offices, they sit at desks for extended periods. In kitchens and laboratories, they may be required to stand for a significant part of the day.

Relevant Skills and Abilities

Analytical Skills
- Analyzing information
- Solving problems

Communication Skills
- Speaking and writing effectively

Interpersonal/Social Skills
- Cooperating with others
- Providing support to others
- Working as a member of a team

Organization & Management Skills
- Coordinating tasks
- Managing people/groups
- Performing duties that change frequently

Planning & Research Skills
- Creating and laying out a plan
- Researching information

Technical Skills
- Performing scientific, mathematical, or technical work

Human Environment

Dietitians and nutritionists interact with patients and their families, and with fellow staff members such as doctors, nurses, and dietetic technicians.

Technological Environment

Dietitians and nutritionists take measurements using scales, calorimeters, glucose meters, skinfold calipers, and bioelectric impedance machines. Financial and medical software, databases, and office suites help them track patient information such as weight, diet, medications, protein supplements, and lab results.

EDUCATION, TRAINING, AND ADVANCEMENT

High School/Secondary

High school students interested in becoming dietitians and nutritionists should focus on math, science, health, and communication courses. In addition, students should prepare themselves by participating in relevant extracurricular activities. To learn what dietitians and nutritionists do each day, interested students may find it useful to seek an internship. High school career counselors often have lists of internship opportunities. Aspiring dietitians and nutritionists should apply to college or university programs.

Suggested High School Subjects
- Applied Biology/Chemistry
- Applied Communication
- Applied Math
- Biology
- Chemistry
- College Preparatory
- Computer Science
- English
- Family & Consumer Sciences
- Food Service & Management
- Foods & Nutrition
- Health Science Technology
- Mathematics
- Physiology
- Science
- Sociology

Famous First

The first nationwide food labeling standards for nutritional information appeared in 1992, the result of the Nutrition Labeling and Education Act. According to the act, packaged foods were required to bear labels identifying their ingredients, nutritional values, and serving sizes, among other information. Also newly regulated was the use of promotional terms such as "low fat" and "light."

College/Postsecondary

A college degree provides the best opportunities for employment or advancement. College and university students looking to enter the field should study biology, food sciences, math, chemistry, medicine, physiology, administration and institution management, education, psychology, and counseling, in pursuit of an undergraduate degree in dietetics, nutrition, food service, or a related discipline. Students may gain experience and build connections through internships and co-ops that integrate clinical work with university-level coursework. Many dietitians and nutritionists choose to pursue a graduate degree after completing their undergraduate studies.

Related College Majors
- Dietetics/Human Nutritional Services
- Foods & Nutrition Science
- Foods & Nutrition Studies, General
- Human & Animal Physiology

Adult Job Seekers

Adults with a bachelor's or master's degree will have better job opportunities in this field. By joining professional associations such as the American Dietetic Association, adult job seekers can benefit from ongoing networking, professional development services, food and nutrition information, and mentorships to establish career and educational options. These professional organizations generally maintain job lists and advertise open dietitian and nutritionist positions.

Professional Certification and Licensure

For dietitians and nutritionists, licensure, certification, and registration requirements vary by state; therefore, candidates need to determine what the requirements are in the state or states where they want to work. Some states require that all practitioners of dietetics and nutrition be licensed, a process which entails doing specific coursework, passing an exam, and completing a supervised internship. Where certification is mandatory, those without it can still practice but cannot use certain titles.

The Commission on Dietetic Registration provides voluntary certification that is completely distinct from state licensure or certification. Registered dietitians (RDs) must fulfill education and work experience requirements in order to qualify for the certifying exam.

Additional Requirements

Dietitians and nutritionists must be resourceful and always willing to research the latest information, as the state of medical knowledge is frequently changing. Specializing in a particular body system or age group may be helpful for advancement in this field.

EARNINGS AND ADVANCEMENT

Earnings depend on the geographic location and size of the employer and the community and the employee's education, specialty area, and number of years in practice. Median annual earnings of dietitians and nutritionists were $56,445 in 2012. The lowest ten percent earned less than $35,330, and the highest ten percent earned more than $80,009.

Dietitians and nutritionists may receive paid vacations, holidays, and sick days; life and health insurance; and retirement benefits. These are usually paid by the employer.

Metropolitan Areas with the Highest Concentration of Jobs in this Occupation

Metropolitan area	Employment(1)	Employment per thousand jobs	Hourly mean wage
New York-White Plains-Wayne, NY-NJ	2,970	0.58	$29.11
Los Angeles-Long Beach-Glendale, CA	1,740	0.45	$32.00
Chicago-Joliet-Naperville, IL	1,430	0.39	$24.38
Minneapolis-St. Paul-Bloomington, MN-WI	1,170	0.67	$26.75
Philadelphia, PA	1,050	0.57	$25.58
Boston-Cambridge-Quincy, MA	910	0.53	$29.62
Pittsburgh, PA	720	0.64	$20.67
Washington-Arlington-Alexandria, DC-VA-MD-WV	700	0.30	$29.54

(1)Does not include self-employed. Source: Bureau of Labor Statistics, 2012

EMPLOYMENT AND OUTLOOK

Dietitians and nutritionists held about 58,000 jobs in 2012. More than half of all jobs were in hospitals, nursing care facilities, outpatient care centers or offices of physicians. Employment of dietitians and nutritionists is expected to grow faster than the average for all occupations through the year 2020, which means employment is projected to increase 20 percent. This is due to increased emphasis on the prevention of disease by improved dietary habits. A growing and aging population will increase demand for meals and nutritional counseling in nursing homes, schools, prisons, community health programs and home health care agencies.

Employment Trend, Projected 2010–20

Health Diagnosing and Treating Practitioners: 26%

Dietitians and Nutritionists: 20%

Total, All Occupations: 14%

Note: "All Occupations" includes all occupations in the U.S. Economy. Source: U.S. Bureau of Labor Statistics, 2012.

Related Occupations
- Cook/Chef
- Food Service Manager
- Dietitian
- Food Service Manager

Conversation With . . .
JESSICA WAGNER
Nutritionist/Health Coach, 6 years

1. What was your individual career path in terms of education, entry-level job, or other significant opportunity?

Eight years prior to my nutrition and health counseling education, I had obtained a Bachelor's degree in East Asian Studies from Wittenberg University. There's a huge connection between how to live a healthy lifestyle and the philosophy of East Asian Studies. Then I worked for 10 years in international education, advising and counseling individuals, and learned that one-on-one counseling is my thing. During this time, I also realized I was not healthy in the workplace and other people weren't either. We weren't getting the basics, like fresh air and sunlight every day, in our cubicles. We were eating cafeteria food, or too busy to cook dinner. I got very sick, and wanted to cure myself naturally. So I received a post-bachelor's certificate in Health Counseling through The Center for Educational Outreach and Innovation at Teacher's College Columbia University and The Institute for Integrative Nutrition (IIN) in New York City. For nine months, I traveled there once a month for intensive study all day Saturday and Sunday and, quite often, Monday. Upon graduation, I was prepared to open my own health and nutritional counseling practice. A year later, I completed the Integrative Nutrition Immersion Graduate Program.

2. Are there many job opportunities in your profession? In what specific areas?

The most valuable opportunity in this profession is to open your own practice. I have created my own niche. I do workshops, I've done group programs, and I do one-on-one counseling, which is where I think my talent is. I offer one-on-one relationships to clients who need serious help. They can email or text me between sessions. I'm holding them by the hand and I think that's really needed. In addition to operating a business, there are opportunities in doctors' offices, yoga studios, gyms, chiropractic or other wellness practices. Corporations regularly look for health and nutrition coaches to provide workshops and counseling to employees.

3. What do you wish you had known going into this profession?

Only hands-on experience could prepare me to work effectively with people. Each person, depending on their personality and fears, will respond differently to your guidance. Most people are afraid to break old habits and will try to hold onto unhealthy patterns. With sensitivity, care, and respect, you can learn how to guide even the most fearful people. Nutritional knowledge alone doesn't make you a good health and nutrition coach. You need to be a good listener and a patient teacher.

4. How do you see your profession changing in the next five years?

I see this profession becoming much more mainstream. The public interest in conventional medicine is shifting to holistic-based approaches and preventative services. Doctors simply don't have the time to counsel their clients on how to make healthy lifestyle changes. I see every doctor's office having a health and nutrition coach. I also see health insurance coverage for this kind of preventive wellness service.

5. What role will technology play in those changes, and what skills will be required?

Technology is already playing a large role in this field. Many health and nutrition coaches provide counseling services over the phone and Internet, as I do. In addition, webinars are provided regularly for groups of clients. Being so easily accessible means clients are more apt to hire me.

6. Do you have any general advice or additional professional insights to share with someone interested in your profession?

If you want the flexibility of creating your own work hours and having an important impact on the lives of people, no other career that I know of can provide that in quite the same way that this profession does. Transforming the health and happiness of people is truly the best job anyone could have.

7. Can you suggest a valuable "try this" for students considering a career in your profession?

Call an admission's counselor at a school that offers training in this field and ask to sit in on a class. If you feel inspired, take it a step further by reading a good book recommended by the professor. If you still feel inspired, try out a healthy nutritional lifestyle for a good year or so, following the recommendations in the book. During this time, practice talking to people about your experiences. Offer tips to people looking for answers. Practice having simple conversations with individuals and being a mentor and advocate for their health.

SELECTED SCHOOLS

Many colleges and universities offer programs in health and nutrition; some have degree programs in dietetics. Interested students are advised to consult with a school guidance counselor or research area postsecondary schools. The website of the Commission on the Academy of Nutrition and Dietetics (see below) allows users to search for accredited programs in their stateeld.

MORE INFORMATION

Academy of Nutrition & Dietetics
120 South Riverside Plaza
Suite 2000
Chicago, IL 60606
800.877.1600
www.eatright.org

American Association for Nutritional Consultants
400 Oakhill Drive
Winona Lake, IN 46590
888.828.2262
www.aanc.net

American Society for Nutritional Sciences
9650 Rockville Pike, Suite 4500
Bethesda,MD 20814
301.634.7050
www.nutrition.org

Association for Healthcare Foodservice
455 S. 4th Street, Suite 650
Louisville, KY 40202
888.528.9552
info@healthcarefoodservice.org
www.healthcarefoodservice.org

Dietary Managers Association
406 Surrey Woods Drive
St. Charles, IL 60174
800.323.1908
www.dmaonline.org

Susan Williams/Editor

Exercise Physiologist

Snapshot

Career Cluster(s): Sports & Fitness

Interests: Fitness, science, medicine, athletics, investigation, social interaction, education

Earnings (Yearly Average): $47,010

Employment & Outlook: Faster than average growth expected

OVERVIEW

Sphere of Work

Exercise physiologists, sometimes called kinesiotherapists, develop fitness and exercise programs for patients recovering for diseases or suffering from chronic conditions. Exercise physiologists may work for hospitals, outpatient clinics, or private therapeutic businesses and work with both physicians and patients to develop programs tailored to the needs of each client.

Work Environment

Exercise physiologists may work in office environments as well as in patient homes or in exercise studios. In some cases, exercise physiologists may work with clients in outdoor environments as well. Depending on the details of a physiologist's position, the specialist may work with patients at a single location or may need to travel between locations. Many exercise physiologists work independently and approximately half of all exercise physiologists in the United States were self-employed in 2014, with the other half working for hospitals, physicians, or other healthcare companies. Independent exercise physiologists typically visit patients in their homes.

Profile

Working Conditions: Work both Indoors and Outdoors
Physical Strength: Light to strenuous work
Education Needs: Bachelor's Degree, Master's Degree, Doctorate
Licensure/Certification: Required in some areas
Opportunities For Experience: On-Job Training, Part-Time Work, Internship
Holland Interest Score*: SIR

* See Appendix A

Occupation Interest

Exercise physiologists work in the healthcare field and so should have a strong interest helping patients to achieve healthy lifestyles and wellness. Physiology is also a scientific discipline and professionals in the field will benefit from an interest in biology and scientific investigation. Whether working independently or through a healthcare facility, exercise physiologists work with both patients and medical professionals and should be comfortable with regular daily interaction. Successful exercise physiologists are able to form relationship with their clients, getting to know their client's needs and personality to better tailor fitness programs for the needs of each individual. Those seeking work in the field should therefore had an interest in forming personal relationships, helping others, and promoting health and wellbeing.

A Day in the Life—Duties and Responsibilities

The duties expected of an exercise physiologist may differ depending on the professional's current role. On a given day, a professional in the field might meet with physicians, speaking about patients and strategizing for future programs. Once an exercise physiologist has accepted or been assigned a new patient, the physiologist meets with the patient and reviews the patient's medical history to begin planning an exercise regimen. While working with patients, exercise physiologists perform tests to ensure that the patient is responding to the program and to guide them in changing the program to meet the patient's needs. Exercise physiologists measure blood pressure, oxygen usage, breathing rate, heart rate, and other indicator of the patient's physiological state to develop and alter the fitness regime created for the patient. While working with patients, many exercise physiologists also meet with members of the patient's family to discuss exercise and wellness routines that can help the patient's progress.

When not working with patients, exercise physiologists may spend time researching new techniques, equipment, or theories in their field or may prepare reports for patients or physicians. While most exercise physiologists are not doctors, professionals in the field may also spend time networking in the medical community. Those who are self-employed may spent time marketing their services to hospitals, physicians, or directly to patients.

Duties and Responsibilities

- Create and alter exercise routines and programs for patients
- Meet with physicians and other medical professionals
- Meet with patients and their families.
- Teach patients exercise routines and strategies
- Measure bodily functions and perform tests on patients
- Research new and developing technologies in the field
- Attend networking and professional development programs

OCCUPATION SPECIALTIES

Physiotherapists

Like exercise physiologists, physical therapists are specialists who help patients overcome physical injuries or impairments using therapy, exercise, and other methods. Some physiotherapists may also train in exercise physiology.

Ambulation Specialist

Ambulation specialists are kinesiotherapists who specialize in helping patients with movement and walking disorders such as occur with certain types of brain or spinal injuries. These specialists use specialized equipment to help patients practice and master walking, climbing stairs, and other ambulatory activities.

Prosthetic Rehabilitation

Prosthetic rehabilitation specialists are therapists who work with individuals who, because of either disease or injury, need to learn to use prosthetic limbs. Therapists in the field need detailed knowledge of prosthetics as well as specialized therapeutic techniques for teaching motor control, reflexes, and other skills.

Aquatic Therapist

Aquatic therapists often specialize in patients with movement disorder and help patients to develop muscle control and to build atrophied muscle by exercising in swimming pools or therapeutic water chambers.

WORK ENVIRONMENT

Relevant Skills and Abilities

Communication Skills
- Communicating clearly across cultural/linguistic barriers
- Writing instructions and therapy plans for patients

Interpersonal/Social Skills
- Forming relationships with patients and their families
- Working with doctors and other healthcare professionals

Organization & Management Skills
- Teaching exercise skills and routines to patients
- Managing time and scheduling patient meetings and training sessions
- Managing assistants and students

Research & Planning Skills
- Creating original exercise routines based on individualized treatment
- Researching new developments in physiology and physical therapy

Technical Skills
- Utilizing basic digital technology and personal computers
- Using specialized exercise equipment
- Using patient monitoring equipment

Physical Environment

Exercise physiologists perform most of their work indoors, though some therapists may also guide patients through outdoor therapy, like jogging or walking. Some exercise physiologists who are self-employed may work out of their homes or may have private offices with an exercise room and specialized equipment for measuring patient response to therapy. In some cases, exercise physiologists may work directly in physician's offices or in hospitals. Depending on the needs of the patient, a variety of specialized and sometimes large equipment may be needed, and an exercise physiologist may therefore need to operate or access facilities set up with the necessary tools.

Human Environment

Exercise physiologists work closely with both patients and members of the medical community. For instance, in managing a patient's care, an exercise physiologist may need to work directly with the patient's primary care physician or a specialist and may also need to meet with nutritionists, other therapists, and other members of a medical team. At times, exercise physiologists may work alongside physician's assistants or student therapists while working with a patient. Exercise physiologists also spend much of their time directly interacting with patients and their families.

Technological Environment

Depending on the needs of a specific patient, exercise physiologists may need to know how to sue a variety of equipment. Exercise physiologists use basic fitness tools, including both free weights and hand weights as well as treadmills and other cardiovascular exercise machines. For measuring patient progress, exercise physiologists use monitoring tools used to measure blood pressure, heart rate, breathing capacity, body fat index, and other physiological properties. In some cases, physiologists may also need access to equipment for measuring brain function. In addition to exercise equipment, exercise physiologists typically use computers and other types of digital technology to communicate with physicians and patients and to schedule and monitor their therapy programs.

EDUCATION, TRAINING, AND ADVANCEMENT

High School/Secondary

High school students interested in becoming exercise physiologists should prepare for higher education in the biological sciences or for direct training in the field. Basic familiarity with biology, physiology, anatomy, and fitness science is essential for the field and high school/secondary students can prepare for their career by studying subjects related to both fitness and physiology.

Suggested High School Subjects
- World Languages
- Linguistics
- Computer Technology
- Education
- Biology
- Anatomy
- Physiology
- Physics

Famous First

In 1926, George Williams College in Hyde Park, Chicago, became the first institution in the United States to open a research department specifically devoted to the study of exercise physiology. George Williams College began as a training academy for employees of the YMCA (Young Men's Christian Association), a global organization started in 1844 by George Williams of London, who envisioned the YMCA as an organization that would help people healthy bodies and minds through a combination of exercise, religion, and education. George Williams College, named for the YMCA founder, was established in 1886 in Hyde Park, but, after falling into financial troubles in the 1980s, the college was absorbed into Wisconsin's Aurora University.

College/Postsecondary

Most professional exercise physiologists have at least a bachelor's degree or a related technical degree. According to the 2015 report from the Commission on Accreditation of Allied Health Education Programs (CAAHEP), there were 50 institutions in the United States offering either bachelor's or master's degree programs in exercise physiology. Degree programs in the field typically introduce students to a variety of related fields, including kinesiology, anatomy, nutrition, fitness education, biochemistry, psychology, pharmacology, and gerontology. Programs in the field also typically include clinical studies and clinical work in which students spend time working alongside professionals or working in therapy centers or healthcare institutions that offer exercise physiology services.

Related College Majors
- Bachelor of Science in Exercise Physiology
- Master's in Exercise Physiology
- Ph.D. in Exercise Physiology
- Physical Therapy

Adult Job Seekers

Those with degrees in the field can begin by applying for jobs offered through hospitals, physician's offices, or other institutions offering exercise physiology services. In addition, individuals might seek jobs working with other exercise physiologists in private businesses. Those just starting in their careers might consider applying for assistant positions to train under an experienced professional in the field. Most professional exercise physiologists complete clinical work while studying for their degree and some students may use their clinical assignments to find permanent work after graduation.

Professional Certification and Licensure

As of 2016, only one state, Louisiana, requires exercise physiologists to be licensed by the state, though some other states have considered legislation that would transform exercise physiology into a licensed discipline. The American Society of Exercise Physiologists (ASEP) offers as certification program, the Exercise Physiologist Certified (EPC) program, for individuals with bachelor's degrees in the field. The American College of Sports Medicine (ACSM) offers two certification programs, the Certified Clinical Exercise Physiologist (CEP) program, for those with bachelor's degrees, and an advanced Registered Clinical Exercise Physiologist (RCEP) program for those with master's degrees or higher. Both organization also offer continuing education programs to help professionals maintain their certification as well as staying informed on current developments in the field and related technology.

Additional Requirements

Individuals seeking to become exercise physiologists need to be good at working with others, as professionals in the field must be able to form working relationships with their patients and physicians. In addition, because exercise physiology is a therapeutic field, professionals benefit from a well-developed sense of compassion for their patients and from the ability to empathize, sympathize, and communicate with patients and their families/loved ones while guiding patients through a recovery and fitness program.

Fun Fact

The U.S. military studied whether caffeine is, indeed, dehydrating. The news was good for coffee drinkers: no detrimental impact on 24-hour urine volume was found in regular consumers of the equivalent of a six-ounce cup of joe and, by day's end, urine losses were close between those who did not consume caffeine and those who consume high doses.

Source: www.active.com.

EARNINGS AND ADVANCEMENT

The median annual wage for professional exercise physiologists in the United States was $47,010 in 2015, with those at the lowest-paid 10 percent of the spectrum earning annual salaries of less than $31,540, while those at the higher end earned in excess of $73,840. Advancing in the field can involve transitioning from low-ranking positions within a hospital or other healthcare institution to higher ranking, senior positions, or attempting to become a manager, overseeing other exercise physiologists working within an institution.

Metropolitan Areas with the Highest
Employment Level in this Occupation

Metropolitan area	Employment	Employment per thousand jobs	Hourly mean wage
Washington-Arlington-Alexandria, DC-VA-MD-WV Metropolitan Division	300	0.12	$15.45
Minneapolis-St. Paul-Bloomington, MN-WI	170	0.09	$29.06
Chicago-Naperville-Arlington Heights, IL Metropolitan Division	140	0.04	$28.47
Atlanta-Sandy Springs-Roswell, GA	110	0.05	$21.09
Houston-The Woodlands-Sugar Land, TX	100	0.04	$24.68
Denver-Aurora-Lakewood, CO	100	0.08	$20.79
Dallas-Plano-Irving, TX Metropolitan Division	100	0.04	$20.31
Indianapolis-Carmel-Anderson, IN	100	0.10	$23.81
Los Angeles-Long Beach-Glendale, CA Metropolitan Division	90	0.02	$36.79
Tampa-St. Petersburg-Clearwater, FL	90	0.08	$24.40

Source: Bureau of Labor Statistics

EMPLOYMENT AND OUTLOOK

According to the Bureau of Labor Statistics (BLS), employment in the exercise physiology field was projected to grow by 11 percent between 2014 and 2024, marking faster than average growth in comparison to the 6-7 percent expected for all occupations in the United States. Demand is expected to grow because of increased demand for therapists and physiological specialists in hospitals and physician's offices. Despite high expected growth, there are few available positions in the United States and so competition for available positions is expected to remain high.

Employment Trend, Projected 2014–24

Health diagnosing and treating practitioners: 17%

Exercise physiologists: 11%

Total, all occupations: 7%

Note: "All Occupations" includes all occupations in the U.S. Economy. Source: U.S. Bureau of Labor Statistics, Employment Projections Program

Related Occupations
- Physical Therapists
- Occupational Therapists
- Recreational Therapists
- Respiratory Therapists
- Athletic Trainers
- Nuclear Medicine Technologists

- Physician Assistants
- Research Physiologist

Related Occupations
- Aerospace Physiologist
- Naval Physiologist

Conversation With . . .
PATRICK AYRES

EXECUTIVE VICE PRESIDENT
The American Society of Exercise Physiologists
Minneapolis, Minnesota
Exercise Physiologist, 20 years

1. What was your individual career path in terms of education/training, entry-level job, or other significant opportunity?

A big bike race came to my hometown of Ripon, Wisconsin, every summer when I was a kid. Hundreds of cyclists. That's when "American Flyers," the Kevin Costner bike racing movie, came out. That's initially how I got interested in exercise physiology. In the movie, Costner's got his brother on a treadmill, hooked up to wires and tubes, trying to beat a record. It piqued my interest. I ended up racing bikes competitively for 20 years.

I got my bachelor's degree from the College of St. Scholastic in Duluth, MN, and my master's at Southern Illinois University in Carbondale. Both of my degrees are in exercise physiology. This is really a lab-based science but you're sort of limited doing research unless you have a PhD. My first job was with a guy working on his PhD in sports psychology who started a company focused on mind-body performance enhancement. It ended up flopping, so I found myself in St. Louis with a master's degree and no job. I took a job teaching elementary physical education. In retrospect, it was helpful. Take a very complex exercise physiology topic and explain the concept to an 8-year-old. Simplifying complicated concepts is huge, from an education standpoint.

I did that for two years but moved back to Minneapolis because I wanted to get back to exercise physiology and my fiancé got a job here. I took a job as a personal trainer at a big-box gym, which was the last thing I wanted to do at the time, but I was desperate. I was successful with a full schedule of clients, and also worked for the Minnesota Heart Institute doing public education in schools. Then, out of the blue, I got a call from a woman who owned a small medical fitness center and went to work for her, running a corporate fitness center and developing preventative health programs for people. I went on to work for one of the clients as head exercise physiologist, was transferred to a private club we managed, then left that company and moved into the long-term care arena. My job was to travel to 18 nursing homes in five states to implement a program to prevent falls. We did that for four years until I was laid off for the first time in my life.

Now I am working part-time for the American Society of Exercise Physiologists (ASEP). Our primary goals are to board-certify Exercise Physiologists and to boost our accreditation for bachelor level exercise physiology programs.

2. **What are the most important skills and/or qualities for someone in your profession?**

Excellent critical thinking skills, an analytical mindset, and the desire to help and educate the public on the benefits of exercise.

3. **What do you wish you had known going into this profession?**

That the health and fitness industry is very chaotic. There are hundreds of weekend warrior certifications that give attendees the minimal knowledge necessary to lead group exercise or create an individual exercise prescription. Unfortunately, superior genetics or past athletic achievements are often mistaken as the key requirements needed to make a good exercise physiologist. Nothing compares to a quality four-year degree in exercise physiology—often called exercise science or kinesiology.

4. **Are there many job opportunities in your profession? In what specific areas?**

This is a growing profession. Job opportunities are available in health and fitness centers, rehabilitation clinics, senior living communities and long-term care facilities.

5. **How do you see your profession changing in the next five years, what role will technology play in those changes, and what skills will be required?**

The main change I see is an increase in public awareness of who exercise physiologists are and what they do. Technology may benefit researchers, but I don't see technology creating any big changes for the public except more types of and features on activity monitors. Sometimes, less is more. Data is useless if it cannot be interpreted.

6. **What do you enjoy most about your job? What do you enjoy least about your job?**

I most enjoy helping people and analyzing numbers and data. I least enjoy convincing the public that my knowledge is worth paying for.

7. **Can you suggest a valuable "try this" for students considering a career in your profession?**

Go to a local gym and ask if they offer complimentary equipment orientations. This is often scheduled with staff with an exercise physiology background. Approach it like an informational interview and ask about the daily responsibilities and role of the staff member.

MORE INFORMATION

American College of Sports Medicine (ACSM)
401 W. Michigan Street
Indianapolis, IN 46202
317-637-9200
www.acsm.org

American Society of Exercise Physiologists (ASEP)
info@asep.com
www.asep.org

Committee on Accreditation for the Exercise Sciences (CoAES)
401 W. Michigan Street
Indianapolis, IN 46202
317-777-1135
www.coaces.org

Clinical Exercise Physiology Association (CEPA)
401 W. Michigan Street
Indianapolis, IN 46202
317-637-9200
www.acsm-cepa.org

Micah Issitt/Editor

Fitness Equipment Manufacturer

Snapshot

Career Cluster: Art & Design; Manufacturing

Interests: Design, consumer culture, technological trends, solving problems, being creative

Earnings (Yearly Average): $64,620

Employment & Outlook: Slower than Average Growth Expected

OVERVIEW

Sphere of Work

Fitness Equipment Manufacturers, also known as commercial designers or product designers, plan and create new products that are both functional and stylish. They improve older products by enhancing certain features or by making them safer or more user-friendly. They usually specialize in certain consumer goods, such as cars, toys, housewares, or personal grooming accessories. In addition to designing products, some industrial designers also design packaging for the products or displays for trade shows and may even put their creative skills to work on corporate branding campaigns.

Work Environment

Industrial designers are employed by specialized design firms as well as larger companies and manufacturers. Some are self-employed. They spend much of their time in offices or studios where they design products and in conference rooms with members of product development teams, typically comprised of engineers, strategic planners, financial managers, advertising and marketing specialists, and other creative consultants. They may need to spend some time working in factories and/or testing facilities. Most work a forty-hour week, with additional evening and weekend hours as needed to meet deadlines.

Profile

Working Conditions: Work Indoors
Physical Strength: Light Work
Education Needs: Bachelor's Degree, Master's Degree
Licensure/Certification: Usually Not Required
Opportunities For Experience: Internship
Holland Interest Score*: AES

* See Appendix A

Occupation Interest

Industrial design attracts artistic people who look upon consumer products as potential canvases for their creativity. They take satisfaction in products that look good while also being functional and user-friendly. Industrial designers keep up with the latest trends and stay engaged with contemporary consumer culture, design, and technological trends. They must be technically savvy, with strong spatial, communication, and problem-solving skills. The ability to work under deadlines is important.

A Day in the Life—Duties and Responsibilities

The work performed by an industrial designer depends on the size and type of his or her employer and the particular types of products that employer manufactures or builds. Although many industrial designers work for product manufacturers, others work for specialized businesses like architectural firms and medical companies, and still others are self-employed. The work done by industrial designers is increasingly more commercial as companies focus more closely on consumer trends and market research.

Industrial designers are included early on in the corporate product development phase. They may be asked to sketch products that have already been identified or specific details or components for products that need to be upgraded. In some cases, an industrial designer sees a need for a product and recommends the idea to a research and development team for consideration. During the early stages, the designer may research other products, sometimes attending a trade show to view the competition, or survey potential users for desired features.

Once a product has been conceptualized, the industrial designer sketches out designs, either by hand or with design software. The designs might show a smaller model, a product that is easier to hold or more ergonomic, or some other type of innovation. The designer might also create a model from clay or foam board, often first rendering it in 3-D software. The designer suggests specific colors, materials, and manufacturing processes that are within the limitations of the budget. Those who work for manufacturers might render drawings in computer-aided industrial design (CAID) programs that can direct machines to build the products automatically. Industrial designers also communicate their designs and ideas in writing and give presentations to clients or managers.

Before a product is released for the market, the industrial designer might oversee or participate in its testing, at which time he or she may need to make refinements to the design to correct unforeseen issues or improve the quality of the product.

Duties and Responsibilities

- Studying the potential need for new products
- Studying other similar products on the market
- Consulting with sales and marketing personnel to obtain design ideas and to estimate public reaction to new designs
- Sketching designs
- Making comprehensive drawings of the product

OCCUPATION SPECIALTIES

Package Designers

Package Designers design containers for products, such as foods, beverages, toiletries, cigarettes and medicines.

WORK ENVIRONMENT

Transferable Skills and Abilities

Communication Skills
- Expressing thoughts and ideas
- Speaking effectively

Creative/Artistic Skills
- Being skilled in art, music or dance

Interpersonal/Social Skillss
- Cooperating with others
- Working as a member of a team

Organization & Management Skills
- Making decisions
- Paying attention to and handling details
- Performing routine work

Research & Planning Skills
- Creating ideas
- Setting goals and deadlines
- Using logical reasoning

Technical Skills
- Performing scientific, mathematical and technical work
- Working with data or numbers

Physical Environment

Industrial designers usually work in comfortable offices or studios. Those who regularly oversee product manufacturing might be at some risk for health issues related to their factory environments.

Human Environment

Industrial designers usually report to the creative director of the design firm or manager of a department, and they may oversee an intern or assistant as he or she gains experience. Interaction with clients and other members of a product development team may include lively brainstorming sessions as well as harsh criticism about ideas and designs. Self-employed industrial designers interact with others less often as they usually work from home offices.

Technological Environment

Industrial designers use a variety of art tools and supplies to build models and sketch designs, but much of their work is also performed using computer-aided design (CAD) software, computer-aided industrial design (CAID) software, and modeling, animation, and design software.

EDUCATION, TRAINING, AND ADVANCEMENT

High School/Secondary

Students should take a college-preparatory program that includes courses in English, math, and science, including physics and trigonometry. Electives should include drafting, drawing, and other art courses (sculpture, painting, ceramics, and photography) and/ or industrial arts (woodworking and metalworking). Other useful courses include psychology, engineering, and business. Students need to prepare a portfolio for admission to postsecondary art and design programs. Because this is a hands-on field, students should put together models, visit art museums, and engage in other cultural and educational activities that encourage critical and creative thinking skills.

Suggested High School Subjects
- Algebra
- Applied Communication
- Applied Math
- Applied Physics
- Arts
- Blueprint Reading
- College Preparatory
- Drafting
- English

- Geometry
- Industrial Arts
- Mechanical Drawing
- Photography
- Pottery
- Trigonometry
- Woodshop

Famous First

The first patent for a design was issued in 1844 to George Bruce of New York City for a printing typeface.

College/Postsecondary

A bachelor's degree in industrial design or engineering, ideally with a minor in art or design, is the standard minimum requirement for most entry-level jobs in this field; some employers prefer to hire those with a master's degree. Students must acquire skills in drawing, CAD and design software, and building 3-D models by hand, as well as knowledge about industrial materials and manufacturing processes. Courses that build understanding of humans and society, such as psychology, anthropology, human ecology, and philosophy, are also important. Business skills are required for some jobs. Students should plan to apply for an internship and prepare a portfolio of their best work.

Related College Majors
- Industrial Design
- Industrial/Manufacturing Technology

Adult Job Seekers

Industrial design draws on many different abilities, skills, and knowledge. Adults with a close familiarity with industry-specific products, such as medical equipment or sporting goods, could build upon that experience by taking industrial design classes. Adults with a background in art might simply need to add engineering and/or CAD training to their current skill set. Interested adults should discuss options with college admissions counselors.

Most industrial designers begin their careers as interns. They are given assignments of increasing responsibility and prestige as they become more experienced and prove their abilities. In time, an industrial designer may be able to advance to a supervisory position or establish his or her own design firm. Teaching at the college level, writing books, and consulting are other options for those with adequate experience and education.

Professional Certification and Licensure

No professional license or certification is required. Certificates are sometimes awarded upon completion of associate's degree programs.

Additional Requirements

Designers must have good eyesight, including the ability to see different colors. Problem-solving skills, creativity, self-discipline, awareness of cultural trends, and open-mindedness are all desirable. Industrial designers should develop a strong portfolio of their work, as this is often the deciding factor in the hiring process.

Fun Fact

Red Dot Design Awards are like the Oscars of the industrial design world. A few products that won in 2015 include plastic Birkenstock sandals, the Triumph Magic Wire bra, and the BackBeatFIT sports headset.

Source: http://www.dexigner.com/directory/cat/Industrial-Design/Awards.html and http://red-dot.de/pd/online-exhibition/?lang=en&c=0&a=0&y=2015&i=0&oes=

EARNINGS AND ADVANCEMENT

Earnings of industrial designers depend on the individual's education and experience and the type, size, and geographic location of the employer. Industrial designers who have their own consulting firms may have fluctuating incomes, depending on their business for the year. Some industrial designers may work on retainers, which means they may receive flat fees for given periods of time. During any given period, industrial designers can work on retainers for many different companies.

Median annual earnings of industrial designers were $64,620 in 2014. The lowest ten percent earned less than $37,030, and the highest ten percent earned more than $100,070.

Industrial designers may receive paid vacations, holidays, and sick days; life and health insurance; and retirement benefits. These are usually paid by the employer.

Metropolitan Areas with the Highest
Employment Level in this Occupation

Metropolitan area	Employment	Employment per thousand jobs	Annual mean wage
New York-White Plains-Wayne, NY-NJ	1,920	0.36	$75,240
Warren-Troy-Farmington Hills, MI	1,900	1.66	$78,240
Detroit-Livonia-Dearborn, MI	1,590	2.21	$81,150
Los Angeles-Long Beach-Glendale, CA	1,510	0.37	$64,120
Chicago-Joliet-Naperville, IL	710	0.19	$67,220
Santa Ana-Anaheim-Irvine, CA	560	0.38	$73,180
Atlanta-Sandy Springs-Marietta, GA	540	0.23	$68,490
Columbus, OH	420	0.43	$63,920
Cincinnati-Middletown, OH-KY-IN	420	0.41	$70,890
Minneapolis-St. Paul-Bloomington, MN-WI	390	0.21	$61,700

Source: Bureau of Labor Statistics

EMPLOYMENT AND OUTLOOK

Industrial designers held about 40,000 jobs in 2014. Employment is expected to grow somewhat slower than the average for all occupations through the year 2024, which means employment is projected to increase 0 percent to 4 percent. Demand for industrial designers will stem from continued emphasis on product quality and safety, design of new products that are easy and comfortable to use and high technology products in medicine, transportation and other fields.

Employment Trend, Projected 2014–24

Total, all occupations: 7%

Art and design workers: 2%

Commercial and industrial designers: 2%

Note: "All Occupations" includes all occupations in the U.S. Economy. Source: U.S. Bureau of Labor Statistics, Employment Projections Program

Related Occupations
- Designer
- Graphic Designer
- Merchandise Displayer
- Multimedia Artist & Animator

Conversation With . . .
JONATHAN DALTON, IDSA

CEO and Co-Founder, thrive
Atlanta, Georgia
Industrial design, 20 years

1. What was your individual career path in terms of education/training, entry-level job, or other significant opportunity?

Originally, I wanted to be an aerospace engineer, but I quickly found I wasn't good enough at math. Growing up I was always very creative, always building and drawing things. My grandfather built me my first drawing board when I was nine. With my engineering ambitions shelved, I started thinking about architecture school. One of my mum's cousins, who is an architect, said, "It sounds great, but the reality is you're going to be working on homes and additions and it's all code and very dry." He suggested industrial design. I found the book, Presentation Techniques: A Guide to Drawing and Presenting Design Ideas by English designer Dick Powell. It's basically how to do great product renderings. I thought, "Wow—you get paid to do that?" I'm from England, and I was doing my A Levels—the three big subjects you do at the end of high school. I was doing chemistry, physics, and math at first, but I dropped math and took design instead. That's where it all began.

Out of college, I worked for Electrolux for three years. A lot of my friends had interned in the States and there were great agencies doing great work that turned all our heads. So after three years, I joined Ziba Design in Portland, Oregon—one of the world's best industrial design agencies. It was an incredible experience. In five years, I went from junior designer to creative director. I then joined Altitude Inc. in Boston and from there, I joined Philips Design, the world's largest design group, in Atlanta. I headed up their industrial design group and outside consulting for four years. It helped me understand how to launch my business—thrive—which I did in 2010. Most of my design work has been appliances and medical products, but I've done lots of other stuff over the years.

2. What are the most important skills and/or qualities for someone in your profession?

The biggest one is problem-solving. You have to be a good analytical thinker. Obviously, you've got to be creative. You have to be empathetic and able to walk in someone else's shoes. Design sits between two worlds in many ways. Designers can be consumer advocates in terms of designing products that people love, but also have to consider engineering and marketing needs. "Design thinking" is a big buzzword in the corporate world.

3. What do you wish you had known going into this profession?

To be successful, you have to put a business lens on design. It can't be creativity for creativity's sake.

4. Are there many job opportunities in your profession? In what specific areas?

It's exploding right now. Chief Design Officer is a title that has become more prevalent in the last five years as organizations start to realize that they can't differentiate their products just on technology and features alone; they have to differentiate on experience.

5. How do you see your profession changing in the next five years? What role will technology play in those changes, and what skills will be required?

We're seeing big shifts. There will always be physical products but physical products now are more often a portal to a digital experience. Industrial design principles are being transferred to the services around a product, the product ecosystem, and a lot of that will obviously be more virtual than tangible. It's a real golden age of design right now. Design is being seen as a strategic business tool and that was never the case before. It was always the lipstick on the product at the end of the day.

6. What do you enjoy most about your job? What do you enjoy least about your job?

You never do the same thing twice. I get easily bored and I have never been bored in this profession. There's always a challenge or a problem to solve.

I'm not very good at helping steer design through bureaucracy. I got good at explaining the value of design, because I had to, but in an ideal world it's something you wouldn't have to do because everyone understood it already.

7. Can you suggest a valuable "try this" for students considering a career in your profession?

The Industrial Designers Society of America (idsa.org) has chapters across the country and many run outreach programs for schools, taking a problem and working as a team to solve it, typically over two weekends. It's sponsored by design agencies and corporations that value design. It's all about teaching kids how to think like a designer. My company, thrive, is an ISDA Ambassador of Excellence. Also, many cities hold a "Design Week" event with various activities like open houses at agencies. It's a great way to peek inside and speak to people who work there and get a sense of what the profession's about.

SELECTED SCHOOLS

Many colleges and universities offer programs in design and illustration. The student may also gain initial training at a technical/ community college. Below are listed some of the more prominent institutions in this field.

Art Center College of Design
1700 Lida Street
Pasadena, CA 91103
626.396.2200
www.artcenter.edu

California College of the Arts
1111 Eighth Street
San Francisco, CA 94107
415.703.9523
www.cca.edu

Carnegie Mellon University
5000 Forbes Avenue
Pittsburgh, PA 15213
412.268.2000
www.cmu.edu

Cranbrook Academy of Art
39221 Woodward Avenue
Bloomfield Hills, MI 48303
248.645.3300
www.cranbrookart.edu

Ohio State University
258 Hopkins Hall
Columbus, OH 43210
614.292.5072
art.osu.edu

Pratt Institute
200 Willoughby Avenue
Brooklyn, NY 11205
718.636.3600
www.pratt.edu

Rhode Island School of Design
2 College Street
Providence, RI 02903
401.454.6100
www.risd.edu

Rochester Institute of Technology
73 Lomb Memorial Drive
Rochester, NY 14623
585.475.2239
www.rit.edu

School of the Art Institute of Chicago
37 South Wabash Avenue
Chicago, IL 60603
800.232.7242
www.saic.edu

School of Visual Arts
209 E. 23rd Street
New York, NY 10010
212.592.2100
www.sva.edu

MORE INFORMATION

Association of Women Industrial Designers
P.O. Box 468, Old Chelsea Station
New York, NY 10011
www.awidweb.com

Core77
561 Broadway, 6th Floor
New York, NY 10012
212.965.1998
www.core77.com

Industrial Designers Society of America
45195 Business Court, Suite 250
Dulles, VA 20166-6717
703.707.6000
www.idsa.org

Organization of Black Designers
300 M Street, SW, Suite N110
Washington, DC 20024-4019
202.659.3918
www.core77.com/OBD/welcome.html

University & College Designers Association
199 W. Enon Springs Road, Suite 300
Smyrna, TN 37167
615.459.4559
www.ucda.com

Sally Driscoll/Editor

Fundraiser/ Fundraising Manager

Snapshot

Career Cluster: Business Administration; Hospitality & Tourism

Interests: Working with people, coordinating activities, planning and scheduling

Earnings (Yearly Average): $49,830

Employment & Outlook: Faster Than Average Growth

OVERVIEW

Sphere of Work

Fundraiser/Fundraising Managers coordinate all aspects of professional and social meetings, gatherings, and events. Working with clients, they choose event locations, organize the invitation process, arrange for food and beverages, and coordinate all other details, including transportation and lodging. They may work as employees of a service organization specializing in events and event planning, such as a convention bureau or resort center, or they may work inside a business corporation or nonprofit organization, where they work with departmental heads or managers to plan important meetings, fundraisers, or other special events. They may also work independently. Their work

encompasses planning for such occasions as weddings, reunions, and other private celebrations as well as for functions such as trade shows, conventions, and fundraisers.

Work Environment

Event planners work in office environments most of the time, although they also work onsite at hotels, convention centers, and similar venues. They often travel to visit prospective meeting sites and attend events. During meetings or conventions, event planners may work very long hours. They interact with many different individuals, from musicians and food caterers to facilities managers and technical services personnel, in the course of setting up a large event.

Profile

Physical Strength: Light Work
Education Needs:
Technical/Community College, Bachelor's Degree
Licensure/Certification: Usually Not Required
Physical Abilities Not Required: No Heavy Labor
Opportunities for Experience:
Volunteer Work, Part-Time Work
Holland Interest Score: CES

* See Appendix A

Occupation Interest

This occupation suits people who combine administrative and organizational capabilities with the ability to work with others and satisfy their needs. Event planners have generally proven their administrative capabilities by first excelling in an entry-level administrative position. Successful event planners enjoy working with people and have strong oral communication skills, allowing them to dialogue with clients and provide suggestions with tact and confidence. Although they work largely independently in the role of "broker" or "agent" on behalf of their clients, event planners must also be comfortable collaborating with members of their own team.

A Day in the Life—Duties and Responsibilities

An event planner's day is likely to involve a combination of personal interaction and business administration. This is a job in which success usually requires a blend of skills in several areas, including management, creative awareness, technology, the ability to coordinate with other service organizations, and communication skills.

During a typical day, event planners may meet with clients to understand the purpose of a meeting or event. They may help plan the scope of the event, including time, location, and cost. They might solicit bids from venues and service providers (for example, florists or photographers), inspect venues to ensure that they meet the client's requirements, coordinate event services such as rooms, transportation, and food service, and monitor event activities to ensure the client and event attendees are satisfied.

Whether it is a wedding, educational conference, or business convention, meetings and events bring people together for a common purpose. Event planners work to ensure that this purpose is achieved efficiently and seamlessly. They coordinate every detail of events, from beginning to end. Before a meeting, for example, planners will meet with clients to estimate attendance and determine the meeting's purpose. During the meeting, they handle meeting logistics, such as registering guests and organizing audio/visual equipment for speakers. After the meeting, they may survey attendees to find out how the event was received. They may also review event bills and approve payment to vendors.

Duties and Responsibilities

- Identifying client needs and interests, including scheduling requirements and budget limitations
- Recommending venues, activities, design elements, food items, and logistics arrangements
- Renting rooms or facilities as needed to accommodate planned events
- Inviting attendees or helping client to do so
- Lining up and contracting with outside vendors and suppliers
- Attending events as needed to coordinate efforts and ensure success
- Reviewing post-event data and/or comments for lessons to be learned
- Handling contractor invoices and making payments

OCCUPATION SPECIALTIES

In many cases, they organize speakers, entertainment, or activities. They must also ensure that services such as wheelchair accessibility, interpreters, and other accommodations are in place.

Association Planners

Association Planners organize annual conferences and trade shows for professional associations. Because member attendance is often voluntary, marketing the meeting's value is an important aspect of their work.

Convention Service Managers

Convention Service Managers help organize major events, as employees of hotels and convention centers. They act as liaisons between the meeting facility and the planners who work for associations, businesses, and governments. They present food service options to outside planners, coordinate special requests, and suggest hotel services depending on a planner's budget.

Corporate & Government Meeting Planners

Corporate Planners organize internal business meetings and meetings between businesses. Government Meeting Planners organize meetings for government officials and agencies; being familiar with government regulations, such as procedures for buying materials and booking hotels, is vital to their work.

Nonprofit Event Planners

Nonprofit Event Planners plan large events with the goal of raising donations for a charity or advocacy organization. Events may include banquets, charity races, and food drives.

Wedding & Party Planners

Wedding and Party Planners arrange the details of celebratory events, including weddings, reunions, and large birthday parties.

WORK ENVIRONMENT

Physical Environment

Event planners spend much of their time in comfortable indoor settings such as offices or similar facilities. During meetings and events, they usually work on-site at hotels or convention centers. They travel regularly to attend the events they organize and to visit prospective meeting sites, sometimes in exotic locations around the world. Some events are held outdoors—typically under tents—and event planners should be prepared for weather changes and uneven ground. Planners may have very long workdays, and sometimes work on weekends.

Relevant Skills and Abilities

Communication Skills
- Expressing thoughts and ideas clearly
- Speaking and writing effectively

Interpersonal/Social Skills
- Cooperating with others
- Inspiring confidence in others
- Listening well
- Working both independently and as a member of a team

Organization & Management Skills
- Managing time
- Meeting goals and deadlines
- Paying attention to and handling details

Research & Planning Skills
- Investigating resources
- Laying out a plan

Human Environment

Event planners regularly collaborate with clients, hospitality workers, and event attendees. The work of event planners can be fast-paced and demanding. Planners oversee many aspects of an event at the same time and face numerous deadlines. They must sometimes deal with anxious clients or vendors and try to calm them while ensuring the success of the event.

Technological Environment

Event planners make use of standard office technologies, including computers, telephones, e-mail, photocopiers, and the Internet. They should be proficient in the use of basic office software such as word processing programs, contact management software, spreadsheets, and presentation programs. More recently, planners also consider whether an online meeting can achieve the same objectives as a face-to-face meeting in certain cases; therefore they need to be familiar with online conferencing tools.

EDUCATION, TRAINING, AND ADVANCEMENT

High School/Secondary

High school students can best prepare for a career as an event planner by taking courses in English, composition, and business writing. Courses that develop general business skills may include accounting, entrepreneurship, bookkeeping, business management, and applied mathematics. Administrative and clerical skills may be developed by taking subjects such as business computing, typing, and shorthand. Subjects such as history and social studies help the student to develop his or her general research and analytical skills. Studies in psychology may be beneficial for developing understanding about human behavior and motivation.

Becoming involved in volunteer work at fundraising events while still in high school is an excellent way to gain entry-level experience in the profession. High school students may also gain part-time administrative experience with local business organizations as well as with scholastic clubs and societies. A wide variety of extracurricular activities provide opportunities for enhancing social skills.

Suggested High School Subjects
- Applied Communication
- Bookkeeping
- Business
- Business & Computer Technology
- Business Data Processing
- Business English
- Business Math
- English
- Keyboarding
- Social Studies
- Psychology

Famous First

The first manufacturers' fair was held in Masonic Hall, New York City, in 1828, under the auspices of the American Institute. The purpose of the event was to publicize, encourage, and promote domestic industry. Other organizations soon began hosting similar fairs and expositions, in agriculture, commerce, and the arts. Together they formed the early context for the eventual rise of the profession of event planning.

College/Postsecondary

Many employers prefer applicants who have a bachelor's degree and some work experience in hotels or planning. The proportion of planners with a bachelor's degree is increasing because work responsibilities are becoming more complex and because there are more college degree programs related to hospitality or tourism management. If an applicant's degree is not related to these fields, employers are likely to require at least one to two years of related experience.

Event planners often come from a variety of academic disciplines. Some related undergraduate majors include marketing, public relations, communications, and business. Planners who have studied hospitality management may start out with greater responsibilities than those from other academic disciplines. College students may also gain experience by planning meetings for a university club. In addition, some colleges offer continuing education courses in meeting and event planning.

Related College Majors
- Business Administration & Management
- Hospitality Management
- Meeting & Event Planning

Adult Job Seekers

Adults seeking a career transition or returning to an event planner role are advised to refresh their skills and update their resume. Any relevant administrative skills, project management, or supervisory experience should be highlighted in the candidate's resume and application letter. Networking, job searching, and interviewing are critical, and those without prior experience may find it helpful to obtain specialized training. Aspiring event planners may also find it beneficial to consider related roles, such as office manager, administrative assistant, and any position involving special events.

Professional Certification and Licensure

The Convention Industry Council offers the Certified Meeting Professional (CMP) credential, a voluntary certification for meeting and convention planners. Although the CMP is not required, it is widely recognized in the industry and may help in career advancement. To qualify, candidates must have a minimum of 36 months of meeting management experience, recent employment in a meeting management job, and proof of continuing education credits. Those who qualify must then pass an exam that covers topics such as adult learning, financial management, facilities and services, logistics, and meeting programs.

The Society of Government Meeting Professionals (SGMP) offers the Certified Government Meeting Professional (CGMP) designation for meeting planners who work for, or contract with, federal, state, or local government. This certification is not required to work as a government meeting planner; however, it may be helpful for those who want to show that they know government buying policies and travel regulations. To qualify, candidates must have worked as a meeting planner for at least one year and have been a member of SGMP for six months. To become a certified planner, members must take a three-day course and pass an exam.

Additional Requirements

Event planners are often under pressure to work quickly and efficiently, while at the same time making clients feel that their needs are being attended to. Beyond such business basics, however, the best event planners cultivate an awareness of how not only to satisfy clients but to "wow" them, or exceed their expectations. It is by their reputations that independent event planners, and planning/catering agencies, are known, and it is by their reputations that they will thrive or fail to grow.

EARNINGS AND ADVANCEMENT

Entry-level planners tend to focus on meeting logistics, such as registering guests and organizing audio/visual equipment. Experienced planners manage interpersonal tasks, such as client relations and contract negotiations. With significant experience, event planners can become independent consultants.

Event planners earned mean annual salaries of $49,830 in 2012. The lowest 10 percent had salaries of less than $26,560, and the highest 10 percent had salaries of over $79,270.

Event planners may receive paid vacations, holidays, and sick days; life and health insurance; and retirement benefits. These are usually paid by the employer.

Metropolitan Areas with the Highest Employment Level in this Occupation

Metropolitan area	Employment[1]	Employment per thousand jobs	Hourly mean wage
New York-White Plains-Wayne, NY-NJ	5,680	1.10	$28.45
Washington-Arlington-Alexandria, DC-VA-MD-WV	5,100	2.18	$30.33
Chicago-Joliet-Naperville, IL	2,300	0.63	$22.90
Los Angeles-Long Beach-Glendale, CA	1,840	0.47	$25.49
Atlanta-Sandy Springs-Marietta, GA	1,690	0.75	$22.68
Dallas-Plano-Irving, TX	1,480	0.70	$25.52
Boston-Cambridge-Quincy, MA	1,270	0.74	$29.22
Philadelphia, PA	1,270	0.69	$24.66

[1]Does not include self-employed. Source: Bureau of Labor Statistics

EMPLOYMENT AND OUTLOOK

There were approximately 70,000 event planners employed nationally in 2012. Employment is expected to grow much faster than the average for all occupations through the year 2022, which means employment is projected to increase by over 30 percent. Growth will occur in most all areas, including the business/professional sector, the travel and tourism industry, the nonprofit sector (including colleges and universities), and the arts and entertainment industry.

Employment Trend, Projected 2012–22

Event Planners: 33%

Business and Financial Operations Occupations: 13%

Total, all occupations: 11%

Note: "All Occupations" includes all occupations in the U.S. Economy. Source: U.S. Bureau of Labor Statistics, Employment Projections Program

Related Occupations
- Food Services Manager
- Hotel /Motel Manager
- Property & Real Estate Manager

Fun Facts

The top five states with the largest number of meeting and event planners are California, New York, Texas, Florida and Virginia.

Source: Froomz, from BLS.gov.

The largest athletic fundraiser in the country—the Pan-Mass Challenge bike-a-thon—began when the founder, Billy Starr, was grieving the loss of his mom to cancer in 1977. He pedaled 125 miles from his home outside Boston to the tip of Cape Cod, then caught the ferry home. He asked friends to join him and it evolved into a fundraiser that has donated to $547 million for cancer research.

Source: http://www.pmc.org/

Conversation With . . .
HELEN MENDEL

Certified Marketing Director
President, All Pro Promotions, Palo Alto, California
Fundraising, 25 years

1. What was your individual career path in terms of education/training, entry-level job, or other significant opportunity?

My career path was unusual. I volunteered to do a fundraising event for the American Cancer Society and it was such a success that I continued doing events for other organizations.

I had studied marketing, public relations and communications at San Jose State University and also studied shopping center marketing and management through the International Council of Shopping Centers and earned my Certified Marketing Director (CMD) designation. In 1980, I started my company, All Pro Promotions. We produce special events, including golf tournaments and other sporting events, and offer management consulting and fundraising expertise to non-profits. We work with organizations to fine-tune community outreach and fundraising programs, increase volunteer recruitment and retention, and prepare company executives and board members to function as media spokespersons.

Additionally—and most importantly—I have been Senior Vice President of Marketing & Operations for the Bay Area Sports Organizing Committee (BASOC) and have produced all of their sports and fundraising events for the past 18 years.

Over the years, I have kept my skills sharp by taking several courses in organizational management, going to trade shows, and monitoring other major events for new trends. I've presented to sports marketing classes at the University of San Francisco, San Jose State and University of the Pacific. My clients have included California State Senior Games, San Jose State Men's Golf Western Invitational, NFL Alumni Northern/California Chapter, the 2011 USA Swimming National & Junior National Swim Championships and the 2007 World Junior Table Tennis Championships.

2. What are the most important skills and/or qualities for someone in your profession?

The most important skills are to be very organized, communicative and able to maintain calm during stressful situations. You must have high energy and an outgoing personality.

3. What do you wish you had known going into this profession?

I wish I had known that the hours would be so long. Particularly just before and after a major event, the work days are intense.

4. Are there many job opportunities in your profession? In what specific areas?

It varies with economic times and also according to the sport you're interested in focusing on. Sports with more opportunities for internships would be the major leagues—that is, baseball, soccer, football, basketball, hockey—as well the governing bodies for Olympic sports and golf through the PGA & USGA. Golf tournaments are lucrative, but you need to know the game, and align with the major governing bodies.

There are a variety of specific types of event management you could focus on, with jobs available working for large corporations and for non-profit organizations, or you could strike out on your own.

5. How do you see your profession changing in the next five years? What role will technology play in those changes, and what skills will be required?

Technology already is playing a larger role in events, with new registration systems, online fundraising tools, and on-site acceptance of credit card payments with smart phones at fundraising events. I believe technology will increasingly play a bigger role. You'll have to stay current with emerging trends. One way to do that is to sign up for trainings offered through trade organizations.

6. What do you enjoy most about your job? What do you enjoy least about your job?

What I love about my job is seeing an event begin as a creative idea then come to life and be successful. I do not especially like all the paperwork and constant emails and tax-deductible information required for donors and so on. But it's great when the end result is that the attendees had a great time and the organization made a profit.

7. Can you suggest a valuable "try this" for students considering a career in your profession?

I would highly recommend interning with or shadowing an event manager at a major sports team. If that's not possible, volunteer to spend at least a week at an organization of interest that produces these events. But the ideal situation—especially if you'd like to be hired in the long-term—is to get a full internship with a team.

SELECTED SCHOOLS

Most colleges and universities offer bachelor's degrees in business administration and management; some have programs specifically in hospitality and tourism. The student may also gain initial training at a technical or community college. Below are listed some of the more prominent four-year institutions in this field.

Fairleigh Dickinson University
International School of Hospitality and Tourism Management
285 Madison Avenue
Madison, NJ 07940
973.443.8500
www.fdu.edu

Iowa State University
Apparel, Events, and Hospitality Management
31 MacKay Hall
Ames, IA 50011
515.294.7474
www.aeshm.hs.iastate.edu

Michigan State University
School of Hospitality Business
345 N. Shaw Lane, Rm. 232
East Lansing, MI 48824
517.353.9211
hospitalitybusiness.broad.msu.edu

Penn State University
School of Hospitality Management
201 Mateer Building
University Park, PA 16802
814.865.1853
www.hhd.psu.edu/shm

Purdue University
School of Hospitality and Tourism Management
900 W. State Street
West Lafayette, IN 47907
765.494.4643
www.purdue.edu/hhs/htm

University of Central Florida
Rosen College of Hospitality Management
9907 Universal Boulevard
Orlando, FL 32819
407.903.8000
hospitality.ucf.edu

University of Massachusetts, Amherst
Isenberg School of Management
Department of Hospitality and Tourism Management
121 Presidents Drive
Amherst, MA 01003
413.545.5610
www.isenberg.umass.edu/htm

University of Nevada, Las Vegas
William F. Harrah College of Hotel Administration
4505 S. Maryland Parkway
Las Vegas, NV 89154
702.895.3011
www.unlv.edu/hotel

Virginia Tech
Pamplin College of Business
Department of Hospitality and
Tourism Management
362 Wallace Hall
295 W. Campus Drive
Blacksburg, VA 24061
540.231.1515
www.htm.pamplin.vt.edu

Washington State University
School of Hospitality Business
Management
PO Box 644750
Pullman, WA 99164
509.335.4750
www.business.wsu.edu/academics/
hospitality

MORE INFORMATION

Convention Industry Council
700 N. Fairfax Street
Suite 510
Alexandria, VA 22314
571.527.3116
www.conventionindustry.org

Event Planners Association
25432 Trabuco
Suite 207
Lake Forest, CA 92630
866.380.3372
eventplannersassociation.com

**Meeting Professionals
International**
3030 Lyndon B. Johnson Freeway
Suite 1700
Dallas, TX 75234
972.702.3000
www.mpiweb.org

**Professional Convention
Management Association**
35 E. Wacker Drive
Suite 500
Chicago, IL 60601
312.423.7262
www.pcma.org

**Society of Government Meeting
Professionals**
908 King Street
Suite 200
Alexandria, VA 22314
703.549.0892
www.sgmp.org

Michael Shally-Jensen

Health & Fitness Center Manager

Snapshot

Career Cluster: Business Administration; Hospitality & Tourism; Sales & Service

Interests: Physical activity, managing others, customer service

Earnings (Yearly Average): $53,582

Employment & Outlook: Slower Than Average Growth Expected

OVERVIEW

Sphere of Work

Health and fitness center managers supervise retail, private, and organizational exercise facilities. In addition to ensuring the maintenance of all club equipment and facilities, they also supervise staff and resolve customer complaints and may play a role in small-scale marketing and promotion initiatives. Health and fitness center managers are also responsible for the recruitment, assessment, and billing related to external vendors such as janitorial staff, pool cleaners, vending machine companies, and laundry facilities that help health clubs function every day.

Work Environment

Health and fitness center managers traditionally split their time between interacting with clients in and around health and fitness center facilities and conducting traditional executive duties in administrative settings. Visibility is an important characteristic of successful health and fitness center managers, who must be available to assist staff members as well as customers throughout the day. Many managers of large health and fitness centers also supervise a small staff of assistant managers who share in the center's management responsibilities.

Profile

Working Conditions: Work Indoors

Physical Strength: Light Work

Education Needs: Junior/
Technical/Community College,
Bachelor's Degree

Licensure/Certification:
Recommended

Physical Abilities Not Required: N/A

Opportunities For Experience:
Internship, Volunteer Work, Part-Time
Work

Holland Interest Score*: ESR

* See Appendix A

Occupation Interest

Health center management attracts a wide variety of professionals. Some health and fitness center managers undertake the position as a means of transitional employment while pursuing postsecondary education in the field—such as chiropractic or physical therapy studies— or coursework in business and executive management. Others come to the position through having worked as a fitness trainer or instructor and recognize the job as a significant step up in their career. Health center management almost exclusively attracts health-conscious and physically active individuals who are by nature team players eager to use their knowledge to assist others in a friendly and productive manner.

A Day in the Life—Duties and Responsibilities

The daily responsibilities of health and fitness center managers are diverse. In addition to ensuring that all center equipment is in proper functioning order, they must supervise all staff and also interview, hire, and oversee training for new employees. Health and fitness center managers are also responsible for addressing the concerns and complaints of both staff members and clientele and must act quickly to ensure that such concerns are addressed.

Health and fitness center managers may also have considerable input into their center's financial health, reviewing budgets and maximizing investments in equipment and tools. They may also be responsible for reviewing the center's membership roster to ensure that member dues are organized and up to date. Health and fitness center managers may play an important role in promotional activities and marketing initiatives designed to attract new members.

Health and fitness center managers who oversee exercise facilities that are part of larger organizational hierarchies—such as country clubs, resort hotels, or golf clubs—are typically required to attend occasional manager meetings in which they discuss how they are approaching and meeting the overall goals of the organization with other facility supervisors.

Duties and Responsibilities

- Hiring and firing personnel
- Coordinating staff
- Attending to day-to-day activities of the club
- Making sure staff is well trained, properly qualified, and certified or licensed
- Holding classes or seminars for new club staffers
- Performing administrative duties, such as payroll and bookkeeping
- Marketing the fitness center to attract new customers
- Overseeing all equipment upkeep and general maintenance

WORK ENVIRONMENT

Physical Environment

Health and fitness center managers may work as independent business owners or as executive staff members in larger organizations such as hotels, resorts, and golf clubs. They typically split their time between the health center and an office environment.

Relevant Skills and Abilities

Communication Skills
- Speaking effectively

Interpersonal/Social Skills
- Asserting oneself
- Providing support to others

Organization & Management Skills
- Coordinating tasks
- Managing people/groups
- Paying attention to and handling details

Other Skills
- Understanding and having knowledge of fitness and exercise

Human Environment

Extensive collaboration and communication skills are required of the position. Health and fitness center managers interact with customers, colleagues, and outside vendors on a daily basis and must be skilled in handling customer questions and complaints.

Technological Environment

Health and fitness center managers use a variety of administrative technologies, ranging from telephone, e-mail, and web conferencing to financial-management software. Familiarity with the intricacies of modern exercise equipment is also important.

EDUCATION, TRAINING, AND ADVANCEMENT

High School/Secondary

High school students can best prepare for a career in health and fitness center management with courses in geometry, biology, chemistry, physical education, nutrition, health, and computers. Summer programs, volunteer work, and internships at health centers or similar facilities can familiarize students with the day-to-day procedures of operation.

Suggested High School Subjects
- Applied Communication
- Biology
- Business
- Business English
- Business Math
- First Aid Training

- Geometry
- Health Science Technology
- Physical Education
- Physiology
- Social Studies
- Sociology

Famous First

The first gymnasium to offer systematic instruction was that of the Round Hill School for Boys in Northampton, Mass. It was opened in 1823 by John Cogswell and George Bancroft. The instructor in Latin, Charles Beck, served as the gym instructor. A few years later the first men's collegiate gymnastics program (which included all manner of physical movement and exercise) opened at Harvard University; and in 1862 the first women's gym program was launched at Mount Holyoke College in South Hadley, Mass., just a few miles from Northampton.

Postsecondary

There are several associate- and bachelor-level postsecondary programs in the United States dedicated to health center facilities management. Coursework in health center management instructs students on the basics of small business management as well as fitness program development, equipment maintenance, and basic nutrition. Health and fitness management students should also take courses in anatomy, kinesiology, and exercise physiology.

Related College Majors
- Business Administration & Management
- Health & Physical Education
- Hospitality Management
- Parks, Recreation & Leisure Studies
- Physical Education Teaching & Coaching
- Public Health
- Sport & Fitness Administration/Management

Adult Job Seekers

Health and fitness center managers traditionally work regular business hours, though their responsibilities may require long workdays and occasional weekend work. The increased cultural awareness of health and fitness in the United States has made health and fitness center management a rapidly growing field. Individuals with management experience in other industries can easily parlay their skills into a new position in health center management through supplemental education or certification.

Professional Certification and Licensure

While states do not explicitly require certification or licensure for non-instructional health and fitness center positions, completion of a certificate program can be beneficial for aspiring health center professionals. Such certification can give prospective managers higher visibility in the job market and serve as proof of their experience with customer service, marketing, and gym safety. Prospective health and fitness center managers should consult credible professional associations within the field and follow professional debate as to the relevance and value of any certification program.

Additional Requirements

Health and fitness center management is a people-centric position that requires patience, understanding, and camaraderie with both fellow staff members and center members. Ideal candidates for health and fitness center management positions have proven leadership abilities and are enthusiastic about helping others meet their health and fitness goals.

EARNINGS AND ADVANCEMENT

Advancement for health and fitness center managers occurs by climbing the career ladder in prestigious centers. Many health and fitness center managers also work toward opening their own centers. Earnings of health and fitness center managers depend on the type, size, geographic location and prestige of the center and whether the center is public or private. Earnings also depend on the education, experience, and responsibilities of the individual. Median annual earnings of health and fitness center managers were $53,582 in 2012. Many health and fitness center managers also receive bonuses for bringing in and signing up new members.

Health and fitness center managers may receive paid vacations, holidays, and sick days; life and health insurance; and retirement benefits. These are usually paid by the employer. Health and fitness center managers are also allowed to use the center facilities at no cost.

EMPLOYMENT AND OUTLOOK

General and operations managers, of which health and fitness center managers are a part, held about 1.9 million jobs nationally in 2012. Employment is expected to grow slower than the average for all occupations through the year 2022, which means employment is projected to increase 3 percent to 6 percent. However, as more people begin to recognize the importance of personal fitness, the need for health and fitness center managers may increase and employment prospects improve. Opportunities for employment can be found in traditional health centers and also in places like resort and hotel spas and cruise ships.

Related Occupations
- Fitness Trainer & Instructor
- Recreation Program Director

Conversation With . . .
RYAN GROLL
Health and Fitness Center Manager, 2 years

1. What was your individual career path in terms of education/training, entry-level job, or other significant opportunity?

In high school, I got my first job in a health and fitness center working for minimum wage. When I turned 18, I got my first ACE personal training certification. I got my bachelor's degree from the University of Maryland in kinesiology. To get into the school is extremely difficult, so I had to take classes at Anne Arundel Community College and boost my credentials. When I finished, I pursued personal training at the University of Maryland, at 24 Hour Fitness in Annapolis, and moved up to master trainer. At night, I went to school for my master's in exercise physiology from McDaniel College. The owner of the club where I now work lives on the Eastern Shore of Maryland and used to commute an hour to the gym in Annapolis. I met him, we hit it off, and he would ask me for ideas. He wanted to open his own gym. He liked some of the ideas I had to offer, one thing led to another, and he brought me on as independent contractor to consult on equipment and how the fitness side of the gym would be run. Finally, he asked me if I wanted to be fitness director. At that time we also had a general manager, so the owner, GM and I worked hand-in-hand to build this from scratch, from the HR handbook to how we keep our clients. Six months after the business opened, we were doing phenomenally, the GM moved on and I stepped into that role, too.

Our area has a lot of weekenders and vacationers. It's a completely different crowd on weekends. The second home-owners come in at 10 or 11 o'clock to train, vs. the 9-to-5ers, who want to get in and out.

2. What are the most important skills and/or qualities for someone in your profession?

Being very knowledgeable is very important so your clients will get results and they won't get hurt. Equal or more is your charisma and confidence. You can be the smartest trainer out there, but if your clients don't trust you, you're not going to make a dramatic impact in their life. If you don't practice what you preach your clients can't take you seriously.

3. What do you wish you had known going into this profession?

When I first started, I thought clients would always come to me and that it would be easy as long as I was smart and knew what I was doing. I figured out that with more planning and relationships, years down the road those relationships blossom. Word of mouth is always best. You've got to talk to everybody, give out as much information as you can – and when something clicks and somebody wants to see a trainer, they will come to you.

4. Are there many job opportunities in your profession? In what specific areas?

The opportunity is there if you make it. If you want to be an independent contractor, go to the more dense cities; there's more of a need and want for that kind of service. East Coast and West Coast are big in fitness, and you do have to realize it's a service.

5. How do you see your profession changing in the next five years? What role will technology play in those changes, and what skills will be required?

As technology gets better, it helps and hinders. People think they can do more things on their own, with more apps and forums online, and they utilize that vs. going to a trainer. One thing technology can never erase is the accountability and motivation you get from a personal trainer.

6. What do you enjoy most about your job? What do you enjoy least?

I still love to impact people's lives. That's the whole reason I got into this industry. I'm glad I'm in an industry I'm passionate about. One of the harder things is that you can't really disconnect from your job. You'll have clients emailing you with their questions and concerns on a Saturday, or you'll text them: "Hey, hope you had a good workout." As a manager, the challenging part is to teach what I know to other trainers. Working with clients came naturally for me. I had to step back and realize it takes more than a month or two. You have to let them work out things and be there to help if they have questions.

7. Can you suggest a valuable "try this" for students considering a career in your profession?

Spend more time in the gym. I can't stress it enough. I brought on three new trainers and told them: you don't have clients yet, but be here to build confidence, build experience, and increase your awareness. Clients see you and they talk to you; they talk to you and they want to train with you. Also, you constantly have to stay on top of new trends and technology.

SELECTED SCHOOLS

Although it may not be necessary in every case to have a college degree to obtain work as a health and fitness center manager, many employers do prefer candidates with either an associates' or bachelor's degree in business, sports management, or a similar subject. Below are listed some of the more prominent institutions in this field.

Endicott College
376 Hale Street
Beverly, MA 01915
978.927.0585
www.endicott.edu

Indiana University, Bloomington
107 S. Indiana Avenue
Bloomington, IN 47405
812.855.4848
www.iub.edu

SUNY Cortland
38 Graham Avenue
Cortland, NY 13045
607.753.2011
www.cortland.edu

Tulane University
6823 St. Charles Avenue
New Orleans, LA 70118
504.865.5000
tulane.edu

University of Michigan
500 S. State Street
Ann Arbor, MI 48109
734.764.1817
www.umich.edu

University of Oregon
1585 E. 13th Avenue
Eugene, OR 97403
541.346.1000
uoregon.edu

University of Tampa
401 W. Kennedy Boulevard
Tampa, FL 33606
813.253.3333
www.ut.edu

University of Texas, Austin
1823 Red River Street
PO Box 8058
Austin, TX 78713
512.475.7440
www.utexas.edu

University of Tulsa
800 S. Tucker Drive
Tulsa, OK 74104
918.631.2000
www.utulsa.edu

West Chester University
700 S. High Street
West Chester, PA 19382
610.436.1000
www.wcupa.edu

MORE INFORMATION

American Fitness Professionals and Associates
1601 Long Beach Boulevard
P.O. Box 214
Ship Bottom, NJ 08008
800.494.7782
www.afpafitness.com

Club Managers Association of America
1733 King Street
Alexandria, VA 22314
703.739.9500
www.cmaa.org

Mid-Atlantic Club Management Association
5734 Wheelwright Way
Haymarket, VA 20169
888.596.2262
www.macmaclubs.org

National Gym Association
P.O. Box 970579
Coconut Creek, FL 33097
954.344.8410
www.nationalgym.com

National Independent Health Club Association
165 8th Avenue
Suite 1
Granite Falls, MN 56241
320.722.0084
www.nihca.org

John Pritchard/Editor

Life Coach

Snapshot

Career Cluster(s): Sports and Fitness
Interests: Interpersonal communication, self-employment, creativity, helping others
Earnings (Yearly Average): $61,900
Employment & Outlook: Unknown

OVERVIEW

Sphere of Work

Life coach is an emerging field that requires no specific background or education and involves helping individuals to meet life goals. Life coaches meet with potential clients, helping clients to identify goals, such as getting a better job, quitting smoking, losing weight, or any other life goal, and then help their clients develop strategies for achieving those goals. Life coaches may work with clients for weeks, months, or years depending on the specifics of a client's goals and how long the client wishes to employ the coach's services. Some life coaches have backgrounds in psychology and others have backgrounds in business or economics and

life coaches with different background may help clients in different ways. For instance, some life coaches specialize in helping clients solve personal or emotional issues, while others specialize in businesses or organizations, helping managers or employees to reach higher levels of productivity or communication.

Work Environment

Life coaches work in a variety of environments, but typically work indoors. Most life coaches are self-employed and many work out of their homes or private offices. Life coaching can be a full time or part-time job and many coaches work irregular hours, needing to be on hand for clients in different areas or on different schedules. Life coaches typically meet with individual clients or groups of clients in person, but may also communicate with clients via telephone or email.

Profile

Working Conditions: Work Indoors
Physical Strength: Light work
Education Needs: None
Licensure/Certification: Not Required
Opportunities For Experience: None
Holland Interest Score*: SI

* See Appendix A

Occupation Interest

Life coaching blends business acumen, therapeutic skills, logistics, and planning, and appeals to individuals who are highly organized, adept at research, and have a tendency to empathize and relate to others. Prospective life coaches should have an active interest in communicating with and helping others and should also have a strong interest in creative problem solving and research. In addition, because the vast majority of life coaches are self-employed, individuals interested in the field should be comfortable working alone and motivated enough to market themselves and their services as a coach. Because life coaches are expected to motivate their clients, a life coach should also be energetic and inspirational.

A Day in the Life—Duties and Responsibilities

A typical day for a life coach will depend on the needs of his or her clients. Life coaches specializing in business coaching, sometimes called "executive coaching," might spend part of a typical day meeting with executives or other members of an organization's staff. Life coaches guide clients through the coaching process, meeting with clients to establish goals and strategies for achieving them and then meeting with those same clients periodically to check on their progress and, when necessary, adjust their strategies for problem solving.

When not meeting with clients, life coaches spend time on marketing and other activities to find new clients or generate new business. For their existing clients, life coaches may need to spend time researching and planning for future meetings. Individual clients can present very different and unique goals and issues, and life coaches may often need to learn about the specifics of their clients' jobs, families, or other factors before being able to create a meaningful coaching plan for the client.

Duties and Responsibilities

- Prepare coaching plans and strategies for clients
- Research information needed for specific clients
- Market and advertise one's services as a life coach
- Meet with new clients or existing clients
- Speak with clients over the phone or communicate via email
- Attend professional development programs and networking events

OCCUPATION SPECIALTIES

Executive Coach

Executive coaches specialize in helping executives to organize their time and to better communicate with other executives and employees within an institution. Executive coaches are often hired to help executives plan for earning promotions or to help in institutions with communication problems between the management and workers.

Business Coach

Business coaches help business owners or prospective business owners to succeed in their professional goals. Coaches in this field may help with marketing, networking, workshopping, product development, or a variety of other factors involved in starting and operating a successful business.

Retirement Coach

Retirement coaches help individuals plan for and prepare for retirement. Coaches in this field can help clients decide when to retire, whether to continue working part-time after retirement, or how to make the most of their post-retirement time.

Relationship Coach

A relationship coach specializes in helping individuals or couples work on their relationships. Unlike therapists, who are trained in counseling and provide many of the same services, relationship coaches can help individuals at any stage of a relationship, or who are seeking to succeed in a future relationship, to realize their interpersonal goals.

WORK ENVIRONMENT

Relevant Skills and Abilities

Communication Skills
- Communicating with clients, other professionals, and family members
- Writing clear instructions/plans

Interpersonal/Social Skills
- Discussing sensitive and emotional subjects
- Frequently conversing with clients

Organization & Management Skills
- Creating schedules and plans for clients
- Managing time and scheduling appointments
- Marketing and advertising services

Research & Planning Skills
- Helping clients to organize and systematize coaching programs

Technical Skills
- Utilizing basic digital technology and personal computers

Physical Environment

Life coaches tend to work indoors and in private offices. Some life coaches may work out of their own homes or may visit clients in their homes or businesses. Life coaches typically meet with clients individually, but some life coaches specialize in working with groups, couples, or business teams and so the physical environment for a life coach may vary depending on their specialty and their current client(s).

Human Environment

Life coaches spend much of their time interacting with others. Life coaches meet with clients face-to-face, and also communicate with clients or prospective clients over the phone and through email. In addition to interacting with clients, in order to build business, life coaches may need to spend time meeting with other professionals or participating in professional development activities. In general, life coaching is an interactive discipline and prospective coaches need to be comfortable with frequent and often personal communication.

Technological Environment

While there are no specific technological tools or skills needed for life coaching, most life coaches use digital technology, including cell phones, tablets, or personal computers to communicate with clients, to schedule and organize their time, and for research. Because life coaching is a highly organizational discipline, life coaches will benefit from experience with creating and organizing spread sheets and using other types of organizational software tools.

EDUCATION, TRAINING, AND ADVANCEMENT

High School/Secondary

There are no specific educational requirements for those looking to become life coaches, but a well-rounded high school/secondary education is recommended. In addition, because life coaching involves communication, speaking, and writing, classes in public speaking, composition, English, and other related disciplines are helpful for those seeking to enter the field. For those looking to become financial or business coaches, a background in economics, business, and marketing may also be helpful. Furthermore, life coaching is a psychological discipline and a basic background in psychology is helpful for coaches in any of the various subdisciplines of the field.

Suggested High School Subjects
- English
- Composition
- World Languages
- Social Studies
- Computer Technology
- Psychology
- Business
- Economics

Famous First

The idea of lifestyle coaching became popular in the 1980s, and borrows from the venerable tradition of sports coaching in which a leader helps athletes to develop their athletic skills and to learn to work together as a team. Harvard University tennis player Tim Gallwey has been called a pioneer in the field as Gallwey described the qualities that made, in his opinion, good coaches in his book *The Inner Game of Tennis*. Gallwey went on to apply these same principles to helping individuals lead more fulfilling lives. The essence of Gallwey's concept of coaching is in helping individuals to develop tools to solve their own problems.

College/Postsecondary

While there are no specific degree requirements for life coaching, those with bachelor's or post-graduate degrees in psychology, business, finance, or economics may have an advantage in finding clients. There are specialized institutions, like the International Coach Federation, that offer training and certification programs specifically for those hoping to become life coaches. While such certification is not required, as the field grows and competition increases for clients, those with certification and/or specific training in various types of life coaching might have an advantage in the field. Educational goals may depend on what type of coach a person wishes to become, as those helping businesses, executives, or clients needing financial planning/assistance may want to focus on studying marketing, economics, and finance, while those hoping to help clients with personal or relationship goals may focus on psychology or studying professional counselling and social work. In addition, because most life coaches are self-employed, prospective coaches will benefit from any classes or educational programs that help entrepreneurs learn how to start, operate, and grow a business, including marketing, advertising, web development, and similar subjects.

Related College Majors

- Psychology
- Abnormal psychology
- Business

- Marketing
- Finance
- Economics
- Counseling
- Social Work

Adult Job Seekers

Adults hoping to become life coaches can essentially begin by starting to market their services to potential customers. As there are no specific educational requirements, a life coach can start a successful business as long as the coach is able to market his or her services to clients. To find clients, prospective coaches might consider attending seminars and/or professional workshops for life coaching or related disciplines and networking is often key to finding new clients and growing one's coaching business.

Professional Certification and Licensure

The International Coach Federation offers certificates in various types of life coaching, which can help a coach to stand out from competition when seeking clients. As of 2017, life coaches are not required to have any professional certification or licenses to operate a life coaching business.

Additional Requirements

Life coaches need to be enthusiastic and self-motivated and able to empathize with their clients. More than technical know-how, life coaching is a field that requires emotional and personal connectivity and sensitivity. Life coaches are often required to cope with their clients' stress and so should be able to handle stress well and to come up with creative strategies for coping with stress, fear, and other challenges that clients must face.

Fun Fact

Professional coaching can deliver progress in a surprisingly short amount of time—even three sessions a month for 20 to 45 minutes per session.

Source: cbsnews.com

EARNINGS AND ADVANCEMENT

As of 2017, the Bureau of Labor Statistics (BLS) and the Department of Labor do not collect information on the field of life coaching specifically, but compare the field to the related fields of rehabilitation counselors, educational or vocational counselors and personal care or service workers. School and career counselors earn an average of $53,660 per year, while the BLS estimates the average for all types of coaches at closer to $61,900, with those at the lowest 10 percent of the field earning less than $32,000 and those at the higher end earning over $80,000. Because most life coaches are self-employed, advancing in the industry is typically a matter of finding new clients or gaining sufficient experience and reputation that a coach can begin charging more for his or her services. For executive or business coaches, advancing in the field may involve building a reputation sufficient to be hired as a coach to work in larger or more lucrative companies.

Metropolitan Areas with the Highest
Employment Level in this Occupation

Metropolitan area	Employment	Employment per thousand jobs	Hourly mean wage
New York-Jersey City-White Plains, NY-NJ Metropolitan Division	13,740	2.12	$32.89
Los Angeles-Long Beach-Glendale, CA Metropolitan Division	8,110	1.98	$31.06
Chicago-Naperville-Arlington Heights, IL Metropolitan Division	6,040	1.69	$29.29
Phoenix-Mesa-Scottsdale, AZ	5,880	3.13	$22.40
Atlanta-Sandy Springs-Roswell, GA	5,020	2.03	$28.21
Houston-The Woodlands-Sugar Land, TX	4,610	1.57	$28.52
Washington-Arlington-Alexandria, DC-VA-MD-WV Metropolitan Division	4,520	1.87	$33.14
Dallas-Plano-Irving, TX Metropolitan Division	3,980	1.71	$29.70
Boston-Cambridge-Newton, MA NECTA Division	3,170	1.80	$29.96
Baltimore-Columbia-Towson, MD	2,950	2.25	$27.88

Source: Bureau of Labor Statistics

EMPLOYMENT AND OUTLOOK

According to the International Coach Federation's 2016 ICF Global Coaching Study, there were 17,500 life coaches working in North America in 2015, though the organization has collected no measurements indicating how fast the field is currently growing in comparison with the 6-7 percent average growth of all U.S. occupations expected between 2014 and 2024. Growth in the field may depend on whether life coaching grows to become a standard career path, which might mean that colleges and universities will more often offer training in the field. The U.S. Bureau of Labor Statistics (BLS) does not collect data specifically on life coaches. Instead, BLS counts these workers among rehabilitation counselors; educational, guidance, school, and vocational counselors; and personal care and service workers, all other.

Employment Trend, Projected 2014–24

Counselors, social workers, and other community and social service specialists: 12%

Rehabilitation counselors: 9%

Total, all occupations: 7%

Note: "All Occupations" includes all occupations in the U.S. Economy. Source: U.S. Bureau of Labor Statistics, Employment Projections Program

Related Occupations
- Social Workers
- Human Resource Specialists
- Mental Health Counselors and Marriage and Family Therapists
- Psychologists
- Rehabilitation Counselors
- Social and Community Service Managers
- Social and Human Service Assistants
- Substance Abuse and Behavioral Disorder Counselors

Conversation With . . .
LAUREN SEAMAN

Yoga Teacher, Personal Trainer
Health and Wellness Coach, Honolulu, Hawaii
Fitness field, 8 years

1. What was your individual career path in terms of education/training, entry-level job, or other significant opportunity?

I was an athlete growing up, and went to Louisiana State University on a full tennis scholarship. Right after graduating with a degree in mass communications, I went backpacking in Southeast Asia with two friends and ended up teaching English in Vientiane, Laos for a year. When I returned home to New Orleans, a contact helped me get a job waiting tables in a fine dining establishment in the French Quarter. But I got tired of that, so I started teaching tennis clinics and lessons.

During this time, I fell in love with yoga and completed a one-month training to become certified as a yoga teacher at Nosara Yoga Institute in Costa Rica. I began teaching on the side at the country club where I was already teaching tennis.

Five years ago, I moved to Honolulu after my boyfriend got a job here. I started out working at the Honolulu YWCA as a health and wellness coordinator and member services associate. One day I started talking with a woman who had a business that placed personal trainers and yoga teachers in Waikiki hotels. She asked if I wanted to teach yoga and do personal training, so I started doing that on the side. After being in Hawaii about a year, I got certified as a personal trainer through AFAA (Athletics and Fitness Association of America). Over time, I built up my personal training clients and yoga classes. In addition, I'm back to teaching tennis a couple of times a week.

But I wanted to connect more personally with people and help them take charge of their health and well-being. So, two years ago, I did a nine-month health and wellness coach training program called Wellcoaches based in Boston. I've been certified for a year and am still building my clientele. However, I get to talk to my clients about their hopes, dreams, vision – and their struggles, and how they might be able to overcome them by designing small goals and plans to make incremental change. I'm working to create a thriving health and wellness coaching business that positively changes people's lives.

2. What are the most important skills and/or qualities for someone in your profession?

Friendliness, a positive outlook, caring for the people you work with and having their best interests at heart, and possessing a baseline knowledge of safe movement techniques.

3. What do you wish you had known going into this profession?

That you don't have to know everything or be an amazing yoga teacher when you start. The classes you teach can still provide a gift to others. Also, the better you understand where your clients are coming from, the better you can serve them.

4. Are there many job opportunities in your profession? In what specific areas?

There are always opportunities to teach yoga at a studio or train people at a gym. However, you have to create the better-paying opportunities yourself, like teaching classes outdoors in a park, or in a workplace. That allows you to establish a fixed rate and gives you a dependable income.

5. How do you see your profession changing in the next five years, what role will technology play in those changes, and what skills will be required?

People are busy, so more and more they enjoy online yoga classes either on YouTube or through membership websites. However, there will always be people who love to physically go to a studio or gym and practice with other people, or with a trainer one on one—so I don't see that need lessening as technology evolves. I think it is important for trainers, teachers and coaches to have a website to market themselves. List your credentials, explain your approach and what you have to offer, and include testimonials.

If you can make successful YouTube videos that do well in terms of viewership and the ads contribute to your income, more power to you.

6. What do you enjoy most about your job? What do you enjoy least about your job?

I most enjoy interacting with others in a hands-on, dynamic, positive way, rather than being stuck in a desk, in front of a computer, in a cubicle. I love that my work helps uplift people and makes them feel better. I love that I'm helping them do something that is good for them.

I least enjoy the very early morning wake-up calls that are usually required of personal trainers, since many clients like to work out before work. Those are difficult if you can't go to sleep early in order to get a full night's rest. Also, income can be unstable. For example, if a main training client leaves for two weeks and I can't fill his regularly-scheduled slot, I can't count on that income.

7. Can you suggest a valuable "try this" for students considering a career in your profession?

Ask to shadow a coach, trainer or teacher. Also, many yoga studios offer free classes in exchange for helping out a certain number of hours each week. Just ask!

MORE INFORMATION

American Coaching Association
2141 Birch Drive
Lafayette Hill, PA 19444
610-825-4505
www.americoach.org

International Coach Federation (ICF)
2365 Harrodsburg, Rd, Suite A325
Lexington, KY 40504
888-423-3131
www.coachfederation.org

International Association of Coaching
www.certifiedcoach.org
info@certifiedcoach.org

Micah Issitt/Editor

Marketing Manager

Snapshot

Career Cluster: Business Administration; Media & Communications; Sales & Marketing

Interests: Animals and Animal Maintenance and Training

Earnings (Yearly Average): $123,220

Employment & Outlook: Average Growth Expected

OVERVIEW

Sphere of Work

Marketing managers work as staff members in corporate marketing and advertising departments. They can also work in specialized ad agencies or marketing firms. Their work falls within the communication, information, and business sectors. They serve as one of the main links or points of contact between the marketplace and the company or agency for which they work. Advertising and marketing managers coordinate print, television, radio, and digital media advertising campaigns and projects; in some cases, they may also be responsible for sales and developing new business opportunities.

While advertising and marketing managers contribute to campaign development, they are not technically part of an agency's creative (or design) team. Their primary role is to ensure that campaigns are priced, administered, and executed smoothly and efficiently, and with the company's (or client's) interests in mind. They ensure that campaign milestones are met and elements of the campaign are delivered on time and within budget. Aside from working closely with the director of advertising and marketing, they coordinate the work activities of personnel such as copywriters, graphic designers, production assistants, public relations personnel, and market researchers. They may interact with sales representatives and have additional project management responsibilities, as well. Advertising and marketing managers are generally supervised by a departmental director or client services supervisor.

Work Environment

Advertising and marketing managers work in an office environment within small to large companies or agencies. Air and car travel may be occasionally required to attend trade conferences or meet with clients. Evening and weekend work is also often required. Advertising and marketing managers frequently work under pressure and adhere to strict budgets and tight deadlines.

Profile

Working Conditions: Work Indoors
Physical Strength: Light Work
Education Needs: Bachelor's Degree
Licensure/Certification: Usually Not Required
Physical Abilities Not Required: No Heavy Labor
Opportunities For Experience: Internship, Apprenticeship, Volunteer Work
Holland Interest Score*: AES

* See Appendix A

Occupation Interest

Graduates and professionals with a strong interest in advertising and marketing, mass media and communications, and project management are often attracted to the advertising industry. In particular, the role suits people who have an interest in coordinating multiple activities in a fast-paced environment and who are comfortable working closely with others.

Aside from excellent collaborative, communication, and organizational skills, advertising and marketing managers must also possess strong research and analytical skills and solid business acumen. They may be expected to formulate and execute budgets, monitor expenses, and assist with financial reporting. In some instances, they will be expected to make sales calls or develop and present new business proposals.

Successful advertising and marketing managers must be able to speak and write fluently, work with a diverse range of people, adapt to new industries, clients, products and services, and deliver consistent results under pressure. The role also requires considerable tact and diplomacy.

A Day in the Life—Duties and Responsibilities

The typical work day of an advertising and marketing manager includes frequent meetings with staff, supervisors, department heads, and, in the case of independent agencies, clients. The campaign deliverables, which advertising and marketing managers coordinate, are usually subject to tight timeframes and strict deadlines. Therefore, on a daily basis, the role demands excellent organizational and time management skills. Advertising and marketing managers must be adept at multi-tasking, adapting to change, and problem solving.

Advertising and marketing managers generally gain a high level of exposure to different customer types, industries, products, and services (although some may specialize in specific industries). The role demands high business (and possibly sales) acumen and the ability to analyze new information quickly and effectively. An advertising and marketing manager is expected to thoroughly research and understand the industry in which their company operates, as well as their competitors and any competing products and marketing campaigns. This includes developing a deep understanding of the company's (or client's) customer base, methods and processes, challenges and opportunities, and target markets.

Advertising and marketing managers are expected to have competent computing skills to help them prepare campaign-related and organizational materials, such as financial and marketing reports, budget proposals, "pitches" (presentations) to acquire new business, and other work-related documents. They may also be expected to develop and manage spreadsheets and databases for project management and accounting purposes.

Duties and Responsibilities

- Preparing advertising and marketing campaigns, schedules, and budgets
- Consulting with people in sales, market research, and creative departments
- Overseeing staff in layout, copy, and production

OCCUPATION SPECIALTIES

Advertising Managers

Advertising managers seek to generate interest in a product or service by means of ads placed in various media. They work with sales staff and others to create ideas for an advertising campaign. Some advertising managers specialize in a particular field or type of advertising. For example, media directors determine the way in which an advertising campaign reaches customers; they can use any or all of various media, including radio, television, newspapers, magazines, the Internet, and outdoor signs. Advertising managers known as account executives manage clients' accounts, but they do not necessarily develop or supervise the creation or presentation of the advertising. That is the work of the creative services department.

Marketing Managers

Marketing managers gather and use data to estimate the demand for products and services that an organization and its competitors offer. They identify potential markets, develop pricing strategies to help maximize profits, and ensure that customers are satisfied (by using surveys, etc.). They work with sales, advertising, and product development staffs to identify and target customers and keep the firm's products or services competitive in the marketplace. In smaller firms individuals may function as both marketing and advertising managers as well as promotions managers.

Promotions Managers

Promotions managers oversee programs that combine advertising with purchasing incentives to increase sales. Often, the programs use direct mail, inserts in newspapers, Internet advertisements, in-store displays, product endorsements, or special events to target customers. Purchasing incentives may include discounts, samples, gifts, rebates, coupons, sweepstakes, and contests.

WORK ENVIRONMENT

Relevant Skills and Abilities

Analytical Skills
- Critical thinking and reasoning
- Information processing

Communication Skills
- Listening to others
- Persuading others
- Speaking and writing effectively

Interpersonal/Social Skills
- Being able to work both independently and on a team
- Cooperating with others
- Having good judgment
- Motivating others

Organization & Management Skills
- Making sound decisions
- Managing time and money
- Meeting goals and deadlines
- Paying attention to and handling details
- Solving problems
- Supervising others as necessary

Other Skills
- Appreciating both the business and the creative sides

Physical Environment

Office settings predominate. Advertising and marketing managers work for small to large advertising and marketing departments or agencies, usually in urban or semi-urban locations. Some travel may be required.

Job security is sometimes tenuous in the advertising industry. Economic or sector downturns, changes to a firm's customer base, or reduced customer spending can lead to layoffs. This tends to create an atmosphere of intense competition.

Human Environment

Advertising and marketing manager roles demand strong collaborative and team skills. Advertising and marketing managers interact with sales, advertising, business, and creative specialists, such as brand and product managers, marketing managers, brand strategists, public relations executives, graphic designers, art directors, multimedia technicians, copywriters, production assistants, and editors. They are likely to work with multiple departmental or client contacts, as well as outside service providers or freelancers. They usually report to an agency/department director or owner, or to an area supervisor.

Technological Environment

Advertising and marketing managers use standard business technologies, including computer systems and networks, telecommunications tools, Internet and social media tools, presentation tools and software, and financial and database software. In smaller firms, where greater overlap between marketing and design functions often exists, managers sometimes need to be familiar with graphic design software and basic production technologies (such as desktop publishing).

EDUCATION, TRAINING, AND ADVANCEMENT

High School/Secondary

High school students can best prepare for a career as an advertising and marketing manager by taking courses in business, math (with an accounting focus), computer literacy, and communications (for example, journalism or business communications). Courses such as social studies, history, and economics will also prepare the student for synthesizing research into written materials. The creative aspects of the advertising industry may be explored through art and graphic design. However, it is important to note that advertising and marketing managers work in an administrative, rather than a creative, capacity. In addition, psychology and cultural studies may provide an understanding of group and individual responses to advertising and other forms of communication.

Students should also become involved in extracurricular school activities and projects that develop business and communication skills to gain hands-on experience prior to graduation. Additionally, serving as a club secretary, treasurer, or other office holder will help to develop organizational skills. Participation in student newsletters and similar publications will help to build an understanding of print and multimedia communications.

Suggested High School Subjects
- Business Data Processing
- Business Math
- Communications
- Composition
- Computer Science
- Economics
- English
- Graphic Arts
- Journalism
- Psychology
- Statistics

Famous First

The first use of coupons in a promotional campaign was in 1865, when soap maker B. T. Babbitt of New York City began selling soap bars in wrappers. He printed the word "coupon" on the wrapper and gave away a lithographic print for every 10 coupons returned. The strategy was so successful that Babbitt had to create a "premium department" to manage this and other such giveaways.

College/Postsecondary

At the college level, students interested in becoming an advertising and marketing manager should work toward earning an undergraduate degree in communications, advertising, marketing, or business administration. Alternatively, they should build a strong liberal arts background. Owing to strong competition among professional business candidates, a master's degree is sometimes expected, although practical experience is often more highly regarded than formal qualifications.

A large number of colleges and universities offer advertising, marketing, communications, and business degree programs. Some programs offer internships or work experience with advertising departments or agencies. These experiences may lead to entry-level opportunities. Aspiring advertising and marketing managers can also gain entry into the advertising industry via other roles, such as market research, administration, or sales.

Related College Majors
- Advertising
- Business Administration
- Communications
- Journalism
- Management/Management Science
- Marketing & Merchandising
- Psychology
- Public Relations
- Statistics

Adult Job Seekers

Adults seeking a career transition into or return to an advertising and marketing manager role will need to highlight qualifications, skills, and experience in areas such as business administration, advertising, and marketing. Necessary skills for a successful transition include account coordination, client liaison, and project management.

Marketing and advertising experience with a non-agency corporation is often highly regarded because agency firms value employees who understand the client side of the relationship.

Networking is critical—candidates should not rely solely on online job searches and advertised positions to explore work opportunities. As with recent college graduates, adult job seekers may wish to consider entry to the advertising industry via an alternative route, such as market research, administration, or sales.

Professional Certification and Licensure

There are no formal professional certifications or licensing requirements for advertising and marketing managers.

Additional Requirements

The most important attributes for advertising and marketing managers are a passion for advertising and marketing communications, coupled with excellent business, organizational, and people skills. Advertising and marketing managers must be skilled and diplomatic coordinators, negotiators, and problem solvers. They should be willing to persist under often heavy workloads and with demanding stakeholders.

Fun Facts

Marketers are using Facebook and Twitter more and more to take advantage of the fact that one of every seven minutes users surf the web is spent on Facebook, and 340 million Tweets were posted each day in 2012.
Source: http://www.i7marketing.com/internetmarketing/10-interesting-social-media-facts/

Minor League Baseball was founded in 1901 as the National Association of Professional Baseball Leagues, and has been headquartered out of St. Petersburg, Fla., since 1973.
Source: ircgov.com

EARNINGS AND ADVANCEMENT

Earning potential increases as advancement occurs. Advancement may be quick in corporate ranks, partly because turnover can be high as a result of account success or failure. Many firms provide their employees with continuing education opportunities, either in-house or at local colleges and universities, and encourage employee participation in seminars and conferences.

According to a salary survey by the National Association of Colleges and Employers, graduates with a bachelor's degree in advertising had starting salaries of $47,343 in 2012. Advertising and marketing managers had median annual earnings of $123,220 in 2013. The lowest ten percent earned less than $65,000, and the highest ten percent earned more than $200,000. Performance incentives and bonuses are granted according to the employee's record of performance.

Advertising and marketing managers may receive paid vacations, holidays, and sick days; life and health insurance; and retirement benefits. These are usually paid by the employer. Top executives in the field may receive additional benefits (such as stock options).

Metropolitan Areas with the Highest Employment Level in This Occupation

Metropolitan area	Employment[1]	Employment per thousand jobs	Hourly mean wage
New York-White Plains-Wayne, NY-NJ	11,630	2.22	$85.29
Los Angeles-Long Beach-Glendale, CA	7,360	1.85	$65.55
Chicago-Joliet-Naperville, IL	7,100	1.92	$55.55
Minneapolis-St. Paul-Bloomington, MN-WI	6,460	3.61	$61.66
Boston-Cambridge-Quincy, MA	5,780	3.31	$67.72
San Jose-Sunnyvale-Santa Clara, CA	5,320	5.72	$88.36
San Francisco-San Mateo-Redwood City, CA	4,700	4.50	$83.57
Washington-Arlington-Alexandria, DC-VA-MD-WV	4,330	1.83	$73.15
Atlanta-Sandy Springs-Marietta, GA	4,300	1.86	$64.06
Santa Ana-Anaheim-Irvine, CA	3,570	2.46	$70.23

[1] Does not include self-employed. Source: Bureau of Labor Statistics.

EMPLOYMENT AND OUTLOOK

There were approximately 215,000 advertising and marketing managers employed nationally in 2012. Positions exist not only in advertising agencies, but also with public relations firms, printing and publishing firms, computer services firms, and many others. There is also a strong demand for advertising and marketing managers in the non-profit sector, including colleges/universities and philanthropic organizations. Employment is expected to grow about as fast as the average for all occupations through the year 2022, which means employment is projected to increase 10 percent to 15 percent. Increasingly intense domestic and global competition in products and services offered to consumers should require greater need for this occupation as companies want to maintain and expand their share of the market.

Many of the high-level jobs are very competitive. College graduates with extensive experience, a high level of creativity, and strong communication skills should have the best job opportunities.

Employment Trend, Projected 2012–22

Marketing Managers: 13%

Advertising, Promotions, and Marketing Managers: 12%

Total, All Occupations: 11%

Advertising and Promotions Managers: 7%

Note: "All Occupations" includes all occupations in the U.S. Economy. Source: U.S. Bureau of Labor Statistics, Employment Projections Program.

Related Occupations
- Advertising Director
- Advertising Sales Agent
- Copywriter
- Electronic Commerce Specialist
- Market Research Analyst
- Public Relations Specialist
- Sales Manager

Conversation With . . .
BRANDAN KAISER

Director of Marketing, Bowie Baysox
Bowie, Maryland
Baseball marketing manager, 11 years

1. What was your individual career path in terms of education/training, entry-level job, or other significant opportunity?

I played baseball through high school in Lancaster, PA and after college. I knew I wanted to work in sports, so I studied sport management at Flagler College in St. Augustine, FL. From there, I came to the Bowie Baysox Minor League Baseball team as an intern. I started as Louie, the mascot, and worked my way up from there. I spent a couple of years doing group sales at another Minor League Baseball team in Maryland, the Frederick Keys. Then I returned, selling sponsorships and billboards and doing on-field promotions, and moved up to become the director of marketing.

Flagler is a small school so you get to know the teachers and the department chairs. They knew people, and they really stressed getting experience wherever you can. The World Golf Hall of Fame is up the road and I interned there, which was a good icebreaker to see what it's like on the professional side of sports.

You don't start in marketing. Most people get experience in sales, and that's a springboard to other things.

2. What are the most important skills and/or qualities for someone in your profession?

Good communication skills. A willingness to dive in and do what needs to be done to complete a job.

3. What do you wish you had known going into this profession?

The hours are long. Working in minor league sports, you wear a lot of hats. For instance, I'm the back-up on-field emcee, which started because the regular emcee couldn't make it one day. In marketing, you learn that nothing is beneath you; something always has to be done and somebody has to do it.

4. Are there many job opportunities in your profession? In what specific areas?

There can be a lot of different opportunities. On the minor league side, you have a smaller staff and do a lot of different things. In Major League Baseball or the National Football League, there's a lot more segmentation in a staff. For instance, there might be a vice president of marketing, a separate person who handles promotions, and so on.

Here, I can have a lot of creativity, do a lot more and not be pigeonholed. You have more independence.

5. How do you see your profession changing in the next five years, what role will technology play in those changes, and what skills will be required?

The biggest change will be the role of social media: keeping up with it and seeing what's next. How can we use it to let people know what we're doing and effectively market our games, teams and players? It never ends. You have to pick the platforms that best fit your audience. Do you want 10 spread thin? Or three or four you can focus on and build? We have one or two people working on social media and we have to focus on what makes sense for our organization.

6. What do you enjoy most about your job? What do you enjoy least about your job?

Being a baseball fan, I love being around sports and working at a baseball stadium. Even at lunch, I can walk out of the office and there's a baseball field! Also, every day is different. There's a mascot floating around the office, we may have a celebrity come in, I may interact with the players. But it's a lot of hours and 70 home games, which means a lot of time away from my family. I end up missing a lot in the summer —but that goes with the gig.

7. Can you suggest a valuable "try this" for students considering a career in your profession?

If there's a professional team of any level near your hometown, try to get an unpaid internship with them, or just shadow. It's a way to see what it's like and what you'd be getting into. We have eight or nine students interning every summer, and every year we have some who say, "I had a good time, but maybe that's not for me." For others, the experience solidifies that this is what they want to do.

SELECTED SCHOOLS

Many colleges and universities, especially those with business schools, offer programs in marketing and advertising. The student can also gain initial training at a technical or community college. Below are listed some of the more prominent institutions in this field.

Indiana University, Bloomington
Kelley School of Business
1309 E. 10th Street
Bloomington, IN 47405
812.855.8100
kelley.iu.edu

New York University
Stern School of Business
665 Broadway, 11th Floor
New York, NY 10012
212.998.4500
www.stern.nyu.edu

University of California, Berkeley
Haas School of Business
S450 Student Services
Building #1900
Berkeley, CA 94720
510.642.1421
haas.berkeley.edu

University of Michigan, Ann Arbor
Ross School of Business
701 Tappan Avenue
Ann Arbor, MI 48109
734.763.5796
michiganross.umich.edu

University of North Carolina, Chapel Hill
Kenan-Flagler Business School
Campus Box 3490, McColl Building
Chapel Hill, NC 27599
919.962.3235
www.kenan-flagler.unc.edu

University of Pennsylvania
The Wharton School
1 College Hall
Philadelphia, PA 19104
215.898.6376
www.whatron.upenn.edu

University of Southern California
Marshall School of Business
3670 Trousdale Parkway
Los Angeles, CA 90089
213.740.8674
www.marshall.usc.edu

University of Texas, Austin
McCombs School of Business
1 University Station, B6000
Austin, TX 78712
512.471.5921
www.mccombs.utexas.edu

University of Virginia
McIntire School of Commerce
125 Ruppel Drive
PO Box 400173
Charlottseville, VA 22903
434.924.3176
www.commerce.virginia.edu

University of Wisconsin, Madison
Wisconsin School of Business
Grainger Hall
975 University Avenue
Madison, WI 53706
608.262.1550
bus.wisc.edu

MORE INFORMATION

Advertising Research Foundation
432 Park Avenue South, 6th Floor
New York, NY 10016-8013
212.751.5656
thearf.org

Advertising Women of New York
25 West 45th Street, Suite 403
New York, NY 10036
212.221.7969
www.awny.org

American Advertising Federation
1101 Vermont Avenue, NW
Suite 500
Washington, DC 20005-6306
800.999.2231
www.aaf.org

American Association of Advertising Agencies
405 Lexington Avenue, 18th Floor
New York, NY 10174-1801
212.682.2500
www.aaaa.org

American Marketing Association
311 S. Wacker Drive
Suite 5800
Chicago, IL 60606
312.542.9000
www.marketingpower.com

Association of National Advertisers
708 Third Avenue, 33rd Floor
New York, NY 10017-4270
212.697.5950
www.ana.net

Kylie Grimshaw Hughes/Editor

Occupational Therapist

Snapshot

Career Cluster: Health Care; Human Services
Interests: Health, biology, psychology, anatomy, record keeping, physical therapy
Earnings (Yearly Average): $76,940
Employment & Outlook: Faster Than Average Growth Expected

OVERVIEW

Sphere of Work

Occupational therapists provide therapeutic services aimed at helping variously disabled people perform everyday tasks in their life and work. Occupational therapists treat people with temporary and chronic motor function impairments caused by mental, physical, developmental, or emotional issues. An occupational therapist may help patients with skills such as self-care (dressing, eating), household care (cleaning, cooking), using communication devices such as telephones and computers, and such

basic activities as writing, problem-solving, memory, and coordination. Occupational therapists develop patient treatment plans that attempt to maintain, develop, or recover a patient's daily functioning, productivity, and quality of life.

Work Environment

Occupational therapists work in settings such as rehabilitation facilities, hospitals, nursing homes, occupational therapy clinics, and schools. In medical environments, occupational therapists generally partner with medical and social service professionals, such as doctors and social workers, to increase patients' physical and mental abilities and overall independence. In school settings, occupational therapists partner with educational professionals such as teachers and special education coordinators to address the physical or mental issues of students with special needs. Occupational therapy is a common component of a special needs child's individualized education plan (IEP). Occupational therapists generally work a standard 40-hour week, and scheduled appointments are the norm.

Profile

Working Conditions: Work Indoors
Physical Strength: Medium Work
Education Needs: Master's Degree
Licensure/Certification: Required
Physical Abilities Not Required: No Heavy Labor
Opportunities For Experience: Internship, Military Service, Part-Time Work
Holland Interest Score*: SRE

* See Appendix A

Occupation Interest

Individuals attracted to the field of occupational therapy tend to be physically capable people who enjoy hands-on work and close interaction with others. Individuals who excel as occupational therapists exhibit traits such as intellectual curiosity, problem solving, a desire to help, patience, and caring. Occupational therapists must be good at science and able to work as part of a team to meet patient needs.

A Day in the Life—Duties and Responsibilities

An occupational therapist's daily occupational duties and responsibilities include full days of hands-on patient interaction and treatment as well as administrative duties. Patients seen by occupational therapists include those experiencing physical limitations caused by accident or injury, stroke, or congenital conditions such as cerebral palsy or muscular dystrophy; other patients may require services due to developmental delays, learning disabilities, or mental retardation.

As a medical or therapeutic professional, occupational therapists interact with patients or clients on a daily basis. Daily work responsibilities may include conducting patient assessments; developing patient treatment plans; providing patients with special instruction in life skills; advising patients on the use of adaptive equipment such as wheelchairs or orthopedic aids; providing early intervention services to young children with physical and social delays and limitations; building adaptive equipment for patients with special needs not met by existing options; providing instruction in self-care such as dressing and eating; counseling patients on technical or physical adaptations that will allow the patient to continue to work at his or her chosen occupation; and meeting with patient treatment team or patient families.

An occupational therapist's daily administrative responsibilities include the record keeping involved with patient evaluation and treatment. Occupational therapists must draft treatment plans, record notes following patient treatment sessions, provide written updates to patient treatment teams, and provide insurance companies with patient records and progress notes as required. Independent occupational therapists working outside of a school or medical clinic may also be responsible for patient appointment scheduling and billing.

Duties and Responsibilities

- Testing and evaluating patients' physical and mental abilities
- Designing special equipment to aid disabled patients
- Instructing and informing patients how to adjust to home, work and social environments
- Evaluating patients' progress, attitudes and behavior

OCCUPATION SPECIALTIES

Directors of Occupational Therapy

Directors of Occupational Therapy plan, direct and coordinate occupational therapy programs in hospitals, institutions and community settings to facilitate the rehabilitation of those who are physically, mentally or emotionally disabled.

Industrial Therapists

Industrial Therapists arrange salaried, productive employment in an actual work environment for disabled patients, to enable them to perform medically prescribed work activities and to prepare them to resume employment outside of the hospital environment.

WORK ENVIRONMENT

Physical Environment

Occupational therapists work in rehabilitation facilities, hospitals, nursing homes, therapy clinics, and schools. Therapeutic office settings used by occupational therapists may be shared with other therapeutic professionals such as physical, recreational, or speech and language therapists.

Human Environment

Examples of patients needing occupational therapy to increase their independence and quality of life include people suffering balance and strength issues caused by cerebral palsy, spinal cord injuries, or muscular dystrophy; stroke victims experiencing memory loss or coordination problems; people experiencing mental health problems; and children or adults with developmental disabilities. Occupational therapists usually work as part of a patient treatment team that includes patient families, social workers, teachers, doctors, and other therapists. As a member of a treatment team, occupational therapists participate in frequent team meetings and are responsible for communicating patient progress to fellow team members.

Relevant Skills and Abilities

Interpersonal/Social Skills
- Being able to remain calm
- Cooperating with others
- Teaching others
- Working as a member of a team

Organization & Management Skills
- Coordinating tasks
- Demonstrating leadership
- Making decisions
- Managing people/groups
- Meeting goals and deadlines
- Paying attention to and handling details
- Performing duties that change frequently

Research & Planning Skills
- Creating ideas

Technological Environment

Occupational therapists use a wide variety of technology in their work. Computers and Internet communication tools are a ubiquitous part of occupational therapy work. Occupational therapists often introduce specialized computer programs to patients that need help with their reasoning, problem solving, memory, and sequencing. In addition, occupational therapists generally learn how to use and teach adaptive devices such as wheelchairs, orthopedic aids, eating aids, and dressing aids.

EDUCATION, TRAINING, AND ADVANCEMENT

High School/Secondary

High school students interested in pursuing the profession of occupational therapy in the future should pursue coursework in biology, psychology, anatomy, sociology, and mathematics to prepare for college-level studies. Students interested in the occupational therapy field will benefit from seeking internships or part time work with occupational therapists or people with physical, developmental, or social problems that have an impact on their daily lives.

Suggested High School Subjects
- Algebra
- Applied Biology/Chemistry
- Applied Communication
- Arts
- Biology
- Chemistry
- College Preparatory
- Composition
- Crafts
- English
- Health Science Technology
- Physical Education
- Physical Science
- Physiology
- Psychology
- Science
- Sociology

Famous First

The first occupational therapy program began at Johns Hopkins University, pictured, in the early 20th century. At that time it was called "habit training," and its goal was to provide persons with mental disabilities the basic skills they needed to handle everyday tasks and live a productive life. Patients were given goal-directed activities such as weaving, broom-making, or bookbinding to focus their efforts and allow them to develop industrious habits.

College/Postsecondary

Occupational therapists are typically required to have a master's degree or higher in their field. Interested college students should complete coursework in occupational therapy, if offered by their school, as well as courses in physical therapy, special education, biology, psychology, anatomy, sociology, and mathematics. Students interested in attending graduate school in occupational therapy will benefit from seeking internships or work with occupational therapists, people with impaired functioning, or as occupational therapy assistants or special education aides. A student membership in the American Occupational Therapy Association may provide networking opportunities and connections.

Related College Majors
- Anatomy
- Exercise Science/Physiology/Movement Studies
- Human & Animal Physiology
- Occupational Therapy

Adult Job Seekers

Adult job seekers in the occupational therapy field should generally have completed master's or doctoral training in occupational therapy from an accredited university (as determined by the Accreditation Council for Occupational Therapy Education (ACOTE)), as well as earned the necessary professional licensure. Occupational therapists seeking employment will benefit from the networking opportunities, job workshops and job lists offered by professional occupational therapy associations such as the American Occupational Therapy Association.

Professional Certification and Licensure

Occupational therapists are required to have a professional occupational therapy license prior to beginning their professional practice. Upon completion of an accredited master's or doctoral program in occupational therapy, candidates take a national occupational therapy licensing exam and, if successful, earn the Occupational Therapist Registered (OTR) title. In addition to national licensing, occupational therapists are required to register with their state health board and engage in continuing education as a condition of their license. State licensing boards generally have additional requirements for occupational therapists choosing to specialize in early education, mental health, or gerontological occupational therapy.

Additional Requirements

Occupational therapists fundamentally enjoy helping other people achieve greater freedom and independence in their daily lives. They find satisfaction working in health care or educational environments with special needs populations. High levels of integrity and ethics are required of occupational therapists, as they work with confidential and personal patient information. Membership in professional occupational therapy associations is encouraged among junior and senior occupational therapists as a means of building status within a professional community and networking. Successful occupational therapists engage in ongoing professional development.

Fun Fact

The young profession of occupational therapy became more widely known after World War I, when "restorative activities were found to be beneficial for rehabilitating war veterans with severe injury."

Source: http://www.therapy-directory.org.uk/articles/occupational-therapy.html

EARNINGS AND ADVANCEMENT

Earnings of occupational therapists depend on the individual's education and experience and the type and geographic location of the employer. Those in private practice generally earned more than salaried workers. Occupational therapists in public elementary or secondary schools were sometimes classified as teachers and received pay accordingly, which averaged less than their hospital counterparts.

Median annual earnings of occupational therapists were $76,940 in 2013. The lowest ten percent earned less than $51,310, and the highest ten percent earned more than $109,380.

Occupational therapists may receive paid vacations, holidays, and sick days; life and health insurance; and retirement benefits. These are usually paid by the employer.

Metropolitan Areas with the Highest Employment Level in this Occupation

Metropolitan area	Employment[1]	Employment per thousand jobs	Hourly mean wage
New York-White Plains-Wayne, NY-NJ	4,900	0.93	$39.02
Chicago-Joliet-Naperville, IL	3,200	0.87	$35.45
Boston-Cambridge-Quincy, MA	2,310	1.32	$37.04
Los Angeles-Long Beach-Glendale, CA	2,210	0.56	$44.43
Philadelphia, PA	1,950	1.06	$36.51
Dallas-Plano-Irving, TX	1,770	0.82	$43.77
Atlanta-Sandy Springs-Marietta, GA	1,730	0.75	$35.63
Denver-Aurora-Broomfield, CO	1,570	1.23	$37.45
Houston-Sugar Land-Baytown, TX	1,540	0.56	$37.05
Minneapolis-St. Paul-Bloomington, MN-WI	1,540	0.86	$32.11

[1] Does not include self-employed. Source: Bureau of Labor Statistics

EMPLOYMENT AND OUTLOOK

There were approximately 113,000 occupational therapists employed nationally in 2012. The largest numbers of jobs were in ambulatory healthcare services, which employed about one-third of occupational therapists. Other major employers included hospitals, offices of health care practitioners, school systems and nursing care facilities. Employment is expected to grow much faster than the average for all occupations through the year 2022, which means employment is projected to increase 29 percent or more. Job growth will occur as a result of an aging population that requires increased occupational therapy services and from advances in medicine that allow people to survive serious illness and injury and need rehabilitative therapy.

Employment Trend, Projected 2010–20

Occupational Therapists: 29%

Health Diagnosing and Treating Practitioners: 20%

Total, All Occupations: 11%

Note: "All Occupations" includes all occupations in the U.S. Economy. Source: U.S. Bureau of Labor Statistics, Employment Projections Program

Related Occupations
- Activities Therapist
- Art Therapist
- Music Therapist
- Occupational Therapy Assistant
- Physical Therapist
- Recreational Therapist
- Rehabilitation Counselor
- Respiratory Therapist

Related Military Occupations
- Physical & Occupational Therapist

Conversation With . . .
AMY LAMB

Vice President, American Occupational Therapy Association
Assistant Professor, Eastern Michigan University
Occupational Therapy Program, Ypsilanti, MI
Occupational Therapist, 17 years

1. What was your individual career path in terms of education/training, entry-level job, or other significant opportunity?

When I went to college, I initially studied psychology. I loved it, but felt something was missing. I wanted to do more to help people overcome their challenges, which led me to look at the therapy world. The roots of occupational therapy are in mental health because the mind and body are interconnected and occupational therapy addresses both. I changed my major and got my bachelor's degree in occupational therapy. Today you have to have a master's degree to enter the profession.

After graduating, I worked in a hospital until I was laid off due to significant changes in the healthcare system. I went back to school, got my doctoral degree and started my own practice, which allowed me to use my occupational therapy knowledge in new ways. I practice in a variety of settings, such as in schools, where students might be having challenges focusing. I evaluate what's happening with the students and maybe adapt the environment. Perhaps you get them a standing desk with a little foot shelf so they can swing one of their feet, which provides them with the sensory stimulation they need to focus. You can't jump to the conclusion that a student's issue is behavioral; maybe it's sensory. We also help people in the community "age in place" by doing things such as making sure older drivers know how to use all the bells and whistles on their cars. Occupational therapy is a health and wellness profession; it's much broader than rehabilitation. One of the things that attracted me is that I can move between practice areas without an additional degree. I still have my own practice, but my full-time job now is as a program director and professor, teaching the next generation of occupational therapists.

2. What are the most important skills and/or qualities for someone in your profession?

You have to be adaptable. You may say, 'I'm going to work with this patient with this plan today," but they might not want that. You need plans B, C, and D. This is not a rote profession. You need to be creative and be able to problem solve. You need to be compassionate and to truly want other people to be successful.

3. What do you wish you had known going into this profession?

Nothing prepares you for the fact that you are going to help an individual shower or get dressed, and you're going to see things you didn't anticipate. That's hard for people. You want to protect modesty and dignity, and you're helping a person with their modesty and dignity by helping them learn to do this on their own. You're helping them gain independence, and that's a huge gift.

4. Are there many job opportunities in your profession? In what specific areas?

Occupational therapists are in high demand due to several things. To meet the needs of aging baby boomers, we have to help them stay in their homes and be safe. Then there are changes under the Affordable Care Act, which is projected to add about 31 million people to the healthcare system with no added infrastructure to care for them. And there are jobs working with children and youth, including in schools, helping students be mentally healthy and handle the challenges that everyday life brings.

5. How do you see your profession changing in the next five years, what role will technology play in those changes, and what skills will be required?

Occupational therapy is going to become less of a mystery: we are learning to better define it in ways that are accessible to the general public. You're going to find it used in places such as community-based organizations — not just in rehabilitation centers — to help people develop healthy lifestyles and maintain independence. The forefront of technology is, how we can help people grow old in their homes, rather than enter a nursing home? For instance, a smart mirror installed in your bathroom literally tells you – via voice or screen message – to take your medicine. We can use these sorts of devices to help people who might have mild cognitive challenges stay home longer and be safe.

6. What do you enjoy most about your job? What do you enjoy least about your job?

I most enjoy helping people get to where they need to be, and where they want to be. It's pretty awesome to have that kind of impact on people. My least favorite thing is probably the paperwork. It takes a lot of time to do it right and it's a necessary part of the equation, yet on the surface it doesn't seem like it's where you want to be spending your time. I would much rather be with my clients.

7. Can you suggest a valuable "try this" for students considering a career in your profession?

Volunteer in a community organization where you can begin to understand people's different needs. In a place like a nursing home, for example, you see a bigger picture that what you know from your own life at home and school.

SELECTED SCHOOLS

Many colleges and universities have bachelor's degree programs in counseling and rehabilitation therapy, often with a specialization in occupational therapy. The student may also gain an initial grounding in the field at a technical or community college. Consult with your school guidance counselor or research area post-secondary programs to find the right fit for you. Below are listed some of the more prominent schools in this field.

Boston University
233 Bay State Road
Boston, MA 02215
617.353.2300
www.bu.edu

Colorado State University
Fort Collins, CO 80523
970.491.6444
www.colostate.edu

Indiana University, Bloomington
107 S. Indiana Avenue
Bloomington, IN 47405
812.855.4848
www.iub.edu

Tufts University
419 Boston Avenue
Medford, MA 02155
617.628.5000
www.tufts.edu

University of Florida
Gainesville, FL 32611
352.392.3261
www.ufl.edu

University of Illinois, Chicago
1200 W. Harrison Street
Chicago, IL 60607
312.996.7000
www.uic.edu

University of Kansas
1450 Jayhawk Boulevard
Lawrence, KS 66045
785.864.2700
www.ku.edu

University of Pittsburgh
4200 Fifth Avenue
Pittsburgh, PA 15260
412.624.4141
www.pitt.edu

University of Southern California
University Park Campus
Los Angeles, CA 90089
213.740.1111
www.usc.edu

Washington University, Saint Louis
1 Brookings Drive
Saint Louis, MO 63130
314.935.5000
wustl.edu

MORE INFORMATION

American Occupational Therapy Association
4720 Montgomery Lane
P.O. Box 31220
Bethesda, MD 20824-1220
301.652.2682
www.aota.org

Simone Isadora Flynn/Editor

Personal Trainer

Snapshot

Career Cluster(s): Sports and Fitness
Interests: Language, interpersonal communication, fitness, athletics
Earnings (Yearly Average): $36,160
Employment & Outlook: Average growth expected

OVERVIEW

Sphere of Work

Personal trainers are fitness instructors who work directly with individual clients creating fitness and exercise regimens tailored to the client's needs and goals. Personal trainers need to become

experts in a variety of different types of athletic and fitness training as well as in nutrition. Trainers also spend much of their time meeting individually with clients and forming personal relationships is an important part of the job. Personal training is therefore a job that combines interpersonal communication and athletics.

Work Environment

Personal trainers work in gyms and fitness studios, but may also work outdoors, guiding clients in jogging or other types of outdoor exercise. Many personal trainers are employed directly by fitness studios or gyms, while others work out of their homes or personal offices. Fitness trainers generally need access to fitness equipment like weights or cardiovascular exercise machines and so need access to facilities with this kind of equipment. Personal trainers can work part time or full time and often work irregular hours to organize their training around the schedules of their clients.

Profile

Working Conditions: Work Indoors
Physical Strength: Strenuous work
Education Needs: High School or equivalent
Licensure/Certification: Not required
Opportunities For Experience: On-Job Training, Part-Time Work
Holland Interest Score*: SRE

* See Appendix A

Occupation Interest

Those pursuing work as personal trainers need to have strong interest in fitness and nutrition as well as a desire to work closely with others. Because each client's needs and goals are unique, personal trainers need to be flexible and sometimes creative in designing nutritional and exercise strategies for various clients and prospective trainers will benefit from having an interest in problem solving. In addition, personal trainers need to motivate and encourage their clients and should be interested in leadership, helping others, and interpersonal communication.

A Day in the Life—Duties and Responsibilities

During a typical day, a personal trainer might meet with new prospective clients, speaking to them about their fitness goals and discussing the logistics of a nutritional and fitness routine. When meeting with clients, personal trainers demonstrate various types of exercises and then watch clients exercise to evaluate their technique. During exercise sessions, personal trainers provide encouragement and help clients to stay motivated. Before or after exercise sessions, trainers may help clients evaluate their progress by using equipment to weight the patients, measure body fat or muscle mass, or a variety of other indicators. Personal trainers also instruct clients about nutrition and other lifestyle choices/options that may help the client achieve their goals. When not working directly with clients, personal trainers may spend time practicing various types of exercises or other fitness activities or may take classes to learn about new techniques or to deepen their knowledge of nutrition and fitness trends. Between sessions with clients, personal trainers may also spend time creating programs for new clients or altering programs for existing clients to address their changing fitness needs.

Duties and Responsibilities

- Create and present fitness and exercise programs to clients
- Motivate and guide clients through fitness routines
- Evaluate and measure client progress using measurement tools.
- Meet with new clients and discuss fitness and nutritional goals
- Study new techniques and advances in fitness and nutrition
- Practice new routines and exercises
- Alter programs for clients to meet changing needs

OCCUPATION SPECIALTIES

Strength Coach

Strength coaches are personal trainers who specialize in helping clients gain strength and improve conditioning. Strength coaches often work with professional athletes, guiding them through weight lifting and conditioning routines and must be able to help clients build strength while avoiding injury.

Life Balance Coach

Life balance coaches often focus on a holistic approach to personal fitness, nutrition, and meeting life goals. Often using yoga and other forms of low-impact exercise that also build flexibility and aid in meditation, life coaches are ideal for individuals looking to improve overall fitness and well-being.

Film Fitness Specialist

A film fitness specialist is a personal trainer who works with actors appearing in films and helps clients to achieve the physical skills needed for demanding roles or to achieve the physical appearance needed to play a specific character.

Rehabilitation or Corrective Exercise Specialist

Rehabilitation specialists help individuals suffering from previous injuries or other conditions that result in specific physical impairment. Trainers in this subfield must have knowledge of exercise and other fitness techniques that can help injured clients gain flexibility, strength, or movement ability without exacerbating injuries.

WORK ENVIRONMENT

Relevant Skills and Abilities

Communication Skills

- Communicating with clients from a variety of backgrounds
- Creating simple instructions for clients

Interpersonal/Social Skills

- Engaging in frequent daily interactions with clients and other professionals
- Motivating and encouraging clients and giving constructive feedback

Organization & Management Skills

- Managing class and training schedules
- Helping to keep clients on track for meeting goals
- Creating fitness routines for new clients

Research & Planning Skills

- Researching and learning about new fitness techniques
- Practicing exercises and other fitness activities

Technical Skills

- Utilizing basic technology for communication and scheduling
- Using physical monitoring/measurement equipment

Physical Environment

The physical environment for a personal trainer may vary according to their specialty and personal preferences. Most personal trainers spend at least some of their time working within gyms or fitness studios where they have access to exercise machines and other tools and where there is sufficient room for the trainer to lead clients through exercises or fitness routines. In other cases, personal trainers may work with clients outside, leading them through jogging, sprinting, or other outdoor fitness activities. While some trainers work regular hours through a fitness studio others work directly with clients in their homes or in private studios and may work irregular hours to accommodate client schedules.

Human Environment

Personal trainers are fitness experts and also help clients to develop strategies for overall wellness and happiness. Developing personal connections with clients is an important part of the job as personal trainers must be able to understand their clients' goals and personalities to better tailor fitness and nutrition programs to their needs. Personal trainers spend most of their working time interacting closely with others and should be comfortable with frequent and sometimes personal interaction. In addition, when working as part of a gym or fitness center, personal trainers may need to work alongside other trainers or managers.

Technological Environment

Personal trainers need to be familiar with a variety of different types of exercise equipment, including both manual exercise tools and exercise machines. In addition, personal trainers often use various types of measurement devices to evaluate client's needs and progress towards reaching their goals. This may include using a variety of monitors to evaluate their clients' blood pressure, heart rate, body fat and muscle mass, weight, and other fitness indicators. Increasingly, personal trainers may use digital technology in their jobs, including computers, tablets, and smart phones for communicating with clients and scheduling as well as devices like step counters and other personal monitors to help guide clients through exercise routines.

EDUCATION, TRAINING, AND ADVANCEMENT

High School/Secondary

While most personal trainers and other types of fitness coaches have at least a high school or secondary school diploma or certificate, there are no specific educational requirements for those looking to become personal trainers. High school/secondary students can focus on obtaining a well-rounded education and participating in any available training in various types of exercise and fitness as well as studying human anatomy and physics. Students will also benefit from a basic introduction to computers/digital technology.

Suggested High School Subjects
- English
- World Languages
- Anatomy/Physiology
- Biology
- Track
- Physical Education

Famous First

American fitness and nutrition expert Francois Henri "Jack" LaLanne became one of the first and most famous advocates of personal fitness in the United States. LaLanne opened one of the first fitness centers in the nation in Oakland, California in 1936 and, after gaining fame through television and radio interviews, hosted a television program on fitness, diet, and exercise, *The Jack LaLanne Show*, which ran from 1953 to 1985. LaLanne also lend his name to a number of books on fitness and exercise. Becoming an international celebrity, LaLanne has been honored with a star on the Hollywood Walk of Fame and has been given a variety of honorifit titles including the "Godfather of Fitness.".

College/Postsecondary

While there are no postsecondary or college-level educational requirements for personal trainers, those with advanced degrees in fitness education, nutrition, or related fields might have an advantage on the job market or in building a client base if working independently. Trainers can choose to study exercise science, kinesiology, or physical education at the collegiate level or to obtain certification as a teacher in the physical sciences. Some colleges and universities offer training programs, either bachelor's or associate's degrees, in personal training, which typically introduce students to exercise physiology, kinesiology, massage, rehabilitation therapy and a variety of other related disciplines.

Related College Majors
- Physical education
- Kinesiology
- Exercise science
- Nutrition
- Anatomy/Physiology

Adult Job Seekers

Those seeking work as personal trainers might begin by applying to become a fitness instructor at a fitness center or gym. Some personal trainers begin by teaching fitness or exercise to groups before transitioning to one-on-one instruction with individual clients. A variety of fitness studios and similar exercise-related businesses employ personal trainers as one of their options for customers. Alternatively, personal trainers can attempt to work independently, marketing their services directly to customers through social media, web marketing, or advertisements in print publications or posted at public gyms and fitness centers.

Professional Certification and Licensure

Certification is not required for personal trainers but there are organization that offer certification programs and many employers prefer hiring trainers who have completed certification programs. The National Commission for Certifying Agencies (NCCA) provides a list of organizations, most based in specific regions or states, that offer training and certification programs for potential personal trainers and other types of fitness instructors. Certification exams focus on the prospective client's knowledge of anatomy and physiology, exercise techniques, capability to communicate with clients, and knowledge of how to evaluate their clients' fitness levels to help guide the creation of tailored fitness regimes. In addition, many employers require trainers to obtain certification in basic first aid and in cardiopulmonary resuscitation (CPR) and the use of automatic defibrillators so that they can administer aid to clients who suffer from some serious physical problem during a training session.

Additional Requirements

In addition to knowledge about exercise and fitness, personal trainers need to motivate their clients and should be energetic and comfortable with inspiring and encouraging their clients. In many ways, personal trainers are also teachers and they must be able to clearly teach their clients about nutrition, exercise, and other lifestyle components that contribute to a person's overall fitness level. Before beginning as a personal trainer, it is advisable for the prospective instructor to spend time working alongside another professional trainer. The amount of time a trainer may be required to work as an assistant varies depending on the organizing hiring the trainer.

EARNINGS AND ADVANCEMENT

The Bureau of Labor Statistics (BLS) estimates that the average salary for physical trainers, including aerobics instructors, personal trainers, yoga and pilates instructors, and other types of fitness experts, was $36,160 in 2015. Those at the lower levels of the industry earn less than $18,690, while those at the upper end of the spectrum earn more than $70,180. For trainers working for a fitness studio, opportunities for advancement may involve work experience and advancing to become a senior trainer for the organization. For those working independently, advancement depends on the trainers ability to build a larger client base.

Metropolitan Areas with the Highest Employment Level in this Occupation

Metropolitan area	Employment	Employment per thousand jobs	Hourly mean wage
New York-Jersey City-White Plains, NY-NJ Metropolitan Division	14,330	2.21	$31.65
Chicago-Naperville-Arlington Heights, IL Metropolitan Division	8,970	2.51	$19.70
Los Angeles-Long Beach-Glendale, CA Metropolitan Division	6,230	1.52	$24.50
Washington-Arlington-Alexandria, DC-VA-MD-WV Metropolitan Division	5,950	2.46	$22.18
Boston-Cambridge-Newton, MA NECTA Division	5,020	2.85	$21.33
Seattle-Bellevue-Everett, WA Metropolitan Division	4,350	2.83	$22.17
Phoenix-Mesa-Scottsdale, AZ	4,240	2.26	$19.11
Denver-Aurora-Lakewood, CO	4,090	2.98	$19.85
Houston-The Woodlands-Sugar Land, TX	3,910	1.33	$21.63
Baltimore-Columbia-Towson, MD	3,690	2.81	$20.87

Source: Bureau of Labor Statistics

EMPLOYMENT AND OUTLOOK

The BLS estimates that jobs in the fitness instructor and trainer field are expected to grow by approximately 8 percent between 2014 and 2024, marking average levels of growth when compared to all occupational categories in the United States. Governmental efforts to enhance fitness and health contribute to growth in the industry and the continuing popularity of alternative exercise systems, like yoga and Pilates, and in holistic health and nutrition, also help to increase the need for personal trainers and other types of fitness experts.

Employment Trend, Projected 2014–24

Personal care and service occupations: 13%

Fitness trainers and aerobics instructors: 8%

Total, all occupations: 7%

Note: "All Occupations" includes all occupations in the U.S. Economy. Source: U.S. Bureau of Labor Statistics, Employment Projections Program

Related Occupations
- Athletic Trainers
- Exercise Physiologists
- Physical Therapists
- Physical Therapist Assistants

- Recreation Workers
- Recreational Therapists

Related Occupations
- Drill Sergeant

Conversation With . . .
BRIAN JOHNSON

Fitness Trainer, 3 years

1. What was your individual career path in terms of education/training, entry-level job, or other significant opportunity?

I was in corporate America for almost 20 years. I became unemployable because I topped out on the rate scale. My last job was running a Safeway distribution center. I asked myself: what's the one thing I've always done? And that's go to the gym. So I got my certification and started training people. I had enough money saved up so I was living off my savings, but the motivating piece was, I didn't want to work for anybody else ever again. I did a 12-week online course to get my certification in 8 weeks. I joined networking groups, which is how I got my clients.

I have my own gym. I trained my first client outside at the park across the street. I used an eight foot chain TRX and a five dollar fitness map. I migrated from individual clients into boot camps, which just makes sense because you're leveraging your time and working with 20 people for $15 each, as opposed to one person at $80.

Through all my marketing and networking, I got hooked up with a couple of wedding vendors. The clients walk in there, see my business cards, and the next thing you know I'll have a bridal party boot camp that usually lasts about two months. I also am starting a two-hour ultimate boot camp challenge, that also has a 5K mudrun, live music, vendors…a fitness festival. We have one coming up in May in Annapolis, and I'm talking about doing one with a guy on Long Island, NY, and a guy in Raleigh, NC. My goal is to do one a month across the nation.

2. What are the most important skills and/or qualities for someone in your profession?

The ability to inspire, motivate and hold people accountable, that's the most important piece. Without that, whether you're working in a gym or doing your own gig, you're never going to retain people.

3. What do you wish you had known going into this profession?

How difficult it would be to get clients. I thought it would be easy. In the fitness industry, word of mouth is everything, networking and social media. You've got to get your name out there. I do Business Networking International and other local area mixers. You have to identify the best social media for your industry. For mine, it's Facebook. For a banker, it's LinkedIn. At the end of the day, I have a very extensive and elaborate website but the majority of my clients come from word of mouth.

Also, in hindsight, I would have trained at a gym for two or three months to gain that confidence level to train people. I only charged my first client $30 a session. Now, I charge $80 for a private session. You need to research what other people are charging. You don't want to devalue yourself, or overprice yourself out of business. You've got to find that balance and test the market.

4. Are there many job opportunities in your profession? In what specific areas?

Yes. I say that because I've seen constant turnover at the gyms. They're always looking for quality instructors.

5. How do you see your profession changing in the next five years? What role will technology play in those changes, and what skills will be required?

I think a lot of it's going to go online. I can already see that shift happening. My vision is, you have this ten-by-ten room, you have a nice camera in there, people log in every day, and I instruct them for an hour. For $1, I have 1,000 people logging in for an hour.

6. What do you enjoy most about your job? What do you enjoy least?

Getting people to their goals, whether somebody is morbidly obese or somebody is already fit and training for a tough event. At my gym, we have a whiteboard where everybody writes their goals. I have a 61-year-old lady flipping a 200-pound tractor tire. It helps to motivate everyone.

What I like least is that you're always on. It's hard to shut it off. Not that I ever would, but God forbid if I ever wanted to go to McDonalds and have a cheeseburger. Too many people in this town know me! But it's a blessing. If I was working for a gym training someone, I would leave there at the end of the day and be done.

7. Can you suggest a valuable "try this" for students considering a career in your profession?

Try it at a gym first. Don't try it on your own. Write out all the pros and cons and make sure it's right for you, because it's not right for everybody.

MORE INFORMATION

**National Strength and
Conditioning Association**
1885 Bob Johnson Dr.
Colorado Springs, CO 80906
800-815-6826
www.nsca.com

**National Academy of Sports
Medicine (NASM)**
1750 E. Northrop Blvd, #200
Chandler, AZ 85286
800-460-6276
www.nasm.org

**National Commission for
Certifying Agencies (NCCA)**
2025 M Street NW Suite 800
Washington DC 20036
202-367-1165
www.credentialingexcellence.org

**National Federation of
Professional Trainers (NFPT)**
PO Box 4579
Lafayette, IN 47903
800-729-6378
www.nfpt.com

**United States Registry of
Exercise Professionals (USREPS)**
4400 College Blvd Suite 220
Overland Park, KS 66211
913-222-8658
www.usreps.org

Micah Issitt/Editor

Physical Education Teacher

Snapshot

Career Cluster(s): Education & Training

Interests: Teaching, lesson planning, leading instructional activities, adolescent development, student safety, peer mentoring

Earnings (Yearly Average): $57,200 (high school); $55,860 (middle school)

Employment & Outlook: Average Growth Expected

OVERVIEW

Sphere of Work

Physical education teachers, also called middle and high school teachers, are teaching professionals that focus on the educational needs of adolescents. Secondary and Middle school teachers may be generalists with knowledge and talents in a wide range of subjects, or they may have an academic specialization, such as history, language arts, mathematics, physical science, art, or

music. Secondary and Middle school teachers work in both public and private school settings. They may be assigned student and peer mentoring and administrative tasks in addition to their teaching responsibilities.

Work Environment

Secondary and Middle school teachers work in high schools and middle schools designed to meet the social and educational needs of adolescents. The amounts and types of resources in middle and high schools and middle and high school classrooms such as art supplies, music lessons, physical education facilities, fieldtrips, and assistant teachers, differ depending on the school's financial resources and the educational philosophy directing the curriculum. Middle and high schools may be private or public. They may be an independent entity or part of a larger school that encompasses more grade levels.

Profile

Working Conditions: Work Indoors
Physical Strength: Light Work
Education Needs: Bachelor's Degree, Master's Degree
Licensure/Certification: Required
Opportunities For Experience: Internship, Volunteer Work, Part Time Work
Holland Interest Score*: SAE

* See Appendix A

Occupation Interest

Individuals drawn to the profession of Secondary and Middle school teacher tend to be intelligent, creative, patient, and caring. Secondary and Middle school teachers, who instruct and nurture secondary and middle school students, should find satisfaction in spending long hours instructing and mentoring adolescents. Successful Secondary and Middle school teachers excel at long-term scheduling, lesson planning, communication, and problem solving.

A Day in the Life—Duties and Responsibilities

A Secondary and Middle school teacher's daily duties and responsibilities include planning, teaching, classroom preparation, student care, family outreach, school duties, and professional development.

Secondary and Middle school teachers plan and execute specific teaching plans and lessons. They may also be responsible for buying or securing donations for classroom or project supplies. They assign homework and projects, teach good study habits, grade student work, maintain accurate academic records for all students, and lead and administer activities such as lab sessions, reviews, exams, student clubs, and small group learning.

Classroom preparation and cleaning duties may include labeling materials, organizing desk and work areas, displaying student work on bulletin boards and display boards, and, depending on janitorial support, cleaning up and sanitizing spaces at the end of the school day.

Secondary and Middle school teachers greet students as they arrive in the classroom, promote a supportive learning environment, maintain student safety and health, provide appropriate levels of discipline in the classroom and school environment, build student cooperation and listening skills, and work to present lessons in multiple ways to accommodate diverse learning styles.

Some teachers may provide family outreach by greeting student families at school drop off and dismissal times and using a student school-family communication notebook when required. All teachers must communicate regularly with families regarding student academic performance.

Secondary and Middle school teachers must attend staff meetings, participate in peer mentoring, enforce school policies, and lead open houses for prospective families. Teachers may also be responsible for overseeing students in the school hallways and for supervising school fieldtrips. Their professional development duties include attendance at professional meetings, continued training, and recertification as needed.

Secondary and Middle school teachers must work on a daily basis to meet the needs of all students, families, fellow teachers, and school administrators.

Duties and Responsibilities

- Preparing lesson plans
- Guiding the learning activities of students
- Instructing students through demonstrations or lectures
- Evaluating students through daily work, tests and reports, or through a portfolio of the students' artwork or writing
- Computing and recording grades
- Maintaining discipline
- Counseling and referring students when academic or other problems arise
- Conferring with parents and staff
- Assisting with student clubs, teams, plays and other student activities
- Supplementing lecturing with audio-visual teaching aides

OCCUPATION SPECIALTIES

Resource Teachers

Resource Teachers teach basic academic subjects to students requiring remedial work using special help programs to improve scholastic levels.

WORK ENVIRONMENT

Physical Environment

A Secondary and Middle school teacher's physical environment is the middle and high school classroom. Secondary and Middle school teachers tend to have a fair bit of autonomy in deciding classroom layout and curriculum. Secondary and Middle school teachers generally work forty-hour weeks and follow an annual academic schedule with ample winter, spring, and summer vacations. Summer teaching opportunities in summer school and summer camps are common.

Relevant Skills and Abilities

Communication Skills
- Expressing thoughts and ideas
- Persuading others
- Speaking effectively
- Writing concisely

Interpersonal/Social Skills
- Being patient
- Cooperating with others
- Working as a member of a team

Organization & Management Skills
- Coordinating tasks
- Making decisions
- Managing people/groups

Research & Planning Skills
- Creating ideas
- Using logical reasoning

Human Environment

Secondary and Middle school teachers are in constant contact with adolescents, student families, school administrators, and fellow teachers. Secondary and Middle school teachers may have students with physical and mental disabilities as well as students who are English language learners (ELL). Secondary and Middle school teachers must be comfortable working with people from a wide range of backgrounds and able to incorporate lessons on diversity into their teaching.

Technological Environment

Secondary and Middle school classrooms increasingly include computers for student use. Teachers should be comfortable using Internet communication tools and teaching adolescent students to use educational software. Teachers may also use computers to perform administrative tasks and record student progress. Secondary and Middle school teachers should be comfortable with standard office and audiovisual equipment.

EDUCATION, TRAINING, AND ADVANCEMENT

Middle and high school/Secondary and Middle

Middle and high school students interested in becoming Secondary and Middle school teachers should develop good study habits. Interested middle and high school students should take a broad range of courses in education, child development, science, mathematics, history, language arts, physical education, and the arts. Those interested in the field of education may benefit from seeking internships or volunteer/part-time work with children and teachers at camps and afterschool programs.

Suggested High School Subjects
- Algebra
- Arts
- Audio-Visual
- Biology
- Child Growth & Development
- College Preparatory
- Composition
- Computer Science
- English
- Foreign Languages
- Government
- Graphic Communications
- History
- Humanities
- Literature
- Mathematics
- Political Science
- Psychology
- Science

- Social Studies
- Sociology
- Speech
- Theatre & Drama

Famous First

The first junior high school, or middle school, was the Indianola Junior High School in Columbus, OH, which opened in September 1909. The school served 7th, 8th, and 9th grade students along with "such of the first six grades as might be necessary to relieve neighboring districts."

College/Postsecondary

College students interested in working towards a degree or career in Secondary and Middle school education should consider majoring in education and earning initial teaching certification as part of their undergraduate education program. Aspiring teachers should complete coursework in education, child development, and psychology. Those interested in pursuing a career in secondary education often major in the subject area they wish to teach. Prior to graduation, college students intent on becoming Secondary and Middle school teachers should gain teaching experience through an internship or volunteer/part-time work; prospective teachers should also research master's of education programs and state teaching certification requirements.

Related College Majors
- Agricultural Teacher Education
- Art Teacher Education
- Bilingual/Bicultural Education
- Business Teacher Education (Vocational)
- Computer Teacher Education
- Education Admin & Supervision, General
- Education of the Blind & Visually Handicapped

- Education of the Deaf & Hearing Impaired
- Education of the Specific Learning Disabled
- Education of the Speech Impaired
- Elementary/Pre-Elem/Early Childhood/Kindergarten Teacher Education
- English Teacher Education
- Family & Consumer Science Education
- Foreign Languages Teacher Education
- Health & Physical Education, General
- Health Teacher Education
- Marketing Operations Teacher Education (Vocational)
- Mathematics Teacher Education
- Music Teacher Education
- Physical Education Teaching & Coaching
- Science Teacher Education, General
- Secondary and Middle/Jr. High/Middle School Teacher Education
- Special Education, General
- Speech Teacher Education
- Technology Teacher Education/Industrial Arts Teacher Education
- Trade & Industrial Teacher Education (Vocational)
- Vocational Teacher Education

Adult Job Seekers

Adults seeking jobs as Secondary and Middle school teachers should research the education and certification requirements of their home states as well of the schools where they might seek employment. Adult job seekers in the education field may benefit from the employment workshops and job lists maintained by professional teaching associations, such as the American Federation of Teachers (AFT).

Professional Certification and Licensure

Professional certification and licensure requirements for Secondary and Middle school teachers vary between states and between schools. Secondary and Middle school teachers generally earn a master's in education, with a single-subject teaching concentration in language arts, history, science, political science, music, physical education, or art, and obtain a state teaching license for grades eight through twelve. Single-subject teaching licenses for Secondary and Middle school teachers require academic coursework, supervised student teaching, and successful completion of a general teaching exam.

Background checks are also typically required. State departments of education offer state teaching licenses and require continuing education and recertification on a regular basis. Savvy and successful job seekers will find out the requirements that apply to them and satisfy the requirements prior to seeking employment.

Additional Requirements

Individuals who find satisfaction, success, and job security as Secondary and Middle school teachers will be knowledgeable about the profession's requirements, responsibilities, and opportunities. Successful Secondary and Middle school teachers engage in ongoing professional development. Secondary and Middle school teachers must have high levels of integrity and ethics as they work with adolescents and have access to the personal information of student families. Membership in professional teaching associations is encouraged among beginning and tenured Secondary and Middle school teachers as a means of building status in a professional community and networking.

Fun Facts

Teachers earn 14 percent less than people in other professions that require similar levels of education. They work 52 hours per week.
Source: http://www.theteachersalaryproject.org

Schools started offering physical education—gymnastics, care of the body, and hygiene—around 1820, but it wasn't until after the Civil War that several states passed laws requiring it. It would take another century before federal law mandated that high school and college women had to be allowed to participate in athletic competitions.
Source: http://www.excite.com/

EARNINGS AND ADVANCEMENT

Earnings of Secondary and Middle school teachers depend on their education and experience, and the size and location of the school district. Pay is usually higher in large, metropolitan areas. Secondary and Middle school teachers in private schools generally earn less than public Secondary and Middle school teachers.

Median annual earnings of secondary school teachers was $57,200 in 2014; the comparable figure for middle school teachers was $55,860. Secondary and Middle school teachers receive extra pay for coaching sports and working with students in extracurricular activities. Some Secondary and Middle school teachers earn extra income during the summer working in the school system or in other jobs.

Secondary and Middle school teachers have vacation days when their school is closed, as in during the summer and over holidays. They may also receive life and health insurance and retirement benefits. These are usually paid by the employer.

Metropolitan Areas with the Highest Employment Level in this Occupation

Metropolitan area	Employment	Employment per thousand jobs	Annual mean wage
New York-Jersey City-White Plains, NY-NJ	40,590	6.26	$82,260
Los Angeles-Long Beach-Glendale, CA	29,170	7.11	$76,710
Chicago-Naperville-Arlington Heights, IL	24,010	6.72	$74,960
Houston-The Woodlands-Sugar Land, TX	22,930	7.83	$57,520
Dallas-Plano-Irving, TX	17,080	7.33	$55,330
Washington-Arlington-Alexandria, DC-VA-MD-WV	13,910	5.75	$73,330
Atlanta-Sandy Springs-Roswell, GA	13,300	5.36	$56,620
Minneapolis-St. Paul-Bloomington, MN-WI	12,650	6.73	$67,200
Nassau County-Suffolk County, NY	12,020	9.42	$101,950
Baltimore-Columbia-Towson, MD	11,570	8.80	$64,400

Does not include self-employed.

EMPLOYMENT AND OUTLOOK

There were approximately 1.6 million Secondary and Middle school teachers employed nationally in 2014. Employment is expected to grow about as fast as the average for all occupations through the year 2024, which means employment is projected to increase 4 percent to 8 percent. Most job openings will occur as a result of the expected retirement of a large number of teachers.

The supply of Secondary and Middle school teachers is likely to increase in response to growing student enrollment, improved job opportunities, more teacher involvement in school policy, greater public interest in education and higher salaries. Job prospects are greater in central cities and rural areas. However, job growth could be limited by state and local government budget deficits.

Employment Trend, Projected 2014–24

Total, all occupations: 7%

Preschool, primary, secondary, and special education school teachers: 6%

Secondary and Middle school teachers: 6%

Note: "All Occupations" includes all occupations in the U.S. Economy. Source: U.S. Bureau of Labor Statistics, Employment Projections Program

Related Occupations
- Career/Technology Education Teacher
- College Faculty Member
- Education Administrator
- Elementary School Teacher
- Principal
- Special Education Teacher
- Teacher Assistant

Conversation With . . .
SARA RUSSELL

Physical Education & Health Teacher
Tahoma Junior High School
Maple Valley, Washington
Education, 14 years

1. What was your individual career path in terms of education/training, entry-level job, or other significant opportunity?

I received my undergraduate degree in health & fitness with a teaching certification from Pacific Lutheran University in Tacoma, Washington. After graduating, I was offered a job at Tahoma Junior High in Maple Valley, WA, teaching eighth and ninth grade physical education and health. I went on to earn my Master of Science in Health & Human Performance from Central Washington University. I pursued additional training through the National Board for Professional Teaching Standards and earned my National Board Certification in Physical Education, Early Adolescence through Young Adulthood. I was named 2016 National High School Physical Education Teacher of the Year by the Society of Health and Physical Educators, or SHAPE America.

2. What are the most important skills and/or qualities for someone in your profession?

Flexibility: No matter how perfect a teacher thinks a lesson is, or how prepared for a lesson they are, there will always be things that don't work out. Be ready to go with the flow and adapt as needed.

Communication: Clearly communicating with colleagues, students and parents/guardians is a big part of teacher success. Making sure students know what they're learning and why, and communicating that to families, is crucial. Advocating for physical education is also a big part of our job, and communicating the need for physical education will only help you have more successful programs.

Teamwork: You will be working with a lot of different people as a physical education teacher: other teachers, students, administrators, professional learning communities, etc. You have to be able to be a leader when needed, as well as work together as a team, especially if you work in a department setting as most secondary teachers do.

Passion: You must be passionate about what you do! Passionate about your students, your subject of physical education, and about being a lifelong learner!

3. What do you wish you had known going into this profession?

I didn't know how much getting outside of my own classroom, networking, and getting involved at the local, state, and national level within the field of physical education would impact my career. Meeting and learning from other people is always inspiring. Getting outside of my own gym has made me a better teacher as I've learned from people all over the country.

4. Are there many job opportunities in your profession? In what specific areas?

Yes! Some districts have fewer job openings than others, but there are openings if individuals are willing to move. From what I've heard, there are needs for teachers in many urban schools. The profession is definitely in need of quality physical educators at all levels.

5. How do you see your profession changing in the next five years? What role will technology play in those changes, and what skills will be required?

I definitely see an increase in the use of technology in physical education in upcoming years. New apps, activity trackers, and devices such as heart rate monitors are going to continually change and improve. Physical educators are going to have to stay on top of trends in order to have technology be something that enhances our classes and encourages our students to be physically active. In addition, it's going to be important for us as physical education teachers to enhance our class offerings to meet our students' needs and interests. We can't just keep teaching what we always have been; we have to keep students excited about the activities we teach.

6. What do you enjoy most about your job? What do you enjoy least about your job?

The thing I enjoy most about my job is my students! They constantly make me smile. There's nothing more rewarding than seeing a student succeed. Hearing a student say "I never thought I could do this!" or "I never liked PE before this class!" makes teaching worthwhile.

The thing I enjoy least about teaching is the ever-changing expectations, laws, and initiatives that often come along in education. All of the "outside" things that teachers often have minimal influence over than can get wearing over time.

7. Can you suggest a valuable "try this" for students considering a career in your profession?

Get out and spend time observing quality physical education teachers and programs! Observe all levels—and multiple teachers—to see how teaching truly is an art that can be developed. No two teachers are alike, even when teaching the same curriculum. Find what makes people good teachers, and make it your own! Network with other professionals to learn and grow.

MORE INFORMATION

American Association for Employment in Education
3040 Riverside Drive, Suite 125
Columbus, OH 43221
614.485.1111
www.aaee.org

American Association for Health Education
1900 Association Drive
Reston, VA 20191-1598
800.213.7193
www.aahperd.org/aahe

American Association of Colleges for Teacher Education
1307 New York Avenue, NW
Suite 300
Washington, DC 20005-4701
202.293.2450
www.aacte.org

American Federation of Teachers
Public Affairs Department
555 New Jersey Avenue, NW
Washington, DC 20001
202.879.4400
www.aft.org

National Association for Sport and Physical Education
1900 Association Drive
Reston, VA 20191
800.213.7193
www.aahperd.org/naspe

National Board for Professional Teaching Standards
1525 Wilson Boulevard, Suite 500
Arlington, VA 22209
800.228.3224
www.nbpts.org

National Council for Accreditation of Teacher Education
2010 Massachusetts Avenue, NW
Suite 500
Washington, DC 20036-1023
202.466.7496
www.ncate.org

National Council of Teachers of English
1111 W. Kenyon Road
Urbana, Illinois 61801-1096
877.369.6283
www.ncte.org/second

National Council of Teachers of Mathematics
1906 Association Drive
Reston, VA 20191-1502
703.620.9840
www.nctm.org

National Education Association
1201 16th Street, NW
Washington, DC 20036-3290
202.833.4000
www.nea.org

National Science Teachers Association
1840 Wilson Boulevard
Arlington, VA 22201
703.243.7100
www.nsta.org

Simone Isadora Flynn/Editor

Physical Therapist

Snapshot

Career Cluster: Health Care, Health and Wellness

Interests: Anatomy and Physiology, Sports Medicine, Physical Education

Earnings (Yearly Average): $80,889

Employment & Outlook: Faster Than Average Growth Expected

OVERVIEW

Sphere of Work

Physical therapists (PTs) provide therapeutic services to patients who have temporary or chronic physical conditions or illnesses that limit physical movement and mobility, thereby negatively affecting patients' life and work. When working with patients, a physical therapist may use techniques such as therapeutic exercise, manual therapy techniques, assistive devices, adaptive devices, hydrotherapy, and electrotherapy. Physical therapists develop patient treatment plans designed to help maintain or recover a patient's physical mobility, lessen pain, increase productivity and independence, and improve quality of life.

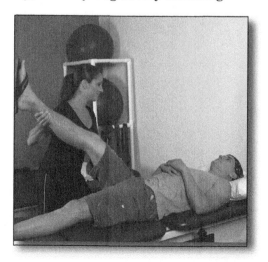

Work Environment

Physical therapists work in rehabilitation facilities, hospitals, nursing homes, physical therapy clinics, and schools. In medical environments, physical therapists work with a team of medical and social service professionals to increase a patient's physical abilities and overall independence. In school settings, physical therapists partner with educational professionals, such as teachers and special education coordinators, to address a student's physical issues. Physical therapists generally work a standard forty-hour workweek, and scheduled appointments are the norm.

Profile

Working Conditions: Work Indoors
Physical Strength: Light Work
Education Needs: Doctoral Degree
Licensure/Certification: Required
Physical Abilities Not Required: No Heavy Labor
Opportunities For Experience: Military Service
Holland Interest Score*: IES

* See Appendix A

Occupation Interest

Individuals attracted to the field of physical therapy tend to be physically strong people who enjoy hands-on work and close interaction with people from diverse backgrounds. Those who excel as physical therapists exhibit traits such as physical stamina, problem solving, empathy, patience, and caring. Physical therapists should enjoy learning, stay knowledgeable about changes in therapeutic techniques, and expect to work as part of a team to effectively address patient needs.

A Day in the Life—Duties and Responsibilities

A physical therapist's daily duties and responsibilities include full days of hands-on patient interaction and treatment, as well as administrative duties. Physical therapists' patients include those experiencing physical limitations and effects from neck and spinal cord injuries, traumatic brain injury, arthritis, burns, cerebral palsy, muscular dystrophy, strokes, limb or digit amputation, or work- or sports-related injuries.

As medical or therapeutic professionals, physical therapists interact with patients or clients on a daily basis and strive to understand the particular challenges faced by each individual. Treatment typically includes a blend of physical techniques and emotional encouragement, since the patient may be in the process of adjusting to a major life change. Some of a physical therapist's daily responsibilities include conducting patient assessments, developing patient treatment plans, and providing physical treatment to patients with severe physical limitations. Physical therapists frequently advise patients on the use of adaptive equipment, such as wheelchairs and orthopedic aids. Some provide early intervention services to young children experiencing physical delays and limitations. Others may offer consultation on or participate in building customized adaptive equipment for patients with special needs not met by existing options. Physical therapists also instruct individuals and groups on physical exercises to prevent injury, lead fitness and health classes and workshops, and counsel patients on physical adaptations that can help the patient to continue to work at his or her chosen occupation. They may also supervise the activities of physical therapy assistants and aides.

During the course of treatment, a physical therapist will consult with a team of physicians, educators, social workers, mental health professionals, occupational therapists, speech therapists, and other medical professionals to help ensure that each patient receives comprehensive care.

A physical therapist's administrative responsibilities include documenting treatment sessions and ongoing patient evaluation. Physical therapists must draft treatment plans, record notes following patient treatment sessions, provide written updates to the other members of a patient's treatment team, and provide insurance companies with patient records and progress notes as required. Independent physical therapists who do not work as part of a school or medical clinic may also be responsible for scheduling appointments and for submitting bills to insurance companies or patients.

Duties and Responsibilities

- Evaluating the physician's referral and the patient's medical records to determine the treatment required
- Performing tests, measurements, and evaluations such as range-of-motion and manual-muscle tests, gait and functional analyses, and body-parts measurements
- Administering manual therapeutic exercises to improve or maintain muscle function
- Administering treatments involving the application of such agents as light, heat, water, and ice massage techniques
- Recording patients' treatments, responses, and progress

OCCUPATION SPECIALTIES

Physical Therapist Assistants

Physical Therapist Assistants help physical therapists provide care to patients. Under the direction and supervision of physical therapists, they give therapy through exercise; therapeutic methods, such as electrical stimulation, mechanical traction, and ultrasound; massage; and gait and balance training. Physical therapist assistants record patients' responses to treatment and report the results of each treatment to the physical therapist.

Physical Therapist Aides

Physical Therapist Aides help make therapy sessions productive, under the direct supervision of a physical therapist or physical therapist assistant. They usually are responsible for keeping the treatment area clean and organized and for preparing for each patient's therapy. They also help patients who need assistance moving to or from a treatment area.

Directors of Physical Therapy

Directors of Physical Therapy plan, direct, and coordinate physical therapy programs and make sure the program complies with state requirements.

WORK ENVIRONMENT

Physical Environment

Physical therapists work in rehabilitation facilities, hospitals, nursing homes, therapy clinics, and schools. Therapeutic office settings used by physical therapists may be shared with other therapeutic professionals, such as occupational, recreational, or speech and language therapists.

Human Environment

Physical therapists work with patients who use physical therapy to improve their strength and mobility, as well as their independence and quality of life. This may include people experiencing balance and strength issues caused by cerebral palsy, spinal cord injuries, or muscular dystrophy; stroke victims experiencing coordination problems or paralysis; and children or adults suffering the physical effects of injuries, abuse, or accidents. Physical therapists usually work as part of a patient treatment team that includes patient families, social workers, teachers, doctors, and additional therapists.

Relevant Skills and Abilities

Communication Skills
- Expressing thoughts and ideas
- Speaking and writing effectively

Interpersonal/Social Skills
- Being patient
- Being sensitive to others
- Cooperating with others
- Working as a member of a team

Organization & Management Skills
- Coordinating tasks
- Managing people/groups
- Paying attention to and handling details
- Performing duties that may change frequently

Planning & Research Skills
- Developing evaluation strategies

Technical Skills
- Performing technical work
- Working with your hands

Technological Environment

Physical therapists use a wide variety of technology in their work. Computers and Internet communication tools are widely used in physical therapy work and practice. Specialized therapies, such as electrotherapy, hydrotherapy, and ultrasound therapy, require technical equipment and training. In addition, physical therapists must learn how to use and teach the use of adaptive devices, such as wheelchairs and orthopedic aids.

EDUCATION, TRAINING, AND ADVANCEMENT

High School/Secondary

High school students interested in pursuing the profession of physical therapy in the future should develop good study habits. High school courses in biology, psychology, anatomy, sociology, and mathematics will prepare students for college- and graduate-level studies. Students interested in the physical therapy field will benefit from seeking internships or part-time work with physical therapists or with people who have physical issues that affect their range of movement or daily life.

Suggested High School Subjects
- Algebra
- Applied Communication
- Applied Math
- Applied Physics
- Biology
- Chemistry
- College Preparatory
- English
- Geometry
- Health Science Technology
- Humanities
- Physical Education
- Physics
- Physiology
- Psychology
- Science
- Trigonometry

Famous First

The first physical therapy school was formed at Walter Reed Army Hospital in Washington, D.C., following the United States' entry into World War I. In 1921 the first research journal in physical therapy, *The PT Review*, was published, and in that same year the first professional organization for physical therapists, the American Physical Therapy Association, was established.

Library of Congress

College/Postsecondary

Postsecondary students interested in becoming physical therapists should complete coursework in physical therapy, if possible, as well as courses on occupational therapy, special education, biology, psychology, anatomy and physiology, sociology, and mathematics. Prior to graduation, college students interested in joining the physical therapy profession should apply to graduate-level physical therapy programs or secure physical therapy-related employment. Those who choose to pursue a master's degree tend to have better prospects for employment and advancement in the field. Membership in the American Physical Therapy Association may help provide postsecondary students with networking opportunities and connections.

Related College Majors
- Adapted Physical Education/Therapeutic Recreation
- Anatomy and Physiology
- Exercise Science/Physiology/Movement Studies
- Health & Physical Education, General
- Physical Therapy
- Sports Medicine & Athletic Training

Adult Job Seekers

Adult job seekers in the physical therapy field should have a master's degree in physical therapy from a college or university accredited by the Commission on Accreditation in Physical Therapy Education. They must also earn the necessary professional licensure. Physical therapists seeking employment may benefit from the networking opportunities, job workshops, and job lists offered by professional physical therapy associations, such as the American Physical Therapy Association and American Board of Physical Therapy Specialties. Advancement in the physical therapy field often depends on the individual's education and specialty certification.

Professional Certification and Licensure

Physical therapists are required to have earned a professional physical therapy (PT) license prior to beginning their professional practice. Upon completion of an accredited master's or doctoral program in physical therapy, candidates take the National Physical Therapy Examination (NPTE) administered by the Federation of State Boards of Physical Therapy. In addition to passing the NPTE, physical therapists are required to register with their state health board, pass a state exam, and engage in continuing education as a condition of their PT license.

Physical therapists may choose to pursue additional, specialized physical therapy certification from the American Board of Physical Therapy Specialties. Certification is available for the following specialties: cardiovascular and pulmonary, clinical electrophysiology, geriatrics, neurology, pediatrics, sports, and women's health.

Additional Requirements

Individuals who find satisfaction, success, and job security as physical therapists will be knowledgeable about the profession's requirements, responsibilities, and opportunities. Successful physical therapists engage in ongoing professional development related to changes in therapeutic techniques, ethical standards, and new technology. Because physical therapists work with vulnerable people and share confidential patient information with other medical professionals, adherence to strict professional and ethical standards is required.

Both entry-level and senior-level physical therapists may find it beneficial to join professional associations as a means of building professional community and networking.

Fun Fact

Brief bouts of dizziness with changes in position or movement of the head – positional vertigo – the most common cause of dizziness, is caused by dysfunction of the inner ear, and can successfully be treated in as little as one session with a physical therapist.

Source: http://www.athletico.com/2011/09/27/the-top-10-things-you-did-not-know-about-physical-therapy

EARNINGS AND ADVANCEMENT

Earnings of physical therapists depend on the type and size of the employer and the physical therapist's length of employment and level of responsibility. Physical therapists in private practice tend to earn more than salaried workers. Salaries are usually higher in rural areas as employers try to attract physical therapists to where there are severe shortages.

Median annual earnings of physical therapists were $80,889 in 2012. The lowest ten percent earned less than $56,837, and the highest ten percent earned more than $114,395.

Physical therapists may receive paid vacations, holidays, and sick days; life and health insurance; and retirement benefits. These are usually paid by the employer. Some employers also provide for paid educational leave.

Metropolitan Areas with the Highest Employment Level in this Occupation

Metropolitan area	Employment (1)	Employment per thousand jobs	Hourly mean wage
New York-White Plains-Wayne, NY-NJ	7,610	1.48	$40.46
Chicago-Joliet-Naperville, IL	6,740	1.85	$37.33
Los Angeles-Long Beach-Glendale, CA	4,880	1.26	$42.51
Boston-Cambridge-Quincy, MA	3,430	2.00	$37.08
Philadelphia, PA	3,000	1.64	$36.78
Phoenix-Mesa-Glendale, AZ	2,960	1.71	$39.40
Dallas-Plano-Irving, TX	2,830	1.35	$45.41
Nassau-Suffolk, NY	2,570	2.10	$41.68

(1) Does not include self-employed. Source: Bureau of Labor Statistics, 2012

EMPLOYMENT AND OUTLOOK

There were approximately 192,000 physical therapists employed nationally in 2012. Another 120,000 worked as physical therapist assistants or aides. Employment of physical therapists is expected to grow much faster than the average for all occupations through the year 2020, which means employment is projected to increase 35 percent or more. As new medical technologies allow more people to survive accidents and illnesses, but who then require physical therapy, employment opportunities will increase. The rapidly growing elderly population will also contribute to this demand. A growing number of employers are using physical therapists to evaluate work sites, develop exercise programs and teach safe work habits to employees in the hope of reducing injuries.

Employment Trend, Projected 2010–20

Physical Therapists: 39%

Health Diagnosing and Treating Practitioners: 26%

Total, All Occupations: 14%

Note: "All Occupations" includes all occupations in the U.S. Economy. Source: U.S. Bureau of Labor Statistics, Employment Projections Program

Related Occupations
- Activities Therapist
- Athletic Trainer
- Chiropractor
- Occupational Therapist
- Recreational Therapist
- Respiratory Therapist

Related Military Occupations
- Physical & Occupational Therapist

Conversation With . . .
ASHLEY BURNS

Physical Therapist/Certified Orthopedic
Manual Therapist, 5 years

1. What was your individual career path in terms of education, entry-level job, or other significant opportunity?

I completed an entry-level 5½-year Master's in Science physical therapy program at Springfield College. The first two years were spent completing prerequisites; the last three years were the graduate school portion of the program. After graduating with a Master's in Physical Therapy (PT) in 2008, I passed my boards, and began working at Brigham & Women's Hospital. After working for two years, I entered the transitional Doctorate in Physical Therapy program at Massachusetts General's Institute of Health Professions, while still working full-time. Before and after my Doctor in Physical Therapy (DPT), I completed continuing education classes through Maitland Australian Physiotherapy Seminars (MAPS) and passed a two-day exam with three parts: practical, short-answer, and multiple-choice. With this completion, I earned the degree of Certified Orthopedic Manual Therapist. While working at the Brigham, I have had many educational opportunities, including teaching courses, lecturing at outside athletic programs, attending rounds/clinical education series, and publishing articles.

2. Are there many job opportunities in your profession? In what specific areas?

There are many job opportunities in the physical therapy profession, which can be broken down into four different areas: outpatient, inpatient, rehabilitation, and home-care. Within these areas, there are different categories, such as orthopedics, geriatric, neurological, oncology, and cardiopulmonary. There are job openings in all of these areas, but the biggest area in terms of available jobs currently is home care. This is due to the growing geriatric population, which is a result of people living longer, people living healthier lifestyles, and the effects of ever-changing and improving health care.

3. What do you wish you had known going into this profession?

I can honestly say that my education prepared me well for the job, and there weren't a lot of big surprises.

4. How do you see your profession changing in the next five years?

I think in the next five years, patients will be able to come directly to physical therapy without being required to have a referral from their primary care physician to satisfy health insurance requirements. Physical therapists will be more respected for having a doctorate in their field, and will have the ability to screen patients for red flags and determine whether they are appropriate for PT or require further diagnostic screening by a different specialist. (By 2015, all degree programs for physical therapists will be doctorate programs.) In addition, I think physical therapists will eventually be allowed to directly order imaging and to refer patients to other specialists as appropriate.

5. What role will technology play in those changes, and what skills will be required?

Technology is already changing the manner in which health care professionals interact with their patients, charge for billing, and record visits. We have to walk a fine line when seeing patients—typing in all the required information while also listening to a patient, making eye contact, and thinking critically: what is this patient's diagnosis? Physical therapists will need to be computer savvy to ensure all information is recorded accurately.

6. Do you have any general advice or additional professional insights to share with someone interested in your profession?

Physical therapy school is not easy. It is very hard work. You will go to class for eight hours some days, like a job. But it is worth all your time and effort. You will change people's lives by teaching them how to walk again, how to work without pain, return to their sport, or live more comfortably. The rewards of this profession are difficult to put into words. You will have patients who change your own perspective on life, who give you a greater insight into life and give your life meaning. You may think that you are changing their lives, but they effect change in yours. Each day is different from the next, full of variety and challenges. I am constantly learning. As more research is being produced, my evidence-based practice changes. You are keeping your mind active at all times. I honestly wouldn't want to be in any other profession.

7. Can you suggest a valuable "try this" for students considering a career in your profession?

I would suggest observing a physical therapist in a clinic for a few weeks. This will give you a better idea of what physical therapy is all about.

SELECTED SCHOOLS

Many colleges, universities, and professional schools offer programs in physical therapy. Below are listed some of the more prominent institutions in this field.

Emory University
Division of Physical Therapy
1462 Clifton Road NE, Suite 312
Atlanta, GA 30322
404.727.4002
www.rehabmed.emory.edu/pt

MGH Institute of Health Professions
Graduate Program in Physical Therapy
36 First Avenue
Boston, MA 02129
617.726.8009
www.mghihp.edu/academics/physical-therapy

Northwestern University
Department of Physical Therapy and Human Movement Science
645 N. Michigan Avenue, Suite 1100
Chicago, IL 60611
312.908.8160
www.medschool.northwestern.edu/nupthms

University of Delaware
Department of Physical Therapy
301 McKinly Laboratory
Newark, DE 19716
302.831.8910
www.udel.edu/PT

University of Iowa
Graduate Program in Physical Therapy
1-252 Medical Education Building
Iowa City, IA 52242
319.335.9791
www.medicine.uiowa.edu/physicaltherapy

University of Miami
Department of Physical Therapy
5915 Ponce de Leon Boulevard
Coral Gables, FL 33146
305.284.4535
pt.med.miami.edu

University of Pittsburgh
School of Health and Rehabilitation Sciences
4020 Forbes Tower
Pittsburgh, PA 15260
412.383.6558
www.shrs.pitt.edu

University of Southern California
Biokinesiology and Physical Therapy
1540 Alcatraz Street, CHP 155
Los Angeles, CA 90089
323.442.2900
pt/usc.edu

U.S. Army-Baylor University
Physical Therapy Department
3151 Scott Road
Fort Sam Houston, TX 78234
210.221.8410
www.baylor.edu/graduate/pt

Washington University, St. Louis
Program in Physical Therapy
4444 Forest Park Boulevard
St. Louis, MO 63108
314.286.1400
physicaltherapy.wustl.edu

MORE INFORMATION

American Physical Therapy Association
1111 N. Fairfax Street
Alexandria, VA 22314-1488
800.999.2782
www.apta.org

Commission on Accreditation of Allied Health Education Programs
1361 Park Street
Clearwater, FL 33756
727.210.2350
www.caahep.org

Federation of State Boards of Physical Therapy
124 West Street S, 3rd Floor
Alexandria, VA 22314
703.299.3100
www.fsbpt.org

Simone Isadora Flynn/Editor

Professional Athlete

Snapshot

Career Cluster(s): Sports and Fitness
Interests: Athletics, fitness, group activities
Earnings (Yearly Average): $44,680
Employment & Outlook: Average growth expected

OVERVIEW

Sphere of Work

Professional athletes and sports competitors are performers who compete in officiated sporting events in front of audiences. While many young athletes around the world aspire to become professional athletes, most will not become members of professional athletics organizations as there are few positions available compared to the number of aspiring athletes. For those who achieve positions in professional athletics associations, careers can be short and difficult as injuries or poor performance can quickly end a professional sports career. However, a small number of those who become professional athletes can achieve national or international fame and can earn extremely high salaries

matched only by other celebrity performers and high-level executive positions.

Work Environment

Most athletes work both indoors and outdoors and athletics is a collaborative discipline. Even athletes that work in single-competitor sports like tennis or boxing work closely with coaches, trainers, practice partners, and others to develop and maintain their athletic abilities. Athletes typically work irregular hours, with work concentrated during playing or performance seasons and the rest of the year spent in training or other types of preparation. During a playing season, athletes may be required to work long hours and may often travel for performances or promotional activities.

Profile

Working Conditions: Work Indoors and outdoors
Physical Strength: Strenuous work
Education Needs: None required
Licensure/Certification: None required
Opportunities For Experience: On the job training, Student experience
Holland Interest Score*: RE

* See Appendix A

Occupation Interest

Individuals looking to become professional athletes should be highly motivated to succeed in their career, due to the extremely high levels of competition for the few positions available for professional athletes. Professional athletes also need to be interested in overcoming obstacles and adversity and should have a strong interest in physical fitness and performance as professional athletes need to be able to craft a public persona as they also struggle to maintain their physical abilities to succeed in their sport.

A Day in the Life—Duties and Responsibilities

A typical day for a professional athlete will differ depending on the time of the year and the specific sport that the athlete takes part in. During the off season, athletes spend time practicing to maintain physical fitness and develop their skills. Athletes often need to participate in scheduled exercise activities and to follow dietary regimes. Athletes also spend time working with coaches, trainers, and teammates to develop their capacity for teamwork and deepen their skills in their chosen sport. During a performing season, athletes continue training and working with coaches and trainers, but also perform in games. During a match or game, the athlete is expected to follow the rules of the game and to follow instructions given by coaches or officials. During and after matches or games, athletes need to evaluate their performance, and the performance of their team in team sports, to identify personal strengths and weaknesses in preparation for future performances. In many cases, during and after playing seasons, athletes also participate in promotional activities that may include meeting with the press or with fans. Whether an athlete is a member of a team or an individual performer, athletes also typically need to spend time working on career development, which may include obtaining and participating in promotional activities or endorsements and participating in contract negotiations when they arise.

Duties and Responsibilities

- Train and practice skills needed for their sport
- Follow exercise, fitness, and nutritional plans
- Work with coaches, trainers, and other game officials
- Participate in promotional activities
- Work with teammates to develop teamwork and other skills
- Perform in official and unofficial matches or games
- Adhere to the rules of their sport during competitions
- Assess their individual performance to identify strengths and weaknesses

OCCUPATION SPECIALTIES

Association Football Player

Football (soccer) players participate in the world's most popular and most watched sport, with an estimated value of more than $600 billion worldwide. Most professional football players begin playing when they are young and continue through secondary school before becoming professional. Association football requires athleticism, endurance, and the ability to work closely with other team members.

Gymnast

Gymnastics is one of the world's oldest sports and is practiced around the world at both the amateur, recreational, and professional levels. Gymnasts need excellent strength, agility, endurance, and coordination and there are numerous specializations within the gymnastics field, such as tumbling, rhythmic gymnastics, and vaulting.

Martial Artist

Martial artists practice one of numerous different types of martial disciplines in competitions and exhibitions around the world. Chinese and Japanese martial arts are the most globally recognized forms of martial arts, while there are a variety of other cultural styles featured in competitions, such as Filipino eskrima and Thai boxing. In addition to competitive matches against other opponents, martial artists can participate in solo exhibitions of weapon or bare handed routines or other skills.

Jockey

Jockeys are athletes who specialize in riding horses and compete in both races and skill competitions where they guide a horse through demonstrations of agility and dexterity. Jockey's need concentration, endurance, and excellent reflexes. Jockeys also need skills with animals as their job requires that they learn to communicate and read the behaviors of the animals that they ride during competitions.

WORK ENVIRONMENT

Relevant Skills and Abilities

Communication Skills
- Communicate with teammates, coaches, and trainers
- Participate in media marketing efforts

Interpersonal/Social Skills
- Developing working relationships with other athletes, coaches, and trainers
- Being able to listen to information from other members of a team.

Organization & Management Skills
- Participating in training and development activities
- Mentoring new teammates or aspiring athletes
- Managing time when performing or practicing

Research & Planning Skills
- Analyzing performances to identify strengths and weaknesses

Technical Skills
- Utilizing basic digital technology and personal computers

Physical Environment

The physical environment for a professional athlete varies according to the type of sport. Winter athletes, for instance, who compete in sports like skiing, skating, and bobsledding, need access to facilities with ice and/or snow and do much of their training outdoors. Many athletes perform some or all of their training outdoors or in specialized training centers. Athletes often need to travel for competitions and to participate in promotional activities or training exercises. In some cases, professional athletes may regularly travel internationally to compete in various types of competitions.

Human Environment

Athletes participating in team sports spend much of their time working closely with others and need to be able to develop strong teamwork and the ability to communicate with officials, coaches, and other members of their team. Individual athletes also spend much of their time working closely with others, including sport professionals and officials, trainers, coaches, and other athletes. For those at the upper end of the spectrum, athletes might also need to spend time promoting their work or their team and so need to develop the skills necessary to act as a spokesperson for their own career.

Technological Environment

Many of the tools used by athletes to develop and improve their athletic prowess not changed significantly in decades or centuries. Athletes regularly use a wide variety of exercise and conditioning equipment to stay in shape and In the 21st century, athletes and athletics organizations also have the option of using complex motion analysis equipment and software, which can be helpful in identifying problems in an athlete's performance or in helping the athlete to visualize his or her technique. Digital technology is also increasingly important for professional athletes, helping them to communicate, schedule, and perform a variety of other necessary activities.

EDUCATION, TRAINING, AND ADVANCEMENT

High School/Secondary

There are no specific high school/secondary requirements for those seeking to be professional athletes, though many athletes get their start by playing for school-sponsored teams. In the United States, aspiring athletes can attempt to join high school baseball, soccer, hockey, and/or football teams as a way of building skills and preparing for a professional career. Though many students play sports at the high school/secondary level, those who become professional athletes often start when younger and few high school/secondary school athletes are able to earn positions with a professional athletics association. Prospective athletes can also use their high school/ secondary education to study subjects that will help in later efforts to develop their professional careers.

Suggested High School Subjects
- Physical education
- Physics
- Mathematics

- English
- Public Speaking
- Marketing
- Introduction to Business
- Introduction to Computers

Famous First

For years, historians have argued about which sport is the oldest. Paleolithic cave drawings in France indicate that wrestling and either running or sprinting existed as early as 7000 BCE and historians believe that these sports were already centuries old before they were commemorated in artistic renditions. Bowling is another of the earliest known sports as evidence of simple bowling sets have been found in the tombs of ancient Egyptians though it is currently unknown where or when the sport originated. While the modern team sports originated far later in history, many of the sports comprising the Olympic Games have been around for thousands of years and represent some of the earliest organized sporting fields in the world.

College/Postsecondary

Athletes who participate in high school/secondary school teams or athletics programs might continue preparing for professional careers by seeking a position on a collegiate team. Many colleges and universities have athletics programs that include sports like baseball, hockey, football, gymnastics, and other sports. Many professional athletes are drafted out of college or university teams, which has made colleges and universities a prime spot for recruitment. Because obtaining a career as a professional athlete is extremely difficult, many college and university advisors will counsel students looking to become athletes to also obtain at least a bachelor's degree in another field. Athletes can choose to focus on athletics or exercise science as an area of concentration or can choose to obtain a degree in any field.

Related College Majors
- Physical Education
- Exercise Science

- Communications
- Business and Marketing
- Education

Adult Job Seekers

Adults looking to become professional athletes can attempt to build a career in professional sports by participating in amateur sports associations, or organizations. Most professional athletes are drafted early in their lives and have short careers as professionals before retiring. As it typically takes many years of training to become a professional athlete, few individuals transition to professional athletics as adults unless they had previous experience earlier in life. Turning professional is the ultimate goal for an aspiring athlete and only a select few are chosen from among thousands of prospective athletes around the world who compete at lower levels.

Professional Certification and Licensure

Licensing for athletes is handled on a state-by-state basis. Some sports do not require athletes to be licensed, while others typically do. Most professional sports have governing organizations that make rules about which athletes are allowed to perform and athletes can lose their certification to perform for violations such as being charged or convicted of a crime, using drugs, or failing to meet safety or performance guidelines. Sports teams may also establish their own guidelines for athletes, requiring athletes to pass certain physical tests before they are allowed to compete or perform with their team.

Additional Requirements

Professional athletics is a difficult goal that typically requires years of concentrated practice. Athletes typically begin playing when young and then compete at lower levels of competition before performing professionally. In addition, athletes must constantly work to maintain and improve their performance and athletes typically dedicate considerable time to exercise and training during a typical year. In addition to athletic skill and talent, athletes need to have coordination, teamwork, stamina, and concentration to perform at the highest levels of their sport.

Fun Fact

You know how baseball games can feel as if they will never end? The actual action lasts a total of 18 minutes, although the game itself lasts for hours.

Source: ftw.usatoday.com

EARNINGS AND ADVANCEMENT

The median annual wages for professional athletes is skewed by the extremely high salaries earned by professional athletes at the top of the profession, who can earn millions each year for their performances. The Bureau of Labor Statistics (BLS) estimated the median annual wage for athletes at $44,680 in 2015, with those at the lowest 10 percent earning less than $19,000 and those in the highest ten percent earning more than $187,000. Advancing in professional sports is a matter of performance and marketability. The highest earning professional athletes are often those considered to be top performers out of all performers in their particular sport or those whose performances attract more attention from fans. Some athletes advance by moving from one team to another after their initial contract has expired. Some athletes are able to increase their annual revenues through promotional endorsements or by using their celebrity to advertise products.

Metropolitan Areas with the Highest Employment Level in this Occupation

Metropolitan area	Employment	Employment per thousand jobs	Hourly mean wage
Philadelphia, PA Metropolitan Division	380	0.44	N/A
Chicago-Naperville-Arlington Heights, IL Metropolitan Division	360	0.10	N/A
Atlanta-Sandy Springs-Roswell, GA	330	0.13	N/A
Orlando-Kissimmee-Sanford, FL	320	0.28	N/A
Denver-Aurora-Lakewood, CO	270	0.20	N/A
Tampa-St. Petersburg-Clearwater, FL	260	0.22	N/A
Charlotte-Concord-Gastonia, NC-SC	260	0.23	N/A
Phoenix-Mesa-Scottsdale, AZ	230	0.12	N/A
Cape Coral-Fort Myers, FL	230	0.96	N/A
Pittsburgh, PA	210	0.19	N/A

Source: Bureau of Labor Statistics

EMPLOYMENT AND OUTLOOK

The BLS estimates that opportunities for professional athletes will increase by 6 percent between 2014 and 2024, marking average or slightly less than average growth compared to the 7-8 percent predicted for all occupations. Growth of urban areas and states may lead to an increase in the number of professional sports teams, thus creating growth. Though the industry is expected to grow over the 2014-2024 period, competition for available positions will remain extremely high. Only 1 in 3,000 collegiate or high school athletes are given the opportunity to play professionally and, even for those who do play professionally, injury and age can quickly end a player's career as professional sports franchises let older or injured players go to begin developing new talent. Competition is highest in the most popular sports, like baseball, hockey, American football, association football, and basketball, and some types of Olympic sports.

Employment Trend, Projected 2014–24

Total, all occupations: 7%

Entertainers and performers, sports and related workers: 6%

Athletes and sports competitors: 6%

Note: "All Occupations" includes all occupations in the U.S. Economy. Source: U.S. Bureau of Labor Statistics, Employment Projections Program

Related Occupations
- Coaches and Scouts
- Fitness Trainers and Instructors
- Recreation Workers
- Umpires, Referees, and other Sports Officials

Related Occupations
- Armed Forces Cross Country Athlete
- Armed Forces Basketball Player
- Armed Forces Baseball Player

Conversation With . . .
ANYA BATTAGLINO

Defense, Connecticut Whale
National Women's Hockey League (NWHL)
Pro athlete, 2 years

1. What was your individual career path in terms of education/training, entry-level job, or other significant opportunity?

My brother played hockey when I was a kid and I wanted to do everything he did. So when I started in a tyke program at age four, I picked the number 16 to be twice as good as him. His number was 8.

I went through the local hockey program in Waltham, MA, and played club AAA hockey. Then I played for Boston University for two years, then played for the Canadian Women's Hockey League for two years for a team called the Boston Blades while I was still in school. I graduated with a bachelor's in marine biology and microbiology. Then the National Women's Hockey League started in 2015 and I came here. We have teams in New York, Boston, Buffalo and Northford, Connecticut, near New Haven. We play nineteen games a year, on Sundays, and practice Tues-Thurs nights. So playing is a 10-hour commitment during weeks we have home games, but it can be up to 30 if we are traveling to Buffalo for a game. We're the first paid women's hockey league, but it's not a livable salary. I work full-time in technology sales for Gartner, Inc.

I'm also the director of our players' association, the governing body to advocate for the betterment of players, fair standards, and where we're going from here. Because I'm in outside sales, I have the flexibility to make my own schedule.

I'll probably play another year or two. Players below me will get better, and I will need to focus on my career, although I haven't really figured that out. I hope one day women's hockey can support more jobs, whether it's as a general manager or administrator...if those things were possible for me now, in the National Hockey League, that would be my dream.

Guys playing hockey have a different life. I work a whole job, try to get in 20 minutes of weight lifting, then go to practice and don't get off the ice until 10:30 p.m. My body doesn't get the recovery I need. A pro guy's day is very different: get a massage, work with the coach, skate, have a nice meal, cool down, and work one-on-one with the athletic trainer. The commitment level for a female is so much higher because she has to do more to make it work. Women's pro sports is so grassroots, we have to be more creative. It makes us that much more qualified to work in sports.

2. What are the most important skills and/or qualities for someone in your profession?

Hard work and dedication. To be a pro athlete in general takes an unrelenting work ethic. As a woman, there's also a huge commitment; a belief that what we are doing is the right thing.

3. What do you wish you had known going into this profession?

When you become a pro athlete, you're a role model. You don't have the flexibility to completely be yourself. You have to think about what other people perceive from your actions and always be on game and represent something bigger than yourself. That, and that I would never sleep.

4. Are there many job opportunities in your profession? In what specific areas?

Not a ton. There are 92 players in our league, which is the only women's hockey league that pays. It's better to think about what this can open up: coaching? Roles in college athletics? Pro athletes have a level of time management and dedication that should open doors.

5. How do you see your profession changing in the next five years, what role will technology play in those changes, and what skills will be required?

Technology plays a huge role, from the "digitized nutritionist" who works with us to heart monitors that track some of the sports-specific parts of our job to market strategies utilizing Twitter or Periscope. It's all about the digital footprint and how you can market online. Also, a lot of coaching pieces to develop youth players are on YouTube. More and more people are going to use athletes to speak to their groups via webinars.

6. What do you enjoy most about your job? What do you enjoy least about your job?

I like playing hockey but I also like watching little kids watch me play, or, at the end of the game, come to get our autographs. It's fun to watch people react to us as we chase and catch our dreams.

I least like that if I were a man, I'd be making millions of dollars and as it is, I won't be making thousands of dollars. It really hurts knowing somebody doing exactly the same thing as me is making so much more.

7. Can you suggest a valuable "try this" for students considering a career in your profession?

Go to as many practices, clinics and coaching opportunities as possible to get feedback. Everyone can get better, and the way to get better is to communicate. If you want to play a pro sport or have sports in your life professionally, you need constant feedback.

MORE INFORMATION

National Collegiate Athletic Association (NCAA)
700 W. Washington Street
P.O. Box 6222
Indianapolis, IN 46206
317-917-6222
www.ncaa.org

National Council of Youth Sports (NCYS)
7185 S.E. Seagate Lane
Stuart, FL 34997
772-781-1452
www.ncys.org

National Federation of State High School Associations (NFHS)
P.O. Box 690
Indianapolis, IN 46206
317-972-6900
www.nfhs.org

Micah Issitt/Editor

Public Relations Specialist

Snapshot

Career Cluster: Business Management, Marketing, Sales & Service

Interests: Mass Communications, Media Relations, Public Opinion, Crisis Management

Earnings (Yearly Average): $55,215

Employment & Outlook: Faster Than Average Growth Expected

OVERVIEW

Sphere of Work

Public relations (PR) specialists are communication professionals who handle a wide range of functions to support clients or employers in their efforts to build and maintain a positive public image, seek positive media exposure, and forge strong relationships with the public. Almost any organization or individual can be a client, such as businesses, industries, non-profit organizations, universities, hospitals, government, or celebrities. Companies employ their own PR specialists, as well. PR specialists are responsible for media and community relations,

consumer and industry relations, investor and employee relations, and interest-group representation, as well as political campaigns, fundraising, and conflict mediation.

As part of these functions, public relations specialists focus on maintaining contact with print and broadcast media, arranging media interviews, setting up speaker engagements, hosting events, writing speeches and press releases, and planning and conducting press conferences. Public relations specialists communicate key messages that have been strategically crafted. These messages must be approved by the client or employer, be clear and understandable to the audience or market, and should align with short- and long-term business goals.

Profile

Working Conditions: Work Indoors
Physical Strength: Light Work
Education Needs: Bachelor's Degree
Licensure/Certification: Required
Physical Abilities Not Required: No Heavy Labor
Opportunities For Experience: Internship, Apprenticeship, Military Service, Volunteer Work, Part-Time Work
Holland Interest Score*: EAS

* See Appendix A

Occupation Interest

The public relations field attracts those who enjoy working with people from all industries and environments—who can easily communicate on many levels. Writing is an essential skill for public relations specialists, as is an ability to gauge public opinion, empathize with particular market segments, and assess the public perception of a given message.

Many colleges and universities offer a degree in public relations. Typical coursework includes core classes in English and writing, with specialty coursework in public relations, journalism, news and speech writing, media relations, communications, planning and analysis, crisis management, and public relations ethics.

A Day in the Life—Duties and Responsibilities

Like all communications experts, public relations specialists are consistently on alert for new and creative ways to achieve client/ employer goals and to protect, preserve, or enhance a company's image. In a typical day, public relations specialists will write and distribute news releases, prepare copy for annual reports, take and manage calls from journalists, plan press conferences or events, line up media interviews, provide executives with media training and debriefing after interviews, and attend strategy meetings with clients or employers and public relations managers. Within a corporation, "clients" may be divisions or areas inside the company, with the public relations specialist preparing and disseminating various types of information for different departments, all under the banner of one key message.

Public relations specialists often face pressure from eager clients, and work frequently with outside reporters, producers, bloggers, and other social media specialists. In order to avoid the label of a "spin doctor"—a pejorative term often assigned to PR professionals in corporate or government communications—successful PR specialists do well to earn the trust of those in the media by maintaining a professional demeanor and a strict code of ethics. Successful PR specialists communicate a client's message by delivering it to the public in a truthful manner that provides positive exposure for the client and useful information to the customer.

Public relations specialists are employed in nearly every industry in some form or fashion, which makes this a flexible career option. Additionally, because of advances in technology, and through the use of email, videoconferencing, and online social media, public relations specialists can work from almost any location. Self-employment is common among PR specialists; however, most entry-level candidates do not yet have the experience required to branch out on their own.

Duties and Responsibilities

- Determining the needs of the organization or individual client
- reparing and distributing fact sheets, photographs, articles, news releases and/or promotional booklets
- Making speeches and conducting background research
- Evaluating and maintaining the client's public image
- Directing advertising campaigns in all types of media
- Coordinating special exhibits, contests or luncheons into the total public relations plan
- Helping clients to communicate with the public

OCCUPATION SPECIALTIES

Lobbyists

Lobbyists contact and confer with members of the legislature and other holders of public office to persuade them to support legislation favorable to their clients' interests.

Fundraising Directors

Fundraising Directors direct and coordinate the solicitation and disbursement of funds for community social-welfare organizations. They establish fund-raising goals according to the financial need of the agency and formulate policies for collecting and safeguarding the contributions.

Media/Communications Specialists

Media specialists, or communications specialists, handle an organization's communication with the public, including consumers, investors, reporters, and other media specialists. In government, public relations specialists may be called press secretaries. They keep the public informed about the activities of government officials and agencies.

Sales-Service Promoters

Sales-Service Promoters generate sales and create good will for a firm's products by preparing displays and touring the country. They call on merchants to advise them of ways to increase sales and demonstrate products.

WORK ENVIRONMENT

Physical Environment

Busy office settings predominate. In an agency environment (i.e., when working for a PR firm), public relations specialists cater to the demands of more than one client and can expect a busy atmosphere with many phone calls and tight deadlines. In-office work includes writing and assistance in strategy sessions with clients and the agency itself. Public relations specialists can also work within a company's larger communication department, often as part of a marketing role. The ability to work as a team, providing a comprehensive communication strategy, is essential.

While most public relations specialists usually work in an office setting, it is not necessarily where they spend all their time. They are often on the road, with clients, meeting with journalists, hosting press conferences or events, and helping executives receive media training. Public relations specialists can be seen at trade shows and conventions, auditoriums, and broadcast or print offices, working with executives from all levels and all industries.

Relevant Skills and Abilities

Analytical Skills
- Assessing social trends

Communication Skills
- Listening attentively
- Speaking and writing effectively
- Persuading others

Interpersonal/Social Skills
- Cooperating with others
- Exhibiting confidence
- Working as a member of a team

Organization & Management Skills
- Coordinating tasks
- Making decisions
- Managing people/groups
- Selling ideas or products

Planning & Research Skills
- Creating ideas
- Developing evaluation strategies
- Solving problems

Human Environment

Public relations specialists must have strong interpersonal skills because they are dealing with a wide variety of environments. They work with fast-paced news reporters and bloggers, broadcast producers, freelance writers, engineers, corporate executives, other business specialists, legal counsel, and the general public. At times, this can produce high stress levels and will require the ability to multitask and delegate. Public relations specialists often work in crisis management, and therefore need to maintain calm while thinking and acting quickly.

Technological Environment

Today, public relations specialists use a wide range of technology to achieve client goals. This technology includes everything from phone and email, to texting, tweeting, blogging, and monitoring online news organizations.

EDUCATION, TRAINING, AND ADVANCEMENT

High School/Secondary

It is best for public relations specialists to have a college degree with some experience, such as an internship. High school students can best prepare to be a public relations specialist through Advanced Placement (AP) English courses that include and encourage non-fiction or news editorial writing, creative writing, reading comprehension, public speaking, critical thinking, and decision making. Extracurricular activities, such as working with the school newspaper, can also help high school students gain admission to the universities they want to attend.

Suggested High School Subjects
- Business
- College Preparatory
- Composition
- English
- Graphic Communications
- Humanities
- Journalism
- Keyboarding
- Literature
- Political Science
- Psychology
- Social Studies
- Sociology
- Speech

Fun Fact

The Stanley Cup, awarded to the National Hockey League's annual champion, has been used as a cereal bowl, tossed into a swimming pool, and accidentally left by the side of the road. A savvy Air Canada employee rescued after it was left on a flight from New Jersey to Vancouver.

Source: onemillionskates.com

Famous First

The first "publicity bureau" is thought to have been founded around 1900 by persons associated with the railroad industry. By the second decade of the 20th century, two prominent pioneers in public relations had emerged: Edward Bernays and Ivy Lee. Both left a lasting imprint on the field, but Bernays outlived Lee by several decades and helped the field to mature.

College/Postsecondary

A bachelor's degree is highly recommended for success as a public relations specialist. Many universities offer communications programs, often specializing in journalism, which can include subspecialties within actual public relations majors.

Universities often provide internship opportunities, with the aim of the internship turning into an official entry-level job offer. College students are encouraged to make use of existing career centers, to question professors with well-thought out ideas, secure mentors, and seek input about studies and the jobs they can lead to.

Advanced degrees, such as a master's or PhD, are not necessary for public relations specialists; after earning a bachelor's degree, most of these professionals move through the job ranks through on-the-job experience and a successful portfolio.

Related College Majors
- Business & Personal Services Marketing Operations
- Business Administration & Management, General
- Liberal Arts
- Mass Communications
- public relations ethics

Adult Job Seekers

It is useful to maintain an up-to-date resume with other credentials, such as scholarships, internships, awards, and grants. Being prepared with a portfolio of accomplishments from previous jobs is a good way to demonstrate relevant skills.

Those who do well as public relations specialists are able to articulate the written and spoken word, have confidence, and relate easily to others. They are quick learners and thinkers, calm in the face of pressure, and are persuasive communicators.

Professional associations are often useful sources for those transitioning from another career to public relations, in that they track job openings and provide unique networking opportunities. The Public Relations Society of America (PRSA) and the International Association of Business Communicators (IABC) are two such professional associations.

Professional Certification and Licensure

Accreditations for public relations can be helpful but are not necessary. Employers have varying outlooks on certification. The PRSA has an accreditation program for members who have at least five years of professional experience. The IABC offers opportunities for professionals to be internationally recognized for their achievements through a variety of awards. Work portfolios that include accomplishments such as press clippings, published speeches, or bylined articles are helpful in receiving certification. Professional accreditation can indicate competence in the field which then can help people find jobs in the highly competitive environment of public relations. Consult credible professional associations within your field and follow professional debate as to the relevancy and value of any certification program.

Additional Requirements

Understanding clients' audiences and target markets is essential for aspiring public relations specialists. Public relations specialists must research client background and objectives, understand the business, and "sell" key messages to those people who will benefit from the specific product or service.

EARNINGS AND ADVANCEMENT

Earnings of public relations specialists depend on the type of industry in which the individual is employed and the size and geographic location of the employer. Private consulting firms generally pay more than companies that have their own public relations departments. Median annual earnings of public relations specialists were $55,215 in 2012. The lowest ten percent earned less than $32,394, and the highest ten percent earned more than $100,912.

Public relations specialists may receive paid vacations, holidays, and sick days; life and health insurance; and retirement benefits. These are usually paid by the employer. Some employers may also provide an expense account.

Metropolitan Areas with the Highest Employment Level in This Occupation

Metropolitan area	Employment[1]	Employment per thousand jobs	Hourly mean wage
New York-White Plains-Wayne, NY-NJ	16,210	3.14	$34.28
Washington-Arlington-Alexandria, DC-VA-MD-WV	13,980	5.97	$42.70
Los Angeles-Long Beach-Glendale, CA	7,800	2.02	$36.18
Boston-Cambridge-Quincy, MA	5,750	3.36	$31.28
Philadelphia, PA	4,620	2.54	$33.58
Chicago-Joliet-Naperville, IL	4,570	1.25	$30.24
Dallas-Plano-Irving, TX	3,660	1.74	$32.65
Houston-Sugar Land-Baytown, TX	3,610	1.37	$27.72

(1) Does not include self-employed or PR managers/executives. Source: Bureau of Labor Statistics, 2012

EMPLOYMENT AND OUTLOOK

Nationally, there were approximately 255,000 public relations specialists employed in 2012. Public relations specialists are concentrated in service-providing industries, such as advertising and related services, health care and social assistance, educational services and government. Employment is expected to grow faster than the average for all occupations through the year 2020, which means employment is projected to increase 16 percent to 23 percent. The need for good public relations in a competitive business environment should create demand for public relations specialists in organizations of all types and sizes. With the increasing demand for corporate accountability, more emphasis will be placed on improving the image of the client, as well as building public confidence.

Employment Trend, Projected 2010–20

Public Relations Specialists: 23%

Public Relations Managers and Specialists: 21%

Public Relations and Fundraising Managers: 16%

Total, All Occupations: -14%

Note: "All Occupations" includes all occupations in the U.S. Economy Source: U.S. Bureau of Labor Statistics, Employment Projections Program

Related Occupations
- Advertising Account Executive
- Advertising Agent
- Copywriter
- Electronic Commerce Specialist
- General Manager and Top Executive
- Online Merchant

Related Military Occupations
- Public Information Officer

Conversation With . . .
ANDY McGOWAN

President, Watkins McGowan & The Ledlie Group
Atlanta, Georgia
Public relations, 28 years

1. What was your individual career path in terms of education/training, entry-level job, or other significant opportunity?

I went to the University of Albany, pre-med, and also played hockey. When I showed up for my work-study assignment freshman year, there were two jobs left. One was to work for the sports information director. They asked, "Can you write?" By the next weekend, I was covering college football. The director taught English part time at the local high school, so I ended up being the de facto sports information director on campus. Pretty good luck! The next year, we got a new director and I trained him. By senior year, I worked directly for the athletic director. I also ran the hockey team, which was a club sport, for two years.

My bachelor's is in biology, but I loved sports and business, so I took business law and other business classes my last year. I went on to get my master's degree in sports management from Springfield College in Massachusetts while interning for the Hartford Whalers. I got to know the reporters and producers, and made as many contacts as I could.

I worked with a sports management team in Albany, N.Y., spent two years in the minors, then was recruited to a top minor hockey league, the International Hockey League in Indianapolis where, for a year and a half, I generated more publicity than some of the NHL markets. The NHL commissioner noticed, and asked: "Who is this kid getting all of this coverage?" I was recruited and flown to New York for a job interview the day the referees went on strike in 1993. They put me to work that night, and offered me a job the next day. I went to the NHL as manager of public relations and was promoted to director a year and a half later.

I later went to the Washington Capitals as Vice President for Communications, then taught sports management and journalism classes at UMass Amherst. In 2007, I went to work for Major League Soccer's New York Red Bulls. They wanted somebody to take over their communications, and I generated more publicity than they'd ever had. When my boss left for Qualcomm, he needed a right-hand man so I joined him in Atlanta. Qualcomm makes chips to make your cell phone run. From a marketing or PR standpoint, it's no different than sports. The same principles apply. I went from Qualcomm to UPS, then started my own communications group. We have one sports client and I'm building up that part of our clientele. I can't get sports out of my blood.

I also still teach. Currently, I teach undergraduate and graduate business courses at Georgia State University.

2. What are the most important skills and/or qualities for someone in your profession?

You need contacts who trust you. I give media people good stories in a timely way, am attentive to detail, and available for follow up. Are you good with people and are you trustworthy? All of this makes your reputation.

You also need to be able to write well, present yourself well, and be comfortable around people. I see people who are uncomfortable with small talk, but you have to have that kind of personality.

3. What do you wish you had known going into this profession?

The hours. Working in sports means that you're busy when everyone else is enjoying leisure time. You work all day, then on game night you set up the pressroom, the media shows up, and you leave at midnight. Hockey is 100-plus games in a season. Baseball is 162.

4. Are there many job opportunities in your profession? In what specific areas?

If you're good at what you do and willing to work hard, you will be successful. Sports doesn't pay well to start. You have to broaden your thinking beyond, "I want to work for the Giants or the Yankees." There are statistics bureaus, TV production companies, and lots of PR and marketing agencies that work with corporate sponsors.

5. How do you see your profession changing in the next five years, what role will technology play in those changes, and what skills will be required?

The big thing I see is analytics, the "Moneyball" kind of idea. The communications tools out there are digital and will continue to change. A friend of mine is doing virtual reality for the NFL. As far as social media: it's great, and it's a nightmare, keeping up with the platforms, understanding them and being able to react and respond. You need to be adaptive.

6. What do you enjoy most about your job? What do you enjoy least?

Working in sports and getting paid for it is fun. I looked forward to getting up and going to work. You're on the ride with the team.

The hours can get long. It takes a lot of time to do an event.

7. Can you suggest a valuable "try this" for students considering a career in your profession?

Volunteer with a team, hang out, and learn. In college, I hung around the athletic department all day long. They'd say, "Hey Andy, we're rolling out the mats for the wrestling match, can you help set up?" And I'd say sure. If you're dependable and reliable, people will trust you.

SELECTED SCHOOLS

Most colleges and universities have bachelor's degree programs in the liberal arts, which is a good foundation for work as a public relations specialist. Other institutions have programs devoted to communications and media, another good foundation. The student may also gain initial training at a community college. Below are listed some of the more prominent four-year institutions in this field.

Columbia University
535 W. 116th Street
New York, NY 10027
212.854.1754
www.columbia.edu

Massachusetts Institute of Technology
77 Massachusetts Avenue
Cambridge, MA 02139
617.253.1000
www.mit.edu

New York University
70 Washington Square S
New York, NY 10012
212.998.1212
www.nyu.edu

Stanford University
450 Serra Mall
Stanford, CA 94305
650.723.2300
www.stanford.edu

University of California, Berkeley
101 Sproul Hall
Berkeley, CA 94704
510.642.6000
www.berkeley.edu

University of California, Los Angeles
405 Hilgard Avenue
Los Angeles, CA 90095
310.825.4321
www.ucla.edu

University of Michigan, Ann Arbor
1032 Green Street
Ann Arbor, MI 48109
734.764.1817
www.umich.edu

University of Pennsylvania
3451 Walnut Street
Philadelphia, PA 19104
215.898.5000
www.upenn.edu

University of Texas, Austin
110 Inner Campus Drive
Austin, TX 78712
512.471.3434
www.utexas.edu

Yale University
P.O. Box 208234
New Haven, CT 06520
203.432.4771
www.yale.edu

MORE INFORMATION

American Association of Advertising Agencies
405 Lexington Avenue, 18th Floor
New York, NY 10174-1801
212.682.2500
www.aaaa.org

Association of Fundraising Professionals
4300 Wilson Boulevard
Arlington, VA 22203
703.684.0410
www.afpnet.org

Public Relations Society of America
33 Maiden Lane, 11th Floor
New York, NY 10038-5150
212.460.1400
www.prsa.org

International Association of Business Communicators
601 Montgomery Street, Suite 1900
San Francisco, CA 94111
415.544.4700
www.iabc.com

Susan Williams/Editor

Radio/TV Announcer & Newscaster

Snapshot

Career Cluster: Media & Communications

Interests: Broadcasting, Mass Communication, Journalism, Public Speaking

Earnings (Yearly Average): $42,925

Employment & Outlook: Slower Than Average Growth Expected

OVERVIEW

Sphere of Work

Announcers and newscasters deliver news and commentary on radio and television. Radio announcers and television newscasters are both also traditionally known as broadcasters. In addition to delivering news information to listeners and viewers, broadcasters conduct interviews, moderate discussions, and provide commentary for live sporting competitions, musical selections, and developing news events. Several broadcasters also veer

into journalism, researching and writing about topics for discussion on their particular programs. As such, broadcasting has broadened into a multidisciplinary profession encompassing mass communication, journalism, and reportage.

Work Environment

Broadcasters operate primarily out of radio and television studios, where they work in concert with technical and production staff to prepare radio and television programs. It is not uncommon for broadcasters to travel to areas where important news events are unfolding, presenting their programs from a diverse array of locales from show to show. Broadcasters are also often called upon to visit interview subjects and develop stories from a variety of locations in and around their region, the country, or even the globe. In the past, most broadcasters worked nontraditional hours, including early mornings, late nights, weekends, and holidays, but newer technology has enabled more broadcasts to be prerecorded.

Occupation Interest

While radio announcers and television newscasters traditionally came from media communications backgrounds, the field is now populated by individuals who come from numerous academic and professional backgrounds, including journalism, politics, science, literature, music, and the arts.

Profile

Working Conditions: Work Indoors
Physical Strength: Light Work
Education Needs: Bachelor's Degree
Licensure/Certification: Recommended
Physical Abilities Not Required: No Heavy Labor
Opportunities For Experience: Internship, Apprenticeship, Military Service, Volunteer Work, Part-Time Work
Holland Interest Score*: SEC

* See Appendix A

Colleges and universities nationwide offer specific academic programs dedicated to both audio and visual broadcasting, which students often reinforce with course work dedicated to their other academic interests, notably English, politics, or sports management. Excellent time management, judgment, and organization are just as imperative as personality and conversational skills.

A Day in the Life—Duties and Responsibilities

Radio and television broadcasters spend their days planning future shows, filming or recording new broadcasts, and editing new recordings for public broadcast. On air, broadcasters generally introduce and close programs, present information, and lead discussions. Many of the specific occupational duties and responsibilities of radio and television broadcasters depend on the nature and frequency of the program for which they work.

Developing programs that air live on a daily basis predominantly involves preproduction tasks such as fact gathering, organizing specific questions, and preparing for guest interviews. Live television and radio production is often completed in a fast-paced environment under strict deadlines. As a result, radio and television broadcasters who work in live programming often must effectively adapt to evolving situations and on-air conversations.

Documentary-style radio and television programs conduct a large amount of investigative research and information gathering. Documentary programs tend to air on a less frequent basis, usually weekly or monthly; thus, much of the focus for developing such programs is placed on gathering video and audio copy, narrative construction, fact checking, and follow-up interviews with subjects. The protracted nature of documentary radio and television broadcasting necessitates a lot of editing work prior to presentation.

Duties and Responsibilities

- Introducing various types of radio or television programs
- Announcing news, commercial breaks, and public service messages
- Interviewing guests
- Describing sports and public events
- Writing scripts and news copy
- Selling commercial time
- Keeping records of programs and preparing program logs
- Reviewing and selecting recordings for air play

OCCUPATION SPECIALTIES

Anchors/Hosts

News Anchors and Program Hosts work in television or radio and specialize in a certain area of interest, such as politics, personal finance, sports, or health. They contribute to the preparation of the program's content, interview guests, and discuss issues with viewers, listeners, or the studio or radio audience.

Commentators

Commentators analyze and write commentaries, based upon personal knowledge and experience with the subject matter, for broadcast. They interpret information on a topic and record their commentary or present it live during the broadcast.

Critics

Critics write and deliver critical reviews of literary, musical, or artistic works and performances for broadcast.

Disc Jockeys (DJs)

Disc Jockeys, or DJs, announce radio programs of musical selections, and choose the selections to be made based upon knowledge of audience preference or requests. They also comment upon the music and other matters of interest to the audience, such as the weather, time, and traffic conditions.

Newsreaders

Newsreaders read prepared news copy over the air. They may or may not be involved in the writing and editing of that copy.

Public Address Announcers

Public Address Announcers provide information to the audience at sporting, performing arts, and other events.

WORK ENVIRONMENT

Physical Environment

Television and radio broadcasting studios are the broadcaster's primary work environment. These spaces are generally bright, soundproof, and temperature controlled. A considerable amount of fieldwork may also be required. Broadcasters may work in a variety of locations, including government buildings, sports arenas, and hospitals. They may also serve as station representatives at public events.

Relevant Skills and Abilities

Communication Skills
- Speaking and writing clearly and effectively
- Being able to pronounce difficult words and phrases with ease
- Being able to speak consistently and at length
- Being able to listen while speaking

Interpersonal/Social Skills
- Being objective
- Being persistent
- Cooperating with others
- Working as a member of a team

Organization & Management Skills
- Paying attention to and handling details
- Performing duties that change frequently

Planning & Research Skills
- Creating ideas
- Laying out a plan
- Researching a topic

Human Environment

Radio and television broadcasters are often the public face of a larger team of technical and production staff with whom they are required to work closely with on a daily basis.

Technological Environment

Radio and television broadcasters use a wide range of communication and broadcasting technology, from microphones and teleprompters to sophisticated editing equipment.

EDUCATION, TRAINING, AND ADVANCEMENT

High School/Secondary

High school students can best prepare for a career in broadcasting with courses in public speaking, composition, the dramatic arts, and computer science. Many high schools have scholastic television and radio stations that instruct students on broadcasting basics. Exposure to local radio and television broadcasting stations through internships or volunteer work may also be highly beneficial. Writing and reporting on local events for a school or community newspaper will provide high school students with reportage and interviewing experience that can benefit a future career in broadcasting.

Suggested High School Subjects
- Applied Communication
- College Preparatory
- Composition
- English
- Foreign Languages
- Journalism
- Literature
- Speech
- Theatre & Drama

Famous First

The first radio station to feature a 24-hour "all-news" format was WINS, 1010 on the AM dial (New York City), beginning in 1965. Other AM stations around the nation quickly followed suit, leading to a spike in the hiring of announcers.

College/Postsecondary

Hundreds of colleges and universities in the United States offer undergraduate- and graduate-level programs in broadcasting. The majority of entry-level radio and television broadcasting positions require a bachelor's degree in communication, broadcasting, or journalism.

Undergraduate programs in journalism outline the techniques and strategies that apply to television and radio reporters while honing students' reporting and storytelling skills. Journalism majors also learn the basic ethical standards that dictate news production across all types and levels of media. Undergraduate work in broadcasting exposes students to the vast array of media technologies and software used in the field and helps them learn the acoustics of speech, vocal delivery, and camera presence.

Graduate-level programs in broadcasting are usually completed in conjunction with an internship at a radio or television news studio. In addition to studying advanced topics such as media law, news production, and directing, graduate students also conduct research for a master's thesis dedicated to an area of their particular interest. Individuals with master's degrees often go on to professional careers as radio and television broadcasters, media researchers, or college-level academic instructors.

Related College Majors
- Acting & Directing
- Broadcast Journalism
- Creative Writing
- Drama/Theater Arts, General
- Film/Cinema Studies
- Journalism
- Music History & Literature
- Music, General
- Radio & Television Broadcasting

Adult Job Seekers

The educational and professional experience requirements of broadcasting can make it a difficult field for adult job seekers to enter. Due to the highly competitive job market and low turnover rate of established broadcasters, landing a professional role as a broadcaster can require several years of lower-level experience, during which one is expected to master the production, reporting, and editing aspects of the role. Advancement to higher-level, higher-paying positions often depends on proven ratings, contributions to the station's marketing efforts, and the station's size. Relocation is common.

Professional Certification and Licensure

Professional certification and licensure is not required of broadcast professionals, although membership and affiliation with national organizations and associations can boost credentials and improve networking opportunities.

Additional Requirements

Radio announcers and television newscasters are also often entertainers. Therefore, those interested in the field should be comfortable speaking and engaging with interviewees and audiences, have a sense of humor, work well under pressure, and adapt quickly to changing situations and circumstances.

Fun Facts

Almost three out of four U.S. adults (71%) view network newscasts over the course of a month, making television the dominant source of news for Americans at home, according to an October 2013 survey.
Source: Pew Research Center analysis of Nielson data.

Basketball, invented by James Naismith in 1891, dispensed with a time-consuming practice in 1936. Up until then, jump balls occurred every time a basket was made!
Source: huffingtonpost.com

EARNINGS AND ADVANCEMENT

Earnings of radio and television announcers and newscasters depend on the employer, the size of the community, the nature of the announcer's or newscaster's work and the announcer's or newscaster's reputation. Salaries are higher in television than in radio, higher in larger markets than in small ones, and higher in commercial than in public broadcasting.

Median annual earnings of announcers were $28,461 in 2012. The lowest ten percent earned less than $17,585, and the highest ten percent earned more than $76,850.

Median annual earnings of newscasters were $57,388 in 2012. The lowest ten percent earned less than $29,214, and the highest ten percent earned more than $155,004.

Radio and television announcers and newscasters may receive paid vacations, holidays, and sick days; life and health insurance; and retirement benefits. These are usually paid by the employer.

Metropolitan Areas with the Highest Employment Level in This Occupation

Metropolitan area	Employment[1]	Employment per thousand jobs	Hourly mean wage
New York-White Plains-Wayne, NY-NJ	1,140	0.22	$28.08
Los Angeles-Long Beach-Glendale, CA	910	0.24	$34.96
Chicago-Joliet-Naperville, IL	480	0.13	$25.39
Boston-Cambridge-Quincy, MA	410	0.24	$42.29
Washington-Arlington-Alexandria, DC-VA-MD-WV	400	0.17	$22.40
Atlanta-Sandy Springs-Marietta, GA	390	0.17	$28.50
Minneapolis-St. Paul-Bloomington, MN-WI	370	0.21	$28.68
Dallas-Plano-Irving, TX	370	0.18	(8)

(1) Does not include self-employed or PR managers/executives. Source: Bureau of Labor Statistics, 2012

EMPLOYMENT AND OUTLOOK

Nationally, there were approximately 31,000 radio and television announcers and newscasters employed in 2012. (An additional 8,000 worked as public address announcers and in similar occupations.) Employment is expected to grow slower than the average for all occupations through the year 2020, which means employment is projected to increase about 7 percent. The slow growth is due to the consolidation of radio and television stations and improving technology.

Employment Trend, Projected 2010–20

Total, All Occupations: 14%

Announcers: 7%

Radio and Television Announcers: 7%

Public Address System and Other Announcers: -5%

Note: "All Occupations" includes all occupations in the U.S. Economy Source: U.S. Bureau of Labor Statistics, Employment Projections Program

Related Occupations
- Actor
- Copywriter
- Journalist
- Writer & Editor

Related Military Occupations
- Broadcast Journalism & Newswriter

Conversation With . . .
ADAM POHL

Director of Broadcast and Corporate Partnerships
Bowie BaySox; Voice of the Mount,
Mount St. Mary's men's basketball
Radio broadcaster, 16 years

1. What was your individual career path in terms of education/training, entry-level job, or other significant opportunity?

I grew up in a musical family, played trumpet, went to the University of North Carolina-Chapel Hill on a scholarship, majored in music and loved it. But, I knew in the back of my mind that music wasn't what I wanted to do for the rest of my life. I had called games when I was a teenager, and that's what I wanted to do.

After junior year, I was a summer intern for the Asheboro Copperheads of the minor league Coastal Plain League. They allowed me to broadcast some of their games. The next year, I interned for UNC's Tarheels Sports Network, and that was a huge help. I did that for two years, which allowed me to get my first job, part-time, with Minor League Baseball's Burlington Royals. I got my first full-time job two seasons later, then went on to Maryland and got a job with the Frederick Keys, another MiLB team. I did PR, sales, and a lot of marketing before I was promoted to assistant general manager. But, the more I did with the Keys, the more I got away from what I wanted to do. I stayed with them seven seasons, then joined the Baysox, also in MiLB, to refocus my career and try to get to a higher level of broadcasting.

During my time in Frederick, I made connections at nearby Mount St. Mary's University. I started doing women's basketball games. Now, I'm the Voice of the Mount, and I do all men's and some women's basketball games. So, I broadcast basketball from mid-November to early March, and baseball from April to September. I'm also the Baysox's business development person, and handle those partnerships.

If you're sitting in your seat at a game, you're not hearing me. But if you're in your car or on the internet, you do. For a minor league baseball team, broadcasting games on the radio is not a big money maker, but it's great marketing.

2. What are the most important skills and/or qualities for someone in your profession?

You have to embrace the fact that you're going to work a lot of hours. This is a 9-to-5 job plus games at night. You must be engaging, able to tell a story, and bring the emotion of the game to those who are listening. It's important to connect with people.

3. What do you wish you had known going into this profession?

That nothing is promised to you. You have to value what you have. When you start, you don't make money. You have to really carve your way and battle for opportunities. I'd love to have that rare, dream job announcing for the Baltimore Orioles, but if, a decade from now, I'm 45 and don't see much forward movement, broadcasting may become a hobby.

4. Are there many job opportunities in your profession? In what specific areas?

You have to network. For all six positions I've had, a connection got my foot in the door. It's unusual to send your demo and get picked over 400 other people.

5. How do you see your profession changing in the next five years, what role will technology play in those changes, and what skills will be required?

Things are moving toward podcasting from AM radio. The ability to make money off what we do is moving from advertising-based to subscriber-based. There will be more content. I'm concerned that there will be fewer outlets to break into the industry but, if you are an established commodity, there will be money to be made.

6. What do you enjoy most about your job? What do you enjoy least about your job?

The thing I love most is the actual calling of the game. That's one fortunate thing about the shelf life of this job, as opposed to being an athlete. I'm going to be able to do this, and do it at a high level, for a long time. I also like working with people in the industry; my colleagues share the same passion and vigor for sports, so being around baseball – and sharing that together – is special.

Because I do baseball and basketball, I'm away from home all the time, including on the road for 120 to 130 games. Broadcasting keeps me away 200 to 220 nights of the year, and that's a lot.

7. Can you suggest a valuable "try this" for students considering a career in your profession?

Work in sports in whatever way you can as soon as you can. Try to create an inroad with a local news or radio station, because that's what it's all about. That doesn't mean getting on the air. Once you're able to get some experience, it's not about how much you get paid. It's all about getting on air. Nobody is good at broadcasting right away. Be your own worst critic. Prepare one or two things to say about a player. You can't be scrolling through looking for a note and leave three seconds of silence. Be ready, be seamless.

SELECTED SCHOOLS

Many colleges and universities have bachelor's degree programs in journalism; some have programs in broadcast journalism, specifically. The student may also gain initial training at a community college. Below are listed some of the more prominent four-year institutions in this field.

Boston University
1 Silber Way
Boston, MA 02215
617.353.2000
www.bu.edu

Emerson College
120 Boylston Street
Boston, MA 02116
617.824.8500
www.emerson.edu

Columbia University
535 W. 116th Street
New York, NY 10027
212.854.1754
www.columbia.edu

Northwestern University
633 Clark Street
Evanston, IL 60208
847.491.3741
www.northwestern.edu

St. Bonaventure University
3261 West State Road
St. Bonaventure, NY 14778
716.375.2000
www.sbu.edu

Syracuse University
900 S. Crouse Avenue
Syracuse, NY 13210
315.443.1870
syr.edu

University of Georgia
100 Green Street
Athens, GA 30602
706.542.3000
www.uga.edu

University of Missouri, Columbia
230 Jesse Hall
Columbia, MI 65211
573.882.7786
www.missouri.edu

University of North Carolina, Chapel Hill
Jackson Hall
Chapel Hill, NC 27599
919.966.3621
www.unc.edu

University of Southern California
850 W. 37th Street
Los Angeles, CA 90089
323.442.1130
www.usc.edu

MORE INFORMATION

American Women in Radio and Television
1760 Old Meadow Road, Suite 500
McLean, VA 22102
703.506.3290
www.awrt.org

Association for Women in Communications
3337 Duke Street
Alexandria, VA 22314
703.370.7436
www.womcom.org

Broadcast Education Association
1771 N Street, NW
Washington, DC 20036-2891
888.380.7222
www.beaweb.org

National Association of Broadcasters
1771 N Street, NW
Washington, DC 20036
202.429.5300
www.nab.org

National Association of Digital Broadcasters
244 Fifth Avenue, Suite 2757
New York, NY 10001-7945
www.thenadb.org

National Cable Television Association
Careers in Cable
1724 Massachusetts Avenue, NW
Washington, DC 20036
202.222.2300
www.ncta.com

John Pritchard/Editor

Recreation Program Director

Snapshot

Career Cluster: Hospitality & Tourism; Human Services; Sports & Entertainment

Interests: Physical education, recreational activities, planning events and programs

Earnings (Yearly Average): $48,215

Employment & Outlook: Faster Than Average Growth Expected

OVERVIEW

Sphere of Work

Recreation program directors work for private institutions as well as municipalities, developing and coordinating recreation needs for residents and visitors, including children, seniors, and adults. Recreation program directors develop these recreation programs by assessing community or service audience recreation needs; hiring and evaluating recreation workers and additional staff; overseeing the safety and maintenance of grounds, equipment, and facilities; promoting the recreation program to the community; planning events; scheduling programs; keeping records on program

happenings and staff; and fundraising through direct solicitation and grant-writing. Recreation program directors manage both public and private recreation programs through a variety of host agencies or institutions such as schools, camps, resorts, public agencies, retirement facilities, and hospitals.

Work Environment

Recreation program directors spend their workdays overseeing recreation programs in a wide variety of indoor and outdoor settings, including schools, public recreation centers, private resorts, indoor childcare centers, playgrounds, sports fields, swimming pools, residential facilities, or day camps. A recreation program director's work environment may involve extremes of heat, cold, or noise. Given the diverse demands of the recreation profession, recreation program directors may need to work a combination of days, evenings, weekends, vacation, and summer hours to ensure program success.

Profile

Working Conditions: Work Both Indoors and Outdoors
Physical Strength: Light Work
Education Needs:
Technical/Community College, Bachelor's Degree
Licensure/Certification:
Recommended
Physical Abilities Not Required: No Heavy Labor
Opportunities For Experience:
Internship, Military Service Part-Time Work
Holland Interest Score*: ESA

* See Appendix A

Occupation Interest

Individuals drawn to the recreation field tend to be charismatic, intelligent, and organized people who have the ability to quickly assess situations, utilize resources, and solve problems. Successful recreation program directors are responsible leaders who display effective time management skills, a strong sense of initiative, and a concern for individuals and society. Recreation program directors should enjoy physical activity and spending time with a wide range of people, including those with special needs and those from diverse cultural, social, and educational backgrounds.

A Day in the Life—Duties and Responsibilities

The daily occupational duties and responsibilities of recreation program directors will be determined by the individual's area of job specialization and work environment. Recreation program directors must be able to assess the recreational needs and abilities of individuals, groups, or the local community. Before their busy season, they typically spend time interviewing, hiring, and evaluating recreation workers and staff, including food service workers and maintenance crews. They spend a portion of each day supervising seasonal and full-time recreation workers, such as lifeguards, coaches, and activity leaders, and overseeing the safety, upkeep, and maintenance of grounds, equipment, and facilities. Recreation program directors promote the recreation program to the local community through flyers, websites, e-mails, and press releases. They also plan and schedule program events such as tournaments, nature studies, leagues, dances, team sports, and classes, and periodically brainstorm new ways to recruit volunteers for all aspects of the recreation program. Conducting program assessment and evaluation through surveys and feedback requests is one way in which recreation program directors can gain an understanding of the success of their programming.

Recreation program directors have many legal, financial, and administrative responsibilities, such as ensuring that their recreation program meets national requirements for safety and the Americans with Disabilities Act, planning the short-term and long-term recreation program budget, and conducting background checks on staff, volunteers, and contractors. Recreation directors are sometimes responsible for raising money for programming through grant-writing, fundraising, and donation requests. Part of the job involves keeping the recreation program in the public eye so that it will continue to attract patrons and contributions. The recreation program director may represent the recreation program at conferences and meetings, including local and national recreation society meetings, or meet periodically with institutional supervisors, such as parks and recreation department commissioners, facility owners, or other stakeholders.

All recreation program directors are responsible for accurate record keeping on program safety, accidents, and staff performance.

Duties and Responsibilities

- Developing and overseeing recreational programs
- Setting up schedules and activities
- Soliciting financial resources
- Coordinating human resources
- Directing specialized activities and events
- Publicizing and promoting programs to the community
- Maintaining facilities in good working order
- Ensuring safety of all patrons and staff
- Dealing with emergencies as necessary

WORK ENVIRONMENT

Physical Environment

The immediate physical environment of recreation program directors varies based on the program's focus and location. Recreation program directors spend their workdays coordinating activities in a wide variety of settings including schools, public recreation centers, indoor childcare centers, ice skating rinks, hospitals, playgrounds, sports fields, pools and aquatic centers, residential facilities, or day camps. Most recreation directors spend part of their work day outdoors, but the majority of their time is spent inside an office.

Human Environment

Recreation program directors work with a wide variety of people and should be comfortable meeting with colleagues, supervisors, program benefactors, staff, children, the elderly, people with physical disabilities, and families. Because they represent the program to the public and function in a supervisory or administrative role, they should enjoy meeting new people and spending much of their job managing others. Excellent communication skills are an advantage.

Relevant Skills and Abilities

Communication Skills
- Promoting an idea
- Speaking effectively

Interpersonal/Social Skills
- Asserting oneself
- Being sensitive to others
- Motivating others

Organization & Management Skills
- Coordinating tasks
- Demonstrating leadership
- Managing people/groups

Other Skills
- Being physically active

Technological Environment

Recreation program directors must be comfortable using computers to access information and records, Internet communication tools for e-mail, social media, and program websites, and cell phones to ensure availability during on-call hours or in case of an emergency. Those recreation program directors coordinating a specialized recreation program, such as metalworking or a ropes course, may also need to be comfortable training others in the use of techniques they have just learned themselves. They should be certified in CPR and other lifesaving techniques, and be at ease using related equipment.

EDUCATION, TRAINING, AND ADVANCEMENT

High School/Secondary

High school students interested in pursuing a career as a recreation program director should prepare themselves by developing good study habits. High school study of physical education, foreign language, public safety, sociology, psychology, and education will provide a strong foundation for work as a recreation program director or college-level work in the field. High school students interested in this career path will benefit from seeking part-time or seasonal work that exposes the students to diverse groups of people and recreational activities. They can also obtain certification in lifesaving techniques through their school or town.

Suggested High School Subjects
- Accounting
- Algebra
- Applied Communication

- Arts
- Business
- Business Law
- Business Math
- Crafts
- English
- Physical Education
- Social Studies

Famous First

The first summer camp for boys was Camp Comfort in Milford, Conn, established in 1861. It was founded by Frederick William Gunn, founder of The Gunnery prep school. The camp took 50 boys on a two-week camping trip. Today there are about 7,000 overnight camps and 5,000 day camps in the United States; together they serve over 10 million children.

College/Postsecondary

Postsecondary students interested in becoming recreation program directors should earn an associate's or bachelor's degree in recreation or physical education. A small number of colleges (accredited by the National Recreation and Park Association) offer the bachelor's of parks and recreation degree. Courses in physical education, education, public safety, business management, accounting, and foreign languages may also prove useful in future recreation work. Postsecondary students can gain work experience and potential advantage in their future job searches by securing internships or part-time employment in parks and recreation departments or private recreation programs.

Related College Majors
- Adapted Physical Education/Therapeutic Recreation
- Parks, Recreation & Leisure Facilities Management
- Parks, Recreation & Leisure Studies
- Physical Education Teaching & Coaching
- Sport & Fitness Administration/Management

Adult Job Seekers

Adults seeking employment as recreation program directors should have, at a minimum, an associate's or bachelor's degree in recreation or a related field and extensive program directing experience. Some recreation programs require their directors to hold a master's degree and second language proficiency. Adult job seekers should educate themselves about the educational and professional license requirements of their home states and the organizations where they seek employment, and may benefit from joining professional associations that offer help with networking and job searches. Professional recreation associations, such as the American Camping Association and the Society of State Directors of Health, Physical Education & Recreation, generally offer job-finding workshops and maintain lists and forums of available jobs.

Professional Certification and Licensure

Professional certification and licensure is not required of general recreation program directors. Directors of specialized recreation programs, such as swimming or parks and recreation, may be required to earn specialized certification as a condition of employment. Lifeguard certification, pool operations certification, and CPR/First Aid certification is offered by the American Lifeguard Association and requires coursework and passing an examination. The National Recreation and Park Association (NRPA) certificate is offered in therapeutic recreation, park management, outdoor recreation, industrial or commercial recreation, and camp management. It also requires a bachelor's degree or its equivalent in education and work experience, as well as passing a national examination. Ongoing professional education is required for continued certification in both lifesaving techniques and NRPA disciplines.

Additional Requirements

Successful recreation program directors will be knowledgeable about the profession's requirements, responsibilities, and opportunities. High levels of integrity and personal and professional ethics are required of recreation program directors, as professionals in this role interact with staff in subordinate roles and have access to personal information. Membership in professional recreation associations is encouraged among all recreation program directors as a means of building status within a professional community and networking.

In most states, the names of those people working in the field of recreation are almost always required to be submitted for a criminal record check. This includes employees, volunteers, and those delivering special programs.

EARNINGS AND ADVANCEMENT

Recreation program directors advance based on their experience. Certification by the National Recreation and Park Association helps advancement. Recreation program directors had mean annual earnings of $48,215 in 2012.

Recreation program directors may receive paid vacations, holidays, and sick days; life and health insurance; and retirement benefits. These are usually paid by the employer.

Metropolitan Areas with the Highest Employment Level in this Occupation (Recreation Workers)

Metropolitan area	Employment	Employment per thousand jobs	Hourly mean wage[1]
New York-White Plains-Wayne, NY-NJ	15,200	2.95	$14.66
Chicago-Joliet-Naperville, IL	10,870	2.99	$12.02
Los Angeles-Long Beach-Glendale, CA	9,640	2.49	$12.21
Washington-Arlington-Alexandria, DC-VA-MD-WV	4,680	1.99	$14.80
Oakland-Fremont-Hayward, CA	4,080	4.20	$13.39
Phoenix-Mesa-Glendale, AZ	4,030	2.33	$12.63
Boston-Cambridge-Quincy, MA	3,980	2.32	$12.20
Philadelphia, PA	3,900	2.14	$13.15

[1]Figures are for all recreation workers, not specifically for directors. Source: Bureau of Labor Statistics

EMPLOYMENT AND OUTLOOK

Recreation workers, of which recreation program directors are a part, held about 310,000 jobs nationally in 2012. About one-third worked in the park and recreation departments of local governments. About another one-fourth worked in nursing and residential care facilities and civic and social organizations, such as the Boy Scouts or Girl Scouts or the YMCA/YWCA. Employment is expected to grow about as fast as the average for all occupations through the year 2022, which means employment is projected to increase 10 percent to 19 percent. This is primarily due to people spending more time and money on recreation. However, employment growth may be limited by budget constraints facing State and local governments over the next decade.

Employment Trend, Projected 2012–22

Personal Care and Service Occupations: 21%

Recreation Workers: 14%

Total, All Occupations: 11%

Note: "All Occupations" includes all occupations in the U.S. Economy. Source: U.S. Bureau of Labor Statistics, Employment Projections Program

Related Occupations
- Fitness Trainer and Aerobics Instructor
- Health Club Manager
- Park Ranger
- Recreation Worker

Related Occupations
- Caseworker & Counselor

Conversation With . . .
DAVID ANDERSON

Recreation Program Director
City of Gatlinburg, Tennessee
Recreation programs, 15 years

1. What was your individual career path in terms of education/training, entry-level job or other significant opportunity?

I went to Lincoln Memorial University in Tennessee where I played Division II baseball and double-majored in physical education/fitness and health. I planned to go into either teaching or recreation. My mom is a teacher and my dad was in recreation. After doing student teaching, I decided recreation was the field for me; I didn't like all the administrative issues the school system has to deal with. And I liked the fact that the people you work with in recreation are there because they want to be there. They're there to have fun, they're there to get healthy, they're there to meet people and make friends.

My first job in the field was as a recreation programmer in Pigeon Forge, Tennessee. I started that in August 2001. The following April, the recreation program director job in Gatlinburg became available and they hired me. I've been here ever since.

2. What are the most important skills and/or qualities for someone in your profession?

It's extremely important to be a people person since you're working with the public and with all age groups. You have to be able to get along with all ages and develop relationships with them. It's important to have knowledge of childhood development. You should also have knowledge about sports although recreation programs encompass more than sports. They also include special events, arts and crafts, summer camps. It's kind of like being a jack of all trades.

3. What do you wish you had known going into this profession?

I wish I'd known that not every program that you put out there is going to be successful. There's a very big difference between running a recreation program in a big city and running one in a small community. I grew up just outside of Toronto. It's a fairly large area and pretty much everything their recreation department offered would become full almost immediately. That's not the case in a smaller community. You really have to work hard to present the best programs available and if something is successful you need to stick with it.

4. Are there many job opportunities in your profession? In what specific areas?

There are definitely job opportunities. It kind of varies and a lot depends on how willing you are to relocate. I would say there are upwards of 50-100 job openings always posted on the National Recreation and Park Association's website. So there are definitely opportunities, especially for people coming out of college. There are lots of internships and lots of entry-level jobs. The higher-level jobs generally don't turn over as much as the others.

5. How do you see your profession changing in the next five years, what role will technology play in those changes and what skills will be required?

We are using social media and technology more to get the word out about our programs and to do registrations. The internet has simplified the registration process. But I don't see the job requirements changing much or technology becoming a bigger factor. We're kind of the alternative to technology because the programs and events we offer are usually outdoors and connected to physical activity. We don't need to be experts in technology.

6. What do you enjoy most about your job? What do you enjoy least about it?

I love that I get to work with different populations and different age groups and in different activities. I meet people from all walks of life. That's a lot of fun. But it can be challenging when a person has a problem with some aspect of a program – for example, if someone has a complaint about a referee. It can also be disheartening if you think a program is going to be tremendously successful and no one signs up. But I love my job and I'm excited to come to work every day. I don't know if a lot of people can say that.

7. Can you suggest a valuable "try this" for students considering a career in your profession?

Internships are a terrific means of getting experience in the field. Other excellent ways to gain experience include getting involved with intramural leagues and volunteering at summer camps, races and similar community activities.

SELECTED SCHOOLS

Many community colleges and four-year colleges and universities offer programs in physical education; a number of them also offer programs in parks and recreation management, arts and crafts management, and related fields. Interested student are advised to consult with a school guidance counselor.

MORE INFORMATION

American Academy for Park and Recreation Administration
P.O. Box 1040
Mahomet, IL 61853
217.586.3360
www.aapra.org

American Alliance for Health, Physical Education, Recreation & Dance
1900 Association Drive
Reston, VA 20192-1598
800.213.7193
www.aahperd.org

American Camping Association
5000 State Road 67 North
Martinsville, IN 46151
765.342.8456
www.acacamps.org

American Lifeguard Association
8300 Boone Boulevard, 5th Floor
Vienna, VA 22182
703.761.6750
www.americanlifeguard.com

Employee Services Management Association
P.O. Box 10517
Rockville, MD 20849
www.esmassn.org

National Council for Therapeutic Recreation Certification
7 Elmwood Drive
New City, NY 10956
845.639.1439
nctrc@NCTRC.org
www.nctrc.org

National Recreation and Park Association
22377 Belmont Ridge Road
Ashburn, VA 20148-4501
800.626.6772
www.nrpa.org

Society of State Directors of Health, Physical Educ. & Recreation
1900 Association Drive, Suite 100
Reston, VA 20191-1599
703.390.4599
www.thesociety.org

YMCA of the USA
101 N. Wacker Drive
Chicago, IL 60606
800.872.9622
www.ymca.net

Simone Isadora Flynn/Editor

Recreational Therapist

Snapshot

Career Cluster: Human Services

Interests: Recreational therapy, physical therapy, human development, psychology, assistive technology, physiology

Earnings (Yearly Average): $43,180

Employment & Outlook: Average Growth Expected

OVERVIEW

Sphere of Work

Recreational therapists provide therapeutic recreational services aimed at helping their patients improve emotional and mental well-being, build interpersonal relations, strengthen social skills, and increase confidence.

Recreational therapists develop and implement medically approved recreational therapies and programs to meet patient needs, abilities, and interests. The range of recreational therapies is vast and includes community integration, stress reduction, fitness, group sports, field trips, and arts and crafts. Recreational

therapists encourage their patients to socialize and use recreational and community resources.

Work Environment

Recreational therapists work in medical settings, such as hospitals, physical rehabilitation centers, substance abuse facilities, and psychiatric facilities, as well as community and institutional settings, including schools, parks and recreation departments, prisons, retirement facilities, and adult day care facilities. In medical environments, recreational therapists generally partner with medical and social service professionals to increase patients' social skills and confidence. In community and institutional settings, recreational therapists partner with educational and therapeutic professionals to address students' or patients' social or recreational needs.

Profile

Working Conditions: Work Indoors
Physical Strength: Light Work
Education Needs: Bachelor's Degree
Licensure/Certification:
Recommended
Physical Abilities Not Required: No
Heavy Labor
Opportunities For Experience:
Internship, Volunteer Work, Part-Time
Work
Holland Interest Score*: SEC

* See Appendix A

Occupation Interest

Individuals attracted to the field of recreational therapy tend to be physically strong and energetic people who have the ability to teach and lead a variety of activities. Individuals who excel as recreational therapists exhibit tact, creativity, problem solving, desire to help, patience, humor, and caring. Recreational therapists must be able to work as part of a team to meet patient needs.

A Day in the Life—Duties and Responsibilities

The daily duties and responsibilities of recreational therapists vary by the individual's area of job specialization and work environment. Recreational therapists attend to the therapeutic needs of their patients. Patients in recreational therapy may be part of inpatient medical facilities or may be seen on an outpatient basis, often by referral. The recreational therapist first conducts patient assessments. Once the patient's needs and abilities have been recorded, the recreational therapist develops patient treatment plans. He or she then provides therapy sessions and workshops that focus on the mental and physical well-being of patients.

Community integration, stress reduction, fitness, group sports, field trips, and arts and crafts are common types of recreational therapies. A recreational therapist might lead individuals and small groups in such community integration exercises as riding public transportation, placing orders in a restaurant, and asking for or giving directions. Recreational therapists might teach patients such stress reduction techniques as massage, meditation, and deep breathing. In various group settings, recreational therapists lead group activities on nature, performing arts, field trips, arts and crafts, stretching, aerobic exercise, strength training, or group sports such as volleyball and baseball. They are responsible for ensuring that all recreation program activities and events meet national requirements for safety and the Americans with Disabilities Act. This may mean overseeing the safety, upkeep, and maintenance of recreational equipment and facilities.

In all cases, recreational therapists must communicate regularly and effectively with patients, patient families, colleagues, and insurers. They interact with patients throughout the day in a friendly and supportive manner and advise patients on the use of recreational equipment. Some provide early intervention services to young children with mental and social delays and limitations. Recreational therapists evaluate, document, and communicate patient progress in therapeutic activities. They then meet with patient treatment teams or patient families and provide insurance companies with patient records and progress notes as required. Recreational therapists may also supervise recreation staff and volunteers.

Independent recreational therapists, who work outside of a medical or educational facility, may also be responsible for scheduling appointments and billing patients.

Duties and Responsibilities

- Observing the physical, mental and social progress of patients
- Contributing information and progress reports for use in meeting treatment goals
- Assisting patients in readjusting recreational needs to activities offered by the community in which they live
- Training groups of volunteers and students in techniques of recreation therapy
- Organizing athletic events, craft workshops, field trips, dances and concerts for patients
- Instructing patients in relaxation techniques
- Instructing patients in calisthenics and individual and group sports
- Developing a treatment plan, leading activities and monitoring patients' progress

WORK ENVIRONMENT

Physical Environment

Recreational therapists work in rehabilitation facilities, hospitals, nursing homes, therapy clinics, and schools. Therapeutic office settings used by recreational therapists may be shared with other therapeutic professionals such as physical, occupational, or speech and language therapists.

Human Environment

Recreational therapists interact with a wide variety of people and should be comfortable meeting with people with physical, mental, and emotional illnesses and special needs, the elderly, and children, as well as colleagues and supervisors. Recreational therapists usually work as part of a patient treatment team that includes families, social workers, teachers, doctors, and other therapists. As a member of a treatment team, recreational therapists participate in frequent team meetings and are responsible for communicating patient progress to fellow team members.

Relevant Skills and Abilities

Communication Skills
- Speaking effectively
- Writing concisely

Interpersonal/Social Skills
- Being sensitive to others
- Counseling others
- Providing support to others

Organization & Management Skills
- Coordinating tasks
- Managing people/groups
- Performing duties that change frequently

Technological Environment

Recreational therapists use a wide variety of technologies and equipment in their work. Recreational therapists use Internet communication tools, word-processing software, and spreadsheets. During therapy sessions, the equipment they use may include musical instruments, sports equipment, and adaptive technology such as wheelchairs.

EDUCATION, TRAINING, AND ADVANCEMENT

High School/Secondary

High school students interested in pursuing the profession of recreational therapy in the future should develop good study habits. High school coursework in physical education, psychology, and sociology can prepare students for undergraduate and master's level studies. Students interested in the recreational therapy field may benefit from seeking internships or part-time or volunteer work in recreational programs or with people with physical, developmental, or social problems that have an impact on their daily life.

Suggested High School Subjects
- Arts
- Biology

- Crafts
- English
- Health Science Technology
- Instrumental & Vocal Music
- Physical Education
- Physiology
- Psychology
- Social Studies

Famous First

The first major statement about the need for recreational therapy was made by Dr. Frank Wynn of Indianapolis in 1909. Wynn, pictured, wrote, "Recreation therapy—a type of psychotherapy—plays an important role in the management of functional neuroses. It is not enough to tell a patient to take a daily walk or to go to the theater. Ascertain what he enjoys. Fortunate is the [patient] who enjoys hunting or fishing; or, still better, the ocean or the mountains. The ceaseless lashing of the sea has a wonderfully calming effect upon the emotions; the inspiring grandeur of the mountains is also quieting and lifts one to higher mental levels."

College/Postsecondary

Postsecondary students interested in recreational therapy should complete coursework in recreational therapy, if offered by their school, and courses in related fields. Such coursework may include physical education, physical therapy, special education, abnormal psychology, human development, ethics, anatomy, physiology, and assistive technology. An internship is typically required for completion of an undergraduate program in recreational therapy. Those interested in attending graduate school in recreational therapy may benefit from seeking internships or work in recreational therapy programs or with people with physical or mental special needs. Membership in the American Therapeutic Recreation Association (ATRA) may provide networking opportunities. Prior to graduating, interested college students should apply to graduate school in recreational therapy or secure related employment as a therapy assistant or special education assistant.

Related College Majors
- Recreational Therapy

Adult Job Seekers

Adult job seekers in the recreational therapy field have generally completed bachelor's or master's degrees in recreational therapy from an accredited university as well as earned necessary professional certification. Recreational therapists seeking employment may benefit from the networking opportunities, job workshops, and job lists offered by professional therapy associations such as the ATRA.

Professional Certification and Licensure

Recreational therapy certification is a voluntary practice and not usually required for general recreational therapy practice. Recreational therapists seeking employment in clinical settings, such as hospital and rehabilitation facilities, will need to be certified by the National Council for Therapeutic Recreation Certification. The Certified Therapeutic Recreation Specialist (CTRS) credential requires completion of a bachelor's degree in recreational therapy, a supervised clinical internship, and a national examination. In addition, recreational therapists who choose a therapeutic specialty, such as art, music or aquatic therapy, need specialized certification as a condition of employment.

Requirements for professional licensure for recreational therapists vary by state. Interested individuals should check the requirements of their home state and the organizations where they seek employment.

Additional Requirements

Individuals who find satisfaction, success, and job security as recreational therapists will be knowledgeable about the profession's requirements, responsibilities, and opportunities. Successful recreational therapists engage in ongoing professional development. Recreational therapists must have a high level of integrity and ethics as they work with vulnerable people and have access to personal patient information. Membership in professional recreational therapy associations is encouraged among all recreational therapists as a means of building professional community and networking.

Fun Facts

Recreational therapy emerged from two schools of thought in the 1940s and 1950s. One held that recreation was a therapeutic tool for treatment. The second viewed recreation as a means to meet a specific human need for people who were institutionalized. The term "therapuetic recreation" was coined in the early 1950s.

Source: Glen E. Van Andel, Re.D

The Egyptians described "diversion and recreation as a means of treating the sick" as early as 2000-1500 BC. In the American colonies, Benjamin Franklin helped found the Pennsylvania Hospital in 1753, where "light manual labor such as spinning and carding wool" were among the therapeutic activities.

Source: http://www.recreationtherapy.com/history/rthistory1.htm

People with disabilities don't just participate in plain old adaptive sports; some of them have moved on to "extreme" adaptive sports: wheelchair bungee jumping, paraclimbing (rock climbing) and sled hockey.

Source: https://ahmexposed.wordpress.com/

EARNINGS AND ADVANCEMENT

Earnings of recreational therapists depend on the type and geographic location of the employer, and the individual's education and experience. Advancement is mainly to supervisory or administrative positions. Median annual earnings of recreational therapists were $43,180 in 2013. The lowest ten percent earned less than $27,120, and the highest ten percent earned more than $68,950.

Recreational therapists may receive paid vacations, holidays, and sick days; life and health insurance; and retirement benefits. These are usually paid by the employer.

Metropolitan Areas with the Highest
Employment Level in this Occupation

Metropolitan area	Employment[1]	Employment per thousand jobs	Hourly mean wage
New York-White Plains-Wayne, NY-NJ	980	0.19	$25.67
Philadelphia, PA	580	0.32	$21.61
Chicago-Joliet-Naperville, IL	560	0.15	$21.94
Boston-Cambridge-Quincy, MA	510	0.29	$18.60
Nassau-Suffolk, NY	380	0.31	$23.94
Los Angeles-Long Beach-Glendale, CA	340	0.09	$30.24
Atlanta-Sandy Springs-Marietta, GA	320	0.14	$19.87
Washington-Arlington-Alexandria, DC-VA-MD-WV	300	0.13	$23.55
Warren-Troy-Farmington Hills, MI	260	0.23	$24.54
St. Louis, MO-IL	230	0.18	$20.05

[1] Does not include self-employed. Source: Bureau of Labor Statistics

EMPLOYMENT AND OUTLOOK

Recreational therapists held about 20,000 jobs nationally in 2012. About one-third worked in nursing care facilities. Others worked in hospitals, residential care facilities, community mental health centers, adult day care programs, correctional facilities, community programs for people with disabilities, substance abuse centers, and state and local government agencies. Employment of recreational therapists is expected to grow about as fast as the average for all occupations through the year 2022, which means employment is projected to increase 9 percent to 16 percent. Job demand will be created by the growing percentage of older adults who will require the services of recreational therapists to manage injuries, illnesses and decreased physical and sometimes mental ability.

Employment Trend, Projected 2010–20

Health Diagnosing and Treating Practitioners: 20%

Recreational Therapists: 13%

Total, All Occupations: 11%

Note: "All Occupations" includes all occupations in the U.S. Economy. Source: U.S. Bureau of Labor Statistics, Employment Projections Program

Related Occupations
- Activities Therapist
- Fitness Trainer & Aerobics Instructor
- Music Therapist
- Occupational Therapist
- Occupational Therapy Assistant
- Physical Therapist
- Sports Instructor/Coach

Conversation With . . .
EILEEN ANDREASSI

Director of Therapeutic Recreation, Helen Hayes Hospital
West Haverstraw, New York
Recreation therapist, 33 years

1. What was your individual career path in terms of education/training, entry-level job, or other significant opportunity?

I double-majored in psychology and sociology for my bachelor's degree. During college, I worked at a camp for people with severe cognitive and physical disabilities. I was introduced to the power of goal-based recreation activities to help people attain a higher quality of life, and decided to get my master's in Therapeutic Recreation (TR). During my graduate studies, the TR director position at the camp opened up and I had the opportunity to work full-time at the managerial level in my chosen field. I love the profession so much I continued to work around the country and with different diagnoses throughout my career. I'm a Certified Therapeutic Recreation Therapist and past chair of the board of the National Council for Therapeutic Recreation Certification.

2. What are the most important skills and/or qualities for someone in your profession?

The three most important qualities for a recreational therapist are flexibility, a love for all types and ages of people, and a sense of humor. These traits simply cannot be taught in a classroom. It's important to learn customer service skills and teaching approaches because much of the job involves working with clients or patients and their families in a teaching role. It's helpful to have strong interests in active and/or passive recreation—sports/physical activities, art, crafts, music, dance, nature, games, literacy (reading, writing, word/number games), technology and home improvement.

3. What do you wish you had known going into this profession?

I wish I had known more about the breadth of the profession, and the opportunities available in the community, health care and corrections sectors. Students now are lucky that they can do in-depth online research into the opportunities available.

4. **Are there many job opportunities in your profession? In what specific areas?**

The job market for Certified Therapeutic Recreation Specialists has been listed in the top 10 growth professions due to the large influx of retiring and aging baby boomers. Senior centers, community recreation centers, assisted living and long term care facilities need trained recreational therapists to develop and provide programs. Also on the horizon is an increase in people diagnosed with dementia and Alzheimer's disease.

Because more people are surviving serious accidents and illnesses, there's a need for recreational therapists working with those who have a spinal cord injury, brain injury, stroke, Parkinson's disease, multiple sclerosis and other neurological disorders. There are also opportunities in the field of corrections, in group homes working with developmentally delayed clients, with camps, outdoor recreation companies and adapted sports and recreation programs.

5. **How do you see your profession changing in the next five years? What role will technology play in those changes, and what skills will be required?**

The therapeutic recreation field is relatively young and still in a period of dynamic change. Research is being conducted to determine the effects of treatments on specific diagnostic groups. The field is probably moving towards a mandatory master's degree, but students who matriculate in the next few years will still qualify to take the national examination and be able to practice with a bachelor's degree.

Technology is being used for treatment modalities across all areas of health care. Assistive devices and prosthetic limbs are all electronic. Patients who have grown up with computers and cell phones interact with their peers and the environment differently than previous generations, so therapeutic approaches are being developed to meet these changing needs.

6. **What do you enjoy most about your job? What do you enjoy least about your job?**

I have been a recreational therapist more than 30 years and have loved every minute of every day of my career. We're trained to work with a large variety of diagnoses, so that has given me flexibility in terms of job choices. I've worked in hospitals, long-term care, group homes, camps and the community and even owned my own community reintegration business when I lived in another state. I've learned as much from my patients as I have taught them and I have had a positive impact on too many people to count. The positive energy of other recreational therapists is always infectious and it is also a really fun, happy job.

As a manager, I must complete administrative paperwork that is required, but not the favorite part of my job.

7. Can you suggest a valuable "try this" for students considering a career in your profession?

Multiple volunteer options are available. Sometimes you may not see people with disabilities but they are there and you can help out in one of the programs. Activity departments in nursing homes always need help and residents brighten up when they see young people willing to do an activity with them. Group homes, hospitals, adapted sports and recreation organizations all are in need of assistance. Each state has a Therapeutic Recreation Association—a simple search can get you a number to call. Recreational therapists are friendly and always willing to help students.

SELECTED SCHOOLS

Many colleges and universities have bachelor's degree programs in recreational therapy or related subjects. The student may also gain an initial grounding at a technical or community college. Consult with your school guidance counselor or research post-secondary programs in your area. The online Therapeutic Recreation Directory (see below) contains a listing of accredited schools and programs.

MORE INFORMATION

American Art Therapy Association
225 North Fairfax Street
Alexandria, VA 22314-1574
888.290.0878
www.arttherapy.org

American Dance Therapy Association
10632 Little Patuxent Parkway
Suite 108
Columbia, MD 21044
410.997.4040
www.adta.org

American Music Therapy Association
8455 Colesville Road, Suite 1000
Silver Spring, MD 20910
301.589.3300
www.musictherapy.org

American Therapeutic Recreation Association
629 North Main Street
Hattiesburg, MS 39401
601.450.2872
www.atra-online.com

National Center on Physical Activity and Disability
1640 W. Roosevelt Road
Chicago, IL 60608-6904
800.900.8086
www.ncpad.org

National Council for Therapeutic Recreation Certification
7 Elmwood Drive
New City, NY 10956
845.639.1439
www.nctrc.org

Simone Isadora Flynn/Editor

Referee, Official, Umpire

Snapshot

Career Cluster(s): Sports and Fitness
Interests: Fitness, sports, practical careers, hands on work
Earnings (Yearly Average): $24,870
Employment & Outlook: Average growth expected

OVERVIEW

Sphere of Work

Umpires, referees, and other sports officials work for professional and amateur sporting associations, companies, and organizations presiding over sporting events to ensure that participants follow the rules of the game. Sports officials are responsible for making determinations in contested incidents, for charging players with penalties for infractions of the rules, and for keeping time during a match or sporting event.

While not as celebrated or well compensates as professional athletes or athletic team managers, trainers, or owners, officials are an essential part of amateur and professional sports and play an important role in making sure that athletes and teams adhere to rules to ensure fair contests.

Work Environment

Referees, umpires, and sports officials may work indoors or outdoors depending on the sport that they officiate and some officials may divide their time between officiating outdoor and indoor contests. Those who officiate sports typically occurring outdoors may work in a variety of weather conditions depending on the timing of the playing season for their sport and the climate of their particular region. Sports officials also tend to work irregular hours as they must follow the playing season of their sport and it is not unusual for officials to work evenings, weekends, and holidays.

Profile

Working Conditions: Work Indoors or outdoors

Physical Strength: Strenuous work

Education Needs: High School/Secondary School

Licensure/Certification: Required for some occupations

Opportunities For Experience: Specialized training, On the job training, Student work

Holland Interest Score*: REC

* See Appendix A

Occupation Interest

Sporting officials need to have a strong interest in their chosen sport and many student or young athletes transition into working as officials or referees rather than pursuing professional sports careers as a way to remain involved in the sport that they enjoy. Officials should have a strong interest in fair play, management, communication, and team work as they work closely with other individuals to ensure that sporting contests are handled fairly and are often called on to enforce rules and to make determinations in situations where some aspect of a game or match is contested between the competitors or teams.

A Day in the Life—Duties and Responsibilities

A typical day for a sports official depends on the official's chosen sport and on the time of the year in seasonal sports. Before games, officials meet with managers, coaches, and other members of a sports team to discuss the rules of the game for the specific event. During a match or game, officials are responsible for watching the contest and enforcing the rules. Officials signal athletes to warn about rule infractions or to make them aware of other regulations. In some sports, officials keep time and signal to athletes and coaches about time restrictions and they may be responsible for stopping and starting contests at set intervals or when an infraction of the rules has occurred. In some cases, officials are responsible for inspecting the playing area or inspecting equipment to ensure the safety of participants and to look for equipment violations and irregularities. In some cases, officials are responsible for determining which player or team wins a contest or they may be required to settle claims about infractions of the rules or when an event is contested between teams or opponents. When infractions of the rules occur, officials assess and assign penalties as required by the rules and they may, in some cases, remove participants from a game or contest because of rule violations.

Duties and Responsibilities

- Officiate sporting events or competitions
- Meet with players, coaches, trainers, and other professionals
- Inspect uniforms and sporting equipment
- Study and explain the rules of a contest to participants
- Enforce the rules of a sport and assign penalties to competitors
- Determine when a contest starts and stops
- Judge claims of infractions made by athletes or coaches
- Keep track of timing and stop and start the contest as needed

OCCUPATION SPECIALTIES

Baseball Umpire

Baseball umpires officiate baseball contests from specific positions on a baseball field and typically work as a member of an umpiring crew that includes several umpires placed in specific positions as well as assistants. In baseball, umpires are responsible for making frequent determinations about the success or failure of a certain aspect of the game.

Boxing Referees

Boxing referees are officials who manage boxing contests, remaining in the ring with the two competitors during a match. Boxing referees are constantly active, being responsible for notifying competitors of rule violations, assigning penalties, and signaling the beginning and end of rounds. Boxing referees are also empowered to stop a contest when he or she believes that one competitor should not continue or if sufficient violations have occurred to invalidate the match.

Gymnastic Judges

Gymnastic judges are sports officials who watch gymnastic performance or exhibitions and are then responsible for judging the performance against the standards established for the sport. Gymnastic judges need to be experts in the sport as they must not only enforce rules but must be capable of qualitatively evaluating performances.

Supervisor of Officials

A supervisor of officials is a manager who manages all referees, umpires, and other officials within a certain region for a specific sport. Supervisors train and mentor officials and also help to develop new rules for the sport and practices for officials working within the sport.

WORK ENVIRONMENT

Relevant Skills and Abilities

Communication Skills
- Communicating clearly across cultural/linguistic barriers
- Communicating using non-verbal cues or signals

Interpersonal/Social Skills
- Working in group environments
- Working closely with athletes and members of athletic teams

Organization & Management Skills
- Managing time and adhering to specific timing rules
- Learning and enforcing rules

Research & Planning Skills
- Researching rules and regulations
- Learning about changes to official rules
- Attending development seminars

Technical Skills
- Utilizing basic digital technology and personal computers
- Using digital recording and playback equipment

Physical Environment

Sports officials work in both outdoor and indoor environments depending on their chosen sport. Most work in specialized arenas or playing areas designed to accommodate a sporting contest, and many who work outdoors may be required to work in a variety of weather conditions, from extreme heat to snow and ice. Most officials work in a single region or area and so do not travel to different states or countries for contests, but may need to travel within their region. Sports officials also work according to the schedule designated for their sport and so may work unusual hours, including weekends and nights. Schedules vary widely for officials involved in different types of sports. Depending on the sport, officials may also need to develop special skills. For instance, judges and officials working in ice sports, like hockey and skating sports, need to have considerable skill with skating.

Human Environment

Depending on the sport, officials may work largely independently or may function as part of a team of officials. Most team sports have more than one official working in each match and the officials work together to ensure that players follow the rules and adhere to the guidelines of the sport. Even when working independently, officials need to communicate with athletes, coaches, trainers and other people involved in a sporting team and so need good interpersonal and communication skills. In many cases, officials learn to use special hand motions to communicate non-verbally with players, audiences, and members of athletic teams.

Technological Environment

Sports officials may use camera recording and playback equipment in cases where determinations are needed to decide the outcome of a play or other event or when some action within a contest is contested by one or the other team. In addition, umpires, referees, and officials may use personal computers and other digital tools for communication, scheduling, and time management.

EDUCATION, TRAINING, AND ADVANCEMENT

High School/Secondary

In some states, and in some sports, officials may be required to have a high school/secondary school diploma though other areas and sports have no educational requirements for prospective officials. Typically, officials must be able to demonstrate extensive knowledge of their sport and the rules involved in the sport and most professional officials begin as young athletes or begin taking an interest in their chosen sport in or before high school/secondary school.

Suggested High School Subjects
- Exercise Science
- Physical Education
- Computer Technology

Famous First

The concept of the "referee" emerged within association football, also known as "soccer," long before there were any set rules for the sport. The first rules of the game were published in 1863, at which time both teams competing in a match supplied an umpire, with the two umpires responsible for debating rules and other issues that came up during the match. In the 1870s, it was decided that the football clubs needed to add a referee who could make the call in the case of a tie vote between the two umpires. By the end of the century, the sport was transitioning away from using umpires for each team and instead entrusted all decisions to impartial referees responsible for upholding the rules and making decisions in the case of contested scores or other issues.

College/Postsecondary

Sports officials are not required to have a postsecondary education, but those who do earn bachelor's or higher degrees may have an advantage in seeking employment. Many sports officials work part time in their fields and so are advised to obtain higher education as a means of finding a career outside of sports officiating. In addition, colleges and universities offer training in fields that can be useful to those looking to enter the field, such as physical education, exercise science, public speaking, and management.

Related College Majors
- Exercise Science
- Sports Education
- Education
- Marketing and Business
- Business Management

Adult Job Seekers

For those with experience in a sport, becoming a sports official typically means participating in specific training programs for sports officials. Many sporting organizations offer training programs for those looking to become umpires, referees, and officials and the educational requirements for entering training programs differ by region and organization. Training clinics introduce students to the rules and practices of officials and give officials work experience and training under professionals in the field. Most professional sports officials begin working at lower levels of the sport, such as amateur or semi-professional leagues, before advancing to professional levels.

Professional Certification and Licensure

Certification and licensing requirements differ according to the specific sport, level of competition, and region. In some states and territories, officials within certain sports need to be licensed by an athletic board or state certifying agency. Officials working with children are more often required to obtain certification. The National Association of Sports Officials helps individuals find and apply for certification programs within their state and is also a helpful tool for professionals looking for work in the field.

Additional Requirements

Sports officials need to have excellent decision making skills and communication skills, as they are often required to make difficult decisions regarding rules violations, scoring disputes, or other contested issues during a contest and must be able to clearly communicate, verbally and non-verbally with competitors. In some sports, referees and officials need to be in good shape as they are required to follow the action of the sport and may need to exert themselves in some circumstances. Vision is also essential for sporting officials who are often required to closely watch the match to identify violations of the rules or to judge player performances.

Fun Fact

Bad call? Twelve-year-old Jeffrey Maier leaned his outstretched glove over the stands during a playoff game at Yankee Stadium, deflecting a Derek Jeter hit that appeared headed for the waiting glove of Tony Tarasco of the Baltimore Orioles. The umps didn't call fan interference and let the home run stand. While playing college baseball a decade later, Maier was belted with rocks.

Source: http://entertainment.howstuffworks.com/

EARNINGS AND ADVANCEMENT

The Bureau of Labor Statistics (BLS) estimated the annual wage for sports officials at $24,870 in 2015, with those at the upper 10 percent of the spectrum earning less than $17,890 and those at the lower end earning over $57,750. Most officials are paid on a per-match or per-game basis and those officiating at higher levels typically earn more than those at lower levels. Because officials are typically paid per-appearance, income is not typically estimated on a per/hour basis. Those looking to advance in their careers need experience to qualify for officiating at higher levels of the sport. Those without certification can enhance their prospects for moving up in the field by attending development programs or certification classes.

Metropolitan Areas with the Highest Employment Level in this Occupation

Metropolitan area	Employment	Employment per thousand jobs	Hourly mean wage
Philadelphia, PA Metropolitan Division	380	0.44	N/A
Chicago-Naperville-Arlington Heights, IL Metropolitan Division	360	0.10	N/A
Atlanta-Sandy Springs-Roswell, GA	330	0.13	N/A
Orlando-Kissimmee-Sanford, FL	320	0.28	N/A
Denver-Aurora-Lakewood, CO	270	0.20	N/A
Tampa-St. Petersburg-Clearwater, FL	260	0.22	N/A
Charlotte-Concord-Gastonia, NC-SC	260	0.23	N/A
Phoenix-Mesa-Scottsdale, AZ	230	0.12	N/A
Cape Coral-Fort Myers, FL	230	0.96	N/A
Pittsburgh, PA	210	0.19	N/A

Source: Bureau of Labor Statistics

EMPLOYMENT AND OUTLOOK

The BLS estimates that the sports official field will grow by 5 percent between 2014 and 2024, representing average or slightly below average growth in comparison to the 6-7 percent growth estimated for all occupations in the United States. Growth in the school-age population can create growth in the field by increasing the demand for officials to manage children's or adolescent sporting organizations. There has also been an increase in interest in women's sports, which has created opportunities for umpires, referees, and other officials at the amateur, semi-pro, and professional levels. Competition will remain high for positions at the upper end of the spectrum and especially for professional sports organizations and only those with prior experience and other qualifications will be likely to obtain positions at this level.

Employment Trend, Projected 2014–24

Total, all occupations: 7%

Entertainers and performers, sports and related workers: 6%

Umpires, referees, and other sports officials: 5%

Note: "All Occupations" includes all occupations in the U.S. Economy. Source: U.S. Bureau of Labor Statistics, Employment Projections Program

Related Occupations
- Athletes and Sports Competitors
- Coaches and Scouts

Related Occupations
- Armed Forces Sports Official

Conversation With . . .
BILL McCALLUM

Umpire Trainer, New England Baseball Umpire Club
Danvers, Massachusetts
Umpiring and teaching, 37 years

1. What was your individual career path in terms of education/training, entry-level job, or other significant opportunity?

Back in the early '80s, I had the opportunity to go to one of two accredited umpire schools, Wendelstedt Umpire School in Florida. They only have so many job openings in professional baseball any given year and you have to qualify to get one of those jobs, so I did that. I went into Minor League Baseball and umpired for nine years. It was one long road trip from April to September. Concurrently with that, I was picked by umpire school founder Harry Wendelstedt to be an instructor. Later, I did collegiate umpiring for about 20 years and started running umpire clinics. I also sold equipment and uniforms for umpires in the Northeast. I also run youth programs. The one I'm most proud of is in Boston. Teens get 40 hours of training, and the city puts them on the summer payroll to umpire youth baseball games. It's very rewarding. The kids learn things like fairness and objectivity and how to handle difficult people. I also work for the NCAA as a regional advisor in the Northeast, evaluating umpires and helping decide who umpires in the post-season. And I'm working with Major League Baseball Umpire Camps, a program they're running across the country to give exposure and access to the profession. If you can't afford financially or time-wise to go to a professional umpire school, they're bringing umpire school to you for a day. Umpires get to show their talents and we offer scholarships to the professional umpire schools.

The path into Major League Baseball is basically the path I took—go to one of the umpire schools, get assigned to the minor leagues and your career begins there. Working in the minor leagues is a full-time job because you're on the road all season. But you don't make enough money to sit at home during the winter. You have a fallback job. Once you get to the major leagues, the money is very, very good. They start at well over $100,000 and I believe the top guy now is making about a half a million dollars.

2. What are the most important skills and/or qualities for someone in your profession?

You have to have some sense of judgment, obviously. You need to have the ability to make fast decisions, to operate under pressure, and to handle difficult people and still stay focused on what you're doing. You need good vision. Contrary to the old stereotype, you do need some athleticism. You have to be able to move around. There are a lot of rules to know. You need to be objective. You need to understand that you can't always have the last word. And we look for people with character.

3. What do you wish you had known going into this profession?

One of the unique things about umpiring is that you establish a lot of great friendships, but at the same time, you're competing with these people for one or two openings. It's an interesting dynamic. I try to instill in umpires that it's important to give the next guy a hand up.

4. Are there many job opportunities in your profession? In what specific areas?

Most opportunities are umpiring locally on a part-time basis. If you work at the youth level you can work your way up to high school varsity baseball, then the collegiate level. Obviously, it's harder to get into professional baseball. But if you're in your early 20s and not married and you don't have children, that's the time to try it. For people who are married and have children, it's a tough life because you're not around for all the milestones that you want to be around for. A number of Major League umpires will be retiring in the next eight to 10 years, which will open up jobs right down the pipeline. One reason Major League Baseball is doing the camps is because they want to find the best umpires. If someone's interested, a camp is the way to explore it.

5. How do you see your profession changing in the next five years? What role will technology play in those changes, and what skills will be required?

They use replay now in Major League Baseball and in some of the minor leagues. In a typical year, there might be one or two rule changes and some are subtle. One of the things they're trying to do is speed up the game because they're getting so long. There's talk about implementing a clock requiring pitchers to pitch within a certain amount of time. They just did away with the intentional walk this year; all you have to do is signal and the guy goes to first base—they don't have to throw four pitches anymore.

6. What do you enjoy most about your job? What do you enjoy least about your job?

I enjoy the teaching, trying to make somebody better. I especially love to see the kids improve. As an umpire, what I really loved was a lot of the guys I worked with.

My least favorite thing is the administrative stuff that goes with money and business. When you're umpiring, you're going to have those battles, those intense confrontations and when you're in the middle of it, it's not fun.

7. Can you suggest a valuable "try this" for students considering a career in your profession?

Get involved with a local umpire association. They run a class every year. They'll give you some games, maybe an entry-level Babe Ruth game. Get your feet wet and see if you like it. If you really feel gung-ho, look at either an umpire school or one of the major league camps.

MORE INFORMATION

National Association of Sports Officials (NASO)
2017 Lathrop Ave.
Racine, WI 53405
262-632-5448
www.naso.org

National Alliance for Youth Sports (NAYS)
2050 Vist Parkway
West Palm Beach, Florida 33411
800-688-5437
www.nays.org

National Federation of State High School Associations (NFHS)
P.O. Box 690
Indianapolis, IN 46206
317-972-6900
www.nfhs.org

Micah Issitt/Editor

Scout

Snapshot

Career Cluster(s): Education & Training; Health Science; Sports & Entertainment
Interests: Physical education, kinesiology, physiology, game preparation, psychology, anatomy
Earnings (Yearly Average): $31,000
Employment & Outlook: Average Growth Expected

OVERVIEW

Sphere of Work

Scouts evaluate athletes' strengths and weaknesses as possible recruits or to improve the athletes' technique to prepare them for competition and help them train in order to achieve success.

Work Environment

Scouts and coaches work with young athletes in a wide range of environments, including athletic fields, gymnasiums, and classrooms. Those who work outdoors will have to factor in the risks or limitations posed by different types of weather. Depending on their level of active participation, instructors and coaches may be at risk for sports-related injuries.

Profile

Working Conditions: Work both Indoors and Outdoors
Physical Strength: Light Work, Medium Work
Education Needs: Bachelor's Degree
Licensure/Certification: Usually Not Required
Opportunities For Experience: Internship, Volunteer Work, Part Time Work
Holland Interest Score*: ESR

* See Appendix A

Occupation Interest

A sports instructor or coach should possess a strong background in, and knowledge of, the various sports for which he or she will be responsible. This includes not only an understanding of the basic physical skills needed to participate in these sports, but also how to teach people to work in a group and develop team goals.

A Day in the Life—Duties and Responsibilities

Scouts and coaching professionals work in a setting that requires tremendous social communication skills, as well as knowledge of motivational and educational techniques. They impart the knowledge and understanding required to effectively participate in an individual or team sport, while teaching young athletes the benefits of working in a group setting toward a common goal. The instructor or coach implements a learning progression, using a variety of repetitive physical drills that allows the athlete to build confidence by properly executing the skills required to compete in the sport being practiced. This is done in team practice sessions, which work progressively from an individual skill development period to a group development period, ending with an exercise in which both individual and group development learning and repetitive drill work are incorporated into the complete team setting. This is essential preparation for athletic contests.

Duties and Responsibilities

- Organizing and running practice sessions
- Developing an individual's athletic talent
- Directing and orchestrating workouts
- Creating and executing game strategy

OCCUPATION SPECIALTIES

Head Coaches

Head Coaches work with groups of athletes through subordinate assistant coaches.

Coaches of Professional Athletes

Coaches of Professional Athletes work with groups of paid professional athletes and paid assistant coaches. Their duties often include not only game preparation and game coaching, but recruiting, assessing and selecting new professional talent.

Physical Instructors

Physical Instructors work with individuals and small groups in beginning or advanced exercises for reducing weight or improving health.

WORK ENVIRONMENT

Physical Environment

Scouts and coaches work in athletic fields, gymnasiums, weight rooms, pools, classrooms, and offices. In certain sports, athletes are introduced to the individual and comprehensive team concepts via classroom instruction.

Relevant Skills and Abilities

Communication Skills
- Speaking effectively
- Writing concisely

Interpersonal/Social Skills
- Being patient
- Cooperating with others
- Motivating others
- Providing support to others
- Teaching others
- Working as a member of a team

Organization & Management Skills
- Coordinating tasks
- Managing people/groups
- Managing time
- Organizing information or materials

Human Environment

Scouts and coaches work with athletes of varying ages and skill levels. They may also work with other coaching professionals, office and teaching personnel, the media, and the community at large.

Technological Environment

Scouts and coaches use a variety of tools, including sports-related physical equipment and audiovisual devices. The physical equipment is designed to improve individual kinetic skills and techniques, which in turn improves the athlete's ability to compete. Audiovisual equipment allows athletes to observe their drill work and exercises, so that they can properly gauge what they need to improve to be competitive.

EDUCATION, TRAINING, AND ADVANCEMENT

High School/Secondary

High school students should study biology, physical education, and computers. English, psychology, and speech communication courses are also helpful, as is participation in whichever sport(s) the student wants to teach. During the summer, students should consider attending athletic camps for further development of individual skills.

Suggested High School Subjects
- English
- First Aid Training
- Health Science Technology
- Physical Education
- Psychology
- Social Studies

Famous First

The first coach of a professional basketball team who as African American was Bill Russell, who began coaching the Boston Celtics in 1966 and, in the following year, led the team to the NBA championship.

College/Postsecondary

Over the years, the job of sports instruction has come to place more of an emphasis on the development of professional standards for those who enter the field. Sports instructors and coaches in schools usually have at least a bachelor's degree, and are often also teachers or other education professionals. Colleges and universities in the United States offer a variety of coaching degree programs, which include courses in subjects such as human kinesiology, biology, physiology, nutrition, sports science and medicine, and professional standards. University programs may also offer internships for interested students, which allow them to observe professionals at work in their chosen sports and develop professional contacts for the future.

Related College Majors
 • Physical Education Teaching & Coaching

Adult Job Seekers

Sports instructors and coaching professionals are generally also educators seeking employment in local school districts. Depending on the economic conditions and availability of qualified teachers, college graduates may be required to work as substitute teachers until a full-time opportunity presents itself. Substitute teacher work does not preclude an individual from working as a sports coach in a school district at the same time, and doing so can afford a recent college graduate the opportunity to further develop his or her individual skills and knowledge, while also becoming familiar with the school district personnel and administration. This can be beneficial in the highly competitive job market, as can being certified to teach multiple disciplines.

Participation in professional associations can also provide good opportunities for employment and personal development of one's professional skills. Each state has an official organization for high school sports, coordinated through the National Federation of State High School Associations (NFHS). Other national organizations, such as the Amateur Athletic Union, may also be helpful.

Professional Certification and Licensure

At the high school level, various states have different requirements for professional certification or endorsements in coaching. Some states may require teaching certification. Students interested in pursuing this profession should investigate the requirements of the state and school district in which they wish to work.

Additional Requirements

As in education, a sports instructor or coaching professional's strong commitment to continued learning and training is important for his or her own professional development, as well as for the safety and instruction of the athletes being coached.

Fun Facts

With 621 wins, John McKissick, former head football coach of Summerville High School in Summerville, South Carolina, holds the record for most wins by a football coach at any level. He coached for 63 years before retiring in 2015.
Source: http://www.postandcourier.com

You could call her the original "girl scout." In 1925, the Chicago White Sox hired a full-time scout with severe hearing problems. His wife, Bessie Largent, was his "secretary," but is credited with being responsible for some great picks, including Hall of Famer Luke Appling.
Source: https://www.nytimes.com/

EARNINGS AND ADVANCEMENT

Earnings in this field span the range from zero to many hundreds of thousands of dollars. Most sports instructors and coaches earn very modest amounts of money and usually must supplement their incomes from other sources. Advancement is based on ability and experience. Median annual earnings of sports instructors and coaches were $31,000 in 2015. The lowest ten percent earned less than $17,930, and the highest ten percent earned more than $70,050.

Only successful professional coaches in established professional organizations or schools can usually expect any fringe benefits. These usually include paid vacations, holidays, and sick days; life and health insurance; and retirement benefits.

Metropolitan Areas with the Highest Employment Level in this Occupation

Metropolitan area	Employment	Employment per thousand jobs	Anuual mean wage
Los Angeles-Long Beach-Glendale, CA	5,490	1.42	$47,000
New York-White Plains-Wayne, NY-NJ	4,320	0.84	$42,880
St. Louis, MO-IL	3,670	2.88	$25,040
Santa Ana-Anaheim-Irvine, CA	3,340	2.37	$41,390
Chicago-Joliet-Naperville, IL	3,320	0.91	$32,290
Seattle-Bellevue-Everett, WA	3,310	2.35	$43,150
Boston-Cambridge-Quincy, MA	3,160	1.85	$47,770
Washington-Arlington-Alexandria, DC-VA-MD-WV	2,840	1.21	$51,510
Denver-Aurora-Broomfield, CO	2,700	2.19	$37,610
Philadelphia, PA	2,600	1.43	$37,780

Source: Bureau of Labor Statistics

EMPLOYMENT AND OUTLOOK

There were about 250,000 scouts and coaches employed nationally in 2014. About half of all scouts and coaches worked part-time, and about one-fourth were self-employed, earning fees for lessons. Employment is expected to grow as fast as the average for all occupations through the year 2024, which means employment is projected to increase 4 percent to 8 percent. Job opportunities are expected for scouts and coaches as more people in our society are becoming interested in physical fitness. Employment will also increase with the growth of school and college athletic programs and demand for private sports instruction. Persons who are certified to teach academic subjects in addition to physical education will have the best chances of finding sports instructor and coach jobs.

Employment Trend, Projected 2014–24

Total, all occupations: 7%

Sports instructors and coaches: 6%

Sports and entertainment occupations: 6%

Note: "All Occupations" includes all occupations in the U.S. Economy. Source: U.S. Bureau of Labor Statistics, Employment Projections Program

Conversation With . . .
DAN JENNINGS

Special Assistant to the General Manager
Washington Nationals, Washington, D.C.
Scouting & other baseball professions, 30 years

1. **What was your individual career path in terms of education/training, entry-level job, or other significant opportunity?**

I played baseball in high school and college. I graduated from William Carey University in Mississippi with a degree in biological science and health physical education. I went to a tryout camp, was signed and went to spring training in 1984 with the NY Yankees. From there, I coached high school until 1986, when I became an associate scout with the Cincinnati Reds. In 1988, I got hired as a full-time scout for the Seattle Mariners. I did that for seven years, then they elevated me to Midwestern cross checker. Essentially, a cross checker is a comparison scout for one-third of the country. I would go see players from Michigan and compare them to players in Kentucky or Tennessee, then go back to Seattle to help set up the draft. After a year, the Tampa Bay Devil Rays hired me as Director of Scouting. I was 35 years old. I did that for seven years. After that, I went to what was then the Florida Marlins as the Vice President of Player Personnel.

I was elevated to assistant general manager after about four years. In 2013, I became general manager of the Miami Marlins until May 2015, when I was asked to go down on the field and be the manager for the remainder of the season. Then I was let go and I became special assistant to the general manager with the Washington Nationals. This is my second year in that capacity. It's been a great ride, very blessed, a lot of fun.

2. **What are the most important skills and/or qualities for someone in your profession?**

First and foremost, people skills are essential. There's a trend in baseball to use a lot of analytics, which basically try to measure things as if it's an exact science. While these things can help in predicting and making proper decisions, we can't forget this is a game played by people, not robots. People skills, organizational skills and communicative skills are the three essentials you have to have.

3. **What do you wish you had known going into this profession?**

I'm thankful that I went into this with a blank canvas, because I was able to draw from veterans who had been around the game in many capacities and formulate my owns thoughts about, "Wow, if I ever get into this capacity … " or "I really like this idea or that idea because it would work with my personality." So there truly are no regrets on what I wish I had known.

4. Are there many job opportunities in your profession? In what specific areas?

I wouldn't use the term "many," but they're out there. I started as an associate scout, helping a full-time scout within a 50- or 100-miles radius. Now intern opportunities are big. There are also scout camps. These avenues can help open a door and all you're looking to do, honestly, is have one door open. You're going to have a lot of grunt jobs, but in doing so you're going to see the intricacies of how things work behind the scenes, which will give you a great frame of reference going forward.

5. How do you see your profession changing in the next five years? What role will technology play in those changes, and what skills will be required?

We're starting to see that push toward the analytical side of measuring skills and trying to predict someone's failure rate and success rate. Understanding the mathematics of these formulas and analytics will be huge. You need to be very proficient and efficient with anything that relates to breaking down statistics and building spreadsheets and charts to prove your points. Also, I see more diversity coming, which is a good thing.

6. What do you enjoy most about your job? What do you enjoy least about your job?

Definitely the camaraderie, the people in and around the game. In scouting, you become your own family out on the road. You can go into a ballpark and see someone you haven't seen for a year and you pick up where you left off.

What I like least are the things you miss at home with your real family. When I was a scouting director, there were times I was on the road staying in a hotel close to 300 nights a year. One of my sons hit his first high school home run when I was out in California. Those are moments that you just don't get back.

7. Can you suggest a valuable "try this" for students considering a career in your profession?

An internship would probably be number one. Number two would be to go to a ballpark where a good player in high school or college will be playing. Get there early and hang out with a scout, create dialogue and have a conversation. Or go to a minor league ballpark and do the same thing, watching from the time the gates open, all the stuff that goes on before the game is played and then the game itself and how the scouts are working in the stands during the game. You can see "a day in the life of" that may help you determine "Yeah, this is for me," or, "Maybe I want to do something else in the game."

MORE INFORMATION

Amateur Athletic Union
P.O. Box 22409
Lake Buena Vista, FL 32830
407.934.7200
www.aausports.org

American Federation of Teachers
555 New Jersey Avenue NW
Washington, DC 20001
202.879.4400
www.aft.org

National Collegiate Athletic Association
700 West Washington Street
P.O. Box 6222
Indianapolis, IN 46206
317.917.6222
www.ncaa.org

National Federation of State High School Associations
P.O. Box 690
Indianapolis, IN 46206
317.972.6900
www.nfhs.org

National High School Athletic Coaches Association
P.O. Box 3181
Clearwater, FL 33767
407.592.9212
www.nhsaca.org

National Junior College Athletic Association
1631 Mesa Avenue, Suite B
Colorado Springs, CO 80906
719.590.9788
www.njcaa.org

Positive Coaching Alliance
1001 North Rengstorff Avenue
Suite 100
Mountain View, CA 94043
866.725.0024
www.positivecoach.org

Chuck Goodwin/Editor

Security

Snapshot

Career Cluster: Law & Criminal Justice; Public Safety & Security
Interests: Public safety, safeguarding property, surveillance, patrolling, investigation, law
Earnings (Yearly Average): $27,240
Employment & Outlook: Average Growth Expected

OVERVIEW

Sphere of Work

Security guards protect property and people from a variety of threats, including theft, vandalism, assault, and other illegal activities. They supervise and control who enters company facilities and ensure the safety of individuals within the facility and grounds. They maintain surveillance of private or public property to prevent theft, especially at night. Security guards are responsible for communicating with emergency services, such as police or fire departments, as needed. Depending on their specific job duties, some may become licensed to carry firearms or other weapons.

Work Environment

Security guards work for private employers, government agencies, or security guard agencies. Some work primarily indoors, while others work outdoors in varying weather. Most security guards either maintain a stationary position, where they monitor one location directly or via closed-circuit television (CCTV), or conduct mobile patrols throughout their designated area during a shift. They spend long hours on their feet. Most security guards work forty to forty-eight hours per week, depending on whether they work for a security company or a company in another industry. Guards at security firms may work as many as sixty hours a week. Though a security guard's job may be tedious or routine at times, it can also be dangerous.

Profile

Working Conditions: Work both Indoors and Outdoors
Physical Strength: Light Work
Education Needs: On-The-Job Training, High School Diploma Or GED
Licensure/Certification: Required
Physical Abilities Not Required: No Heavy Labor
Opportunities For Experience: Apprenticeship, Military Service, Part-Time Work
Holland Interest Score*: ESR, SEC

* See Appendix A

Occupation Interest

People interested in pursuing a career as a security guard should possess a desire to safeguard property and people. They should respond to potential threats according to the training they have received. Prospective security guards should be physically fit and maintain a healthy lifestyle, as part of the success of the job depends on physical speed, dexterity, coordination, and strength. They should demonstrate good judgment and be able to make quick decisions, sometimes based on very little information. Being able to quickly assess possible threats and unusual situations, alert others to what they have observed, and safely investigate to gather more information are other desirable traits in this profession.

A Day in the Life—Duties and Responsibilities

Security guards are responsible for protecting private or public property, as well as ensuring the safety of people on those properties. They perform a wide range of duties to that end. Security guards are employed in many industries, and may work in such varied positions as gate tenders, merchant patrollers, or store detectives. They keep track of visitors and employees who enter and exit the premises. They observe and record daily activities, especially any unusual occurrences, and submit those observations to their employers. Security guards are also responsible for making contact with law enforcement officials in the case of emergencies, such as fires, burglaries, medical emergencies, vandalism, terrorist attacks, and other incidents. They thoroughly investigate all areas of the property they oversee and attend to any disturbances or irregularities they encounter. They protect others from harm partly through their constant presence, which tends to discourage and prevent potential crime.

Security guards ensure that all entrances and exits of a structure, including windows, gates, and doors, are closed and properly secured. Occasionally, they may escort vehicles to specific destinations or provide individuals with personal protection. Some security guards operate detection equipment to screen people for weapons or other prohibited items. They may monitor alarms and electronic security systems.

Security guards must sometimes escort or bodily remove unauthorized personnel from the premises and explain security measures and rules to visitors and employees. They may also inspect incoming mail and packages for suspicious contents. Some security guards monitor and direct parking and traffic. Some are required to collect and verify the authenticity of various forms of identification from visitors or patrons, as well as conduct financial transactions.

Duties and Responsibilities

- Patrolling buildings and grounds at specific times
- Checking doors, windows, gates, locks, and lights
- Checking for proper identification at entrances
- Directing visitors and giving routine information
- Adjusting controls to maintain desired building temperatures or conditions
- Watching for and reporting fire hazards and property damage
- Monitoring video and other electronic security systems

OCCUPATION SPECIALTIES

Security Guards

Security Guards, also called Security Officers, protect property, enforce rules on the property, and deter criminal activity. Some guards are assigned a stationary position from which they monitor alarms or surveillance cameras. Other guards are assigned a patrol area where they conduct security checks.

Gaming Surveillance Officers

Gaming Surveillance Officers act as security agents for casinos. Using audio and video equipment in an observation room, they watch casino operations for suspicious activities, such as cheating and theft, and monitor compliance with rules, regulations, and laws. They maintain and organize recordings from security cameras, which are sometimes used as evidence in police investigations.

Armored Car Guards

Armored Car Guards protect money and valuables during transit. They pick up money and other valuables from businesses and transport them to another location. These guards usually wear bulletproof vests and carry firearms, because transporting money between the truck and the business is potentially dangerous.

Transportation Security Screeners

Transportation Security Screeners conduct screening of passengers, baggage, or cargo to ensure compliance with Transportation Security Administration (TSA) regulations. They may operate basic security equipment such as x-ray machines and hand wands (metal detectors) at screening checkpoints.

Bodyguards

Bodyguards ensure the safety of individual persons—for example, a political figure—or small groups in public spaces and elsewhere. They often are licensed to carry handguns and may also be trained in martial arts.

WORK ENVIRONMENT

Physical Environment

The immediate physical environment of security guards will vary based on the size and type of employer. Some security guards work indoors; others work outdoors in all kinds of weather. Some are stationed at small guard desks inside large buildings, while others work in outdoor guardhouses. Others patrol small stores, large shopping centers, nightclubs and bars (where they are called "bouncers"), museums, movie theaters, banks, hospitals, and office buildings. Some security guards work in airports or at rail terminals, while others are employed by universities, public parks, casinos, or sports stadiums.

Relevant Skills and Abilities

Interpersonal/Social Skills
- Being able to remain calm
- Cooperating with others
- Working as a member of a team

Organization & Management Skills
- Following instructions
- Handling challenging situations
- Meeting goals and deadlines
- Performing routine work
- Working quickly when necessary

Other Skills
- Staying alert

Human Environment

Security guards who work during the day usually interact often with members of the public as well as the staff of the property that they protect. Those who work at night often work alone and do not come into contact with many people. Many security guards also interact with law enforcement personnel, including police officers, firefighters, detectives, and other security officers as needed.

Technological Environment

Security guards may operate patrol cars, golf carts, automobiles, or other vehicles in the course of their work. They often carry cell phones, flashlights, two-way radios, and handcuffs, as well as a personal defense product such as pepper spray, Mace, or a Taser. Some security guards are licensed to carry handguns. Security guards also process documents, which may include witness reports, theft reports, and observation reports. They may use spreadsheet software, the Internet and email, and word processing software.

EDUCATION, TRAINING, AND ADVANCEMENT

High School/Secondary

High school students who are interested in becoming security guards can prepare themselves by taking courses in English, physical education, geography, sociology, and psychology. They should also participate in and maintain ongoing first aid training and certification. Outside of school, students can enroll in extracurricular self-defense courses or one-on-one physical training courses that allow them to understand the foundations of different self-defense techniques. Students can also tour local factories, office buildings, or shopping centers to learn more about the primary duties of a security guard.

Suggested High School Subjects
- English
- First Aid Training
- Physical Education
- Social Studies

Famous First

The first armored car robbery was staged in 1927 by the Flathead gang, a few miles outside of Pittsburgh, Penn. An armored vehicle carrying a $104,250 payroll of the Pittsburgh Terminal Coal Company blew up when it drove over a landmine planted under the roadbed by the bandits. Five guards were badly injured. The gang leader, Paul Jaworski, was later executed for a second payroll robbery that resulted in a murder.

Postsecondary

It is not necessary for security guards to obtain an undergraduate degree; many employers hire security guards who have earned a high school diploma or its equivalent. Other employers, however, may prefer to hire security guards who have some kind of postsecondary training in criminal justice or a related field. Since employer preferences vary widely, it is advisable to check the required education level and experience qualifications before applying for a job.

Employers usually require on-the-job training for newly hired security guards. Depending on a security guard's assignment, he or she may be trained in first aid, emergency procedures, interacting with potentially dangerous individuals, communications skills, and report writing. Security guards who carry weapons receive specific training in the use of force, practical applications of firearms, and weapons retention. The American Society for Industrial Security International provides employers with standard guidelines for the training of security guards, which include suggestions for a written examination covering emergency response techniques, crime prevention, legal issues, and other topics.

Related College Majors
- Corrections/Correctional Administration
- Security & Loss Prevention Services

Adult Job Seekers

Prospective security guards can enter the field by accepting part-time or summer work at local resorts, golf courses, amusement parks, or other seasonal employment venues. They may be able to participate in a job shadowing experience with a local security guard. Other prospective security guards may apply for positions through an employment agency, which then finds them appropriate work.

Professional Certification and Licensure

Security guards are usually required to be licensed by the state in which they seek employment. Licensing requirements vary by state but commonly include a background check, drug test, and practical training in such topics as emergency procedures, property rights, and criminal apprehension. Security guards must also be at least eighteen years of age and possess a valid driver's license. Armed security guards are legally required to obtain special certification in order to carry weapons.

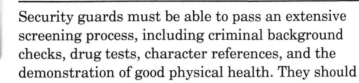

Additional Requirements

Security guards must be able to pass an extensive screening process, including criminal background checks, drug tests, character references, and the demonstration of good physical health. They should possess a clean driving record and have no criminal or police record. Because security guards often work long shifts at night and frequently observe the same area, employers expect guards to be able to stay alert for the duration of a work shift, remain calm enough to follow proper procedures when incidents arise, and react swiftly in emergencies.

Fun Fact

World War II prompted changes all over the country, including in pro football. Because so many players served in the military, the Eagles and Steelers played in 1943 as the Steagles. The next year, the Steelers and the Chicago Cardinals joined forces—but we're not sure what they called themselves.

Source: http://www.huffingtonpost.com

EARNINGS AND ADVANCEMENT

Earnings depend on the geographic location of the employer and the individual's level of experience. Mean annual earnings of security guards were $27,240 in 2012. The lowest ten percent earned less than $17,390, and the highest ten percent earned more than $42,490.

Security guards may receive paid vacations, holidays, and sick days; life and health insurance; and retirement benefits. These are usually paid by the employer.

Metropolitan Areas with the Highest
Employment Level in this Occupation

Metropolitan area	Employment	Employment per thousand jobs	Hourly mean wage
New York-White Plains-Wayne, NY-NJ	78,120	15.15	$14.29
Los Angeles-Long Beach-Glendale, CA	51,950	13.42	$12.61
Chicago-Joliet-Naperville, IL	42,070	11.56	$12.13
Washington-Arlington-Alexandria, DC-VA-MD-WV	33,480	14.28	$17.89
Houston-Sugar Land-Baytown, TX	23,680	8.97	$11.06
Atlanta-Sandy Springs-Marietta, GA	20,590	9.10	$11.60
Dallas-Plano-Irving, TX	19,790	9.44	$12.68
Miami-Miami Beach-Kendall, FL	19,080	19.10	$11.29

Source: Bureau of Labor Statistics

EMPLOYMENT AND OUTLOOK

Security guards held over one million jobs nationally in 2012. Employment is expected to grow about as fast as the average for all occupations through the year 2022, which means employment is projected to increase 8 percent to 15 percent. Increased concern about crime, vandalism and terrorism will heighten the need for security in and around stores, offices, schools, hospitals and other areas. Many opportunities are expected for persons seeking full-time employment, as well as for those seeking part-time or second jobs at night or on weekends.

Employment Trend, Projected 2012–22

Security Guards: 12%

Total, All Occupations: 11%

Gaming Surveillance Officers: 7%

Note: "All Occupations" includes all occupations in the U.S. Economy. Source: U.S. Bureau of Labor Statistics, Employment Projections Program

Related Occupations
- Correctional Officer
- Police Officer
- Private Detective

Related Military Occupations
- Law Enforcement & Security Specialist
- Military Police

Conversation With . . .
PAUL TURNER, CFE CSSP

Senior Director of Event Operations
AT&T Stadium, Dallas Cowboys
Venue management, 27 years
Event security, 17 years

1. What was your individual career path in terms of education/training, entry-level job, or other significant opportunity?

I started as a music major at California State University, Long Beach but earned my degree in speech communication. On campus, I worked as a tech in the recital hall. After graduation, I was hired at a new performing arts center to run the front of the house, which included a small security force. My career shifted to sports when I took a job in arena operations for the Portland Trailblazers. Security was part of what I did, but then 9-11 happened and it went—literally overnight—to a much more specialized and visible part of the operation.

The first thing we did that morning was to assess our standards. We implemented things like walk through metal detectors and pat-down screenings at rock concerts.

I went on to work guest services and facilities security operations for the Philadelphia Eagles, then was hired by the Cowboys in 2008, the year before this stadium opened.

I'm the senior director of event operations and I oversee all public services, including event management, event staff (ticket takers, ushers, guest services), security and police, fire and medical services. I also oversee parking and transportation. Everything is very closely tied with the security function. We have a contracted security provider for daily, 24-7 security and for event security.

Sports security requires specialized training, through courses and organizations like NCS4 (National Center for Spectator Sports Safety and Security). Only recently have academic programs started to prepare people for this.

Here at the stadium, we are still evolving. For instance, we use hand-held wands for screenings but the NFL has a new requirement that all stadiums will have walk through metal detectors, starting in five months. That has implications for line queuing, signage…just a whole different calculus to process the crowd. The vast majority of fans come in the last 45 minutes before kickoff, and we need to get them through in as pleasant and expedient a process as possible.

Some things we do are very visible and intentional so the fans can see we have a show of force, but there are a lot of behind the scenes things we don't talk about. We have a great working relationship with the FBI and the city. We have a pretty robust intelligence network that informs and updates us. We have different layers of screening starting in the parking lots that are encountered as you get closer to the building.

Overall, security concerns arise because of our condensed population and our visibility. We have 98,000 people here on game day. That's a mid-size city. If something bad were to happen, it would be televised worldwide. You wouldn't have to hurt that many people to send shockwaves through our society and world.

2. What are the most important skills and/or qualities for someone in your profession?

You need to be an analytical thinker; good at solving puzzles. You take something as small as one person standing in a specific place and knit him—and all your capabilities—into a big picture.

Consider crowd density. How many people are pressed into what area? Is how to get out intuitive to the crowd? Is the venue kept up clean? Those things influence how crowds operate.

3. What do you wish you had known going into this profession?

I wish I had known security was still in the early phases of development. I stepped in thinking a lot of this had been figured out, but it hadn't. Going to a sporting event today is very different than 20 years ago.

4. Are there many job opportunities in your profession? In what specific areas?

There are a finite number of venues, so there aren't that many. If you can get in and gain experience and be interested in your professional development, you can carve out a career for yourself.

Wages at early stages can be low, hours long. There's really no glamour. It's not about seeing events and hobnobbing with athletes. Your job is to be consumed with taking care of the customers and foreseeing any number of things that could happen and preventing them.

5. How do you see your profession changing in the next five years, what role will technology play in those changes, and what skills will be required?

Formalized education will help people get the skills and knowledge needed to do this work. The body of knowledge is getting more solidified and codified.

Things that are considered cutting edge—like closed-circuit cameras that can identify people with certain behaviors—will become as commonplace as fire sprinklers.

6. What do you enjoy most about your job? What do you enjoy least about your job?

I most enjoy knowing I'm contributing to people's memories and enjoyment of life. There are people in the building for the first time ever, and it's the fulfillment of a dream. Others, it will be their last time. This is a job of service to others, to take a complex environment and run it in a way that is customer-friendly.

I don't necessarily dislike it, but the toughest part of the job is trying to ensure that the people on the very front lines are prepared and capable of doing their very best work.

7. Can you suggest a valuable "try this" for students considering a career in your profession?

Be an usher or a security guard at a stadium or arena. Start at the very bottom. Interested and capable people in a front line role like that will get elevated pretty quickly. What makes you a competent executive someday is having been through that chain of command. Also, when you go to an event, notice how the crowd moves, where people who are working are arranged, how signs are arranged. It's all part of the recipe.

SELECTED SCHOOLS

Training beyond high school is not expected of security guards. However, taking classes in security operations at a vocational school or technical community college will put a candidate in good stead with an employer. Interested students should consult with their school guidance counselor.

MORE INFORMATION

American Society for Industrial Security International
1625 Prince Street
Alexandria, VA 22314-2818
703.519.6200
www.asisonline.org

International Union, Security, Police and Fire Professionals of America
25510 Kelly Road
Roseville, MI 48066
800.228.7492
www.spfpa.org

Service Employees International Union
1800 Massachusetts Avenue, NW
Washington, DC 20036
800.424.8592
www.seiu.org

United Government Security Officers of America
8670 Wolff Court, Suite 210
Westminster, CO 80031
800.572.6103
www.ugsoa.com

Briana Nadeau/Editor

Sports Agent

Snapshot

Career Cluster(s): Sports and Fitness
Interests: Business, marketing, promotion, sports
Earnings (Yearly Average): $60,092
Employment & Outlook: Slower than average growth

OVERVIEW

Sphere of Work

Sports agents are representatives employed directly by athletes or by a managing company to represent athletes in contract and business negotiations. Sports agents advertise and market their clients as performers, help manage a client's public and professional image, network with other agents, team managers and owners, and recruit new clients to build their professional talent portfolio. Sports agents are managers, promotional experts, and financial managers for their clients as well as entrepreneurs who are typically responsible for building their own businesses.

Work Environment

Sports agents spend most of their time working in office environments, whether a private office or one of several offices and conference rooms in a sports agency. Agents are sometimes required to travel extensively to recruit talent or participate in negotiations in different areas. While most sports agents work full time, during certain times of the year, agents may be required to work irregular or unusual hours and overtime work is common in the field.

Profile

Working Conditions: Indoors
Physical Strength: Nonstrenuous work
Education Needs: High School/Secondary School, Bachelor's Degree, Master's Degree
Licensure/Certification: Required in some states and regions
Opportunities For Experience: Internships, On-the-job training
Holland Interest Score*: ES

* See Appendix A

Occupation Interest

Sports agents should be enterprising individuals who enjoy the challenge of marketing their services and building a professional reputation. Successful agents need to have excellent interpersonal skills and the ability to persuade others to see their view on various issues. In addition, sports agents should have a strong interest in sports as intimate knowledge of various types of athletics is helpful in finding talent, handling negotiations, and marketing athletes to various sports franchises. Agents should also be interested in business and finance as they are often involved in helping their clients to manage their earnings.

A Day in the Life—Duties and Responsibilities

Sports agents find and recruit clients and a sports agent may spend part of a typical day researching potential clients or attending games to watch potential clients play. Professional agents report that face-to-face meetings, interviews, and negotiations are a daily part of the job. Agents frequently meet with their clients to advise them on marketing and promotional issues. When it's time for clients to negotiate new contracts, agents meet with representatives of sports franchises and conduct negotiations for their clients. Once a client has signed with an agent, the agent will spend time marketing their clients, which may involve negotiating with companies for product endorsements and advertising deals, negotiating with franchise owners, or organizing press appearances. If an agent works as part of a sports agency, he or she may also spend times in meetings discussing agency strategies. Agents also typically collect payments from sporting franchises and distribute payments to their clients. In some cases, athletes rely on their agents to help them manage their income, setting up investments or arranging for their clients to meet with other financial representatives.

Duties and Responsibilities

- **Research and observe potential clients**
- **Negotiate with athletes and managers to sign new clients**
- **Promote and market clients**
- **Meet with and negotiate with sports franchise officials and recruiters**
- **Collect and distribute payments to clients**
- **Negotiate contracts for clients**
- **Promote their own services or the services of an agency**
- **Meet with clients to discuss media and other image management strategies**

OCCUPATION SPECIALTIES

Agent Manager

An agent manager is a sports agent also serves as a general manager for one or more clients. The agent manager handles negotiations, manages their clients' public image, and also handles other aspects of the client's career, such as scheduling practices, exercise sessions, and other professional development activities.

Booking Agent

A booking agent is an agent who specializes in finding jobs or competitions for their clients and negotiating with organizers and managers to include their clients in an upcoming performance.

Booking agents can work with a variety of performers, including athletes, musicians, actors, and others in the performance fields.

Sports Attorney

A sports attorney can work either for athletes or for professional sports associations handling any legal contract, financial, or other litigation needed by their clients. At times, sports lawyers can handle many of the same functions as a sports agent, in negotiating salary and specifics of a contract, while sports lawyers are also trained in the law and so are able to evaluate and handle the legal needs of their clients.

WORK ENVIRONMENT

Physical Environment

Sports agents spend most of their time working indoors in office environments, though many agents attend sporting events regularly either to watch their existing clients or to research new potential clients. Sports agents may travel regularly to negotiate for their clients or to attend sporting events and many work irregular hours.

Human Environment

Sports agents need to be skilled in communication and negotiation and spend much of their time in meetings with clients, representatives of sports franchises, and others involved in the industry. Agents also need to be effective at marketing their own services and in communicating the value of their experience and expertise to potential clients as well as being able to effectively negotiate on behalf of their clients. Agents working for sports agencies will also work closely with other agents and related professionals to manage clients and should therefore be skilled at working as part of a team.

Relevant Skills and Abilities

Communication Skills
- Communicating with clients, managers, other agents, and recruiters
- Participating in negotiations on contracts

Interpersonal/Social Skills
- Working closely with clients
- Working with other agents, lawyers, and team managers

Organization & Management Skills
- Managing client's public image and marketing
- Organizing meetings, negotiations, and managing time

Research & Planning Skills
- Researching new potential lients
- Planning for upcoming trade negotiations

Technical Skills
- Utilizing basic digital technology and personal computers
- Using video playback and recording equipment
- Using spreadsheet and accounting software

Technological Environment

Sports agents use personal computers and other digital tools like smart phones and tablets to communicate with clients and other individuals, which is a major part of an agent's typical daily activities. In addition, agents should be comfortable using accounting and spreadsheet software to keep track of schedules, payments, and to manage other financial aspects of their business. Agents should also be familiar with photo and video software allowing them to use photos and videos of their clients in promotional presentations. In addition, many agents used video conferencing software to conduct meetings with clients and other professionals from a distance.

EDUCATION, TRAINING, AND ADVANCEMENT

High School/Secondary

Most professional sports agents obtain at least a bachelor's degree and so high school/secondary school students can prepare for a career as a sports agent by working towards obtaining a higher education degree. While in high school/secondary school, students should take classes in finance, economics, management, public speaking, and other disciplines that will help them obtain a degree in management at higher levels.

Suggested High School Subjects
- English
- Economics
- History
- Introduction to Business
- Public Speaking
- Introduction to Marketing
- Mathematics
- Communications
- World Languages
- Sociology

Famous First

In 1925, American football player Red Grange became the first professional athlete to hire a representative to serve as his personal representative in negotiations and other business activities. As a result, Grange became one of the first athletes whose compensation was based on his popularity and the number of fans he attracted to the team's performances. Grange's agent, Charles "C.C." Pyle helped Grange win a contract for $100,000 in his first playing season for the Chicago Bears, while other players on the team were making $100-$200 per appearance. Over the decades, the sports agent field evolved and agents regularly did more than negotiating contracts, helping their clients to build their professional image and popularity with fans which, in turn, allows athletes to command more compensation in future contracts.

College/Postsecondary

Prospective sports agents can earn a degree in a related field, such as sports management or management, though individuals can enter the field with other degree specializations. Sports agents blend economics, advertising and marketing, and management skills and so degrees in any subject related to business management or economics will be helpful for those looking to build a career as a sports agent. Prospective agents can also take their education farther by seeking out master's degree programs in management or, specifically, sports management offered at some colleges and universities. Agents who obtain law degrees or attend seminars in sports law, may have an advantage in understanding the legal aspects of contract negotiations, financial management, and other facets of the field and agents looking to advance in their careers might consider obtaining a degree in law with a specialization in contract law or sports law.

Related College Majors
- Sports Management
- Business
- Business Management
- Advertising
- Marketing
- Sports Law

Adult Job Seekers

Most professional sports agents begin their career by seeking internships or assistant-level positions working under an experienced agent or for an established sports agency. Those seeking to work independently will need to build a list of clients and so can work towards that goal by finding and meeting with athletes who are in the process of building their professional careers.

Professional Certification and Licensure

Licensing requirements differ by region or state and prospective agents need to know the licensing requirements in the state in which they wish to work. In states that require licenses, agents typically need to register, pay fees, and submit to a background check before receiving their licenses. Licensing for sports agents is designed to protect athletes from unscrupulous manipulation rather than to gauge a person's knowledge or skill in the industry.

Additional Requirements

Sports agents need to have excellent critical thinking skills as they must be able to effectively evaluate potential contracts and licensing deals for their clients. They need to have excellent speaking skills and the ability to persuade others and negotiate effectively. In some cases, familiarity with foreign languages can be helpful for managers working with athletes from a variety of different cultural background and of different nationalities. In addition, agents need to be energetic, highly motivated, and driven as most sports agents are required to market and advertise not only their clients, but their own services as they build and grow their careers.

Fun Fact

If Michael Phelps was a country, he'd rank ahead of 97 nations in all-time gold medals won, at 35.

Source: ftw.usatoday.com

EARNINGS AND ADVANCEMENT

The Bureau of Labor Statistics (BLS) estimated the median salary for sports agents at $60,092 in 2915, with agents at the lowest 10 percent of the fields earning less than $28,000 and agents at the highest 10 percent earning in excess of $100,000 annually. Agents managing star athletes or managing athletes for high profile professional sports typically earn the highest salaries in the industry. Agents earn more based on the salaries and contract terms they are able to obtain for clients and based on the number of clients that an agent is representing and so advancement in the field typically involves signing new clients or negotiating on behalf of their clients for higher compensation. Agents who work in agencies may advance in their careers through experience, earning the opportunity to manage higher profile clients and therefore earning more for their work.

Metropolitan Areas with the Highest Employment Level in this Occupation

Metropolitan area	Employment	Employment per thousand jobs	Hourly mean wage
Los Angeles-Long Beach-Glendale, CA Metropolitan Division	4,380	1.07	$56.59
New York-Jersey City-White Plains, NY-NJ Metropolitan Division	2,550	0.39	$49.92
Nashville-Davidson--Murfreesboro--Franklin, TN	400	0.45	$30.08
Washington-Arlington-Alexandria, DC-VA-MD-WV Metropolitan Division	280	0.11	$46.45
Charlotte-Concord-Gastonia, NC-SC	240	0.22	$30.07
Atlanta-Sandy Springs-Roswell, GA	230	0.09	$35.60
Boston-Cambridge-Newton, MA NECTA Division	190	0.11	$52.77
Chicago-Naperville-Arlington Heights, IL Metropolitan Division	170	0.05	$48.59
Warren-Troy-Farmington Hills, MI Metropolitan Division	170	0.14	$36.03
Minneapolis-St. Paul-Bloomington, MN-WI	160	0.09	$41.08

Source: Bureau of Labor Statistics

EMPLOYMENT AND OUTLOOK

The BLS estimates that the sports agent industry will grow by 3 percent between 2014 and 2024, marking slower than average growth in comparison to the 6-7 percent estimates for all U.S. occupations during the same period. Slow growth in the industry is related to slower than average overall growth in professional sports and high competition between existing agents for potential clients. Those with higher education degrees or specializations in contract and sports law may therefore have an advantage in seeking available jobs.

Related Occupations
- Athletes and Sports Competitors
- Coaches and Scouts

Conversation With . . .
JEFFREY D. GUERRIERO

Owner, ProSource Sports Management
Monroe, Louisiana
Sports agent, 19 years

1. What was your individual career path in terms of education/training, entry-level job, or other significant opportunity?

I received a bachelor's degree in liberal arts from Northeast Louisiana University (now ULM) and a master's degree in criminal justice. I went on to earn my J.D. from Tulane Law School and began practicing personal injury law shortly after passing the bar exam, and still do.

I played sports my entire life. I saw many naturally gifted football players in Northeast Louisiana who were unable to enroll in colleges or universities due to grades. Because of this, I started the Bayou Bandits, a semi-professional football team, in 1997. This allowed the athletes to showcase their skills in front of professional teams. The players asked me to negotiate their contracts and manage their careers. Several signed contracts in both the NFL and Canadian Football League (CFL). Since becoming an agent, I've helped more than 200 players sign professional contracts. I realized early on that all some players need is someone to believe in them and the opportunity to show that they have what it takes to play on a big stage.

2. What are the most important skills and/or qualities for someone in your profession?

Being able to communicate effectively, and being honest. I encounter hundreds of athletes from various backgrounds. While everyone wants to make money, I must figure out each player's specific goals for the future—whether it's to purchase their parents a house or to create a charity for a cause that's close to their heart.

These are young men transitioning to adulthood, often focused on the immediate. The average career of an NFL player is about 3 years. So, I need to be proactive in preparing for them for a career after the game. If you're not able to read between the lines and find out exactly what the end game is for these players, they'll find someone who is in tune with their objectives and can help create a clear path to achieving them.

Honesty may be even more important. These young men and women are surrounded by people they may not know very well. They trust me to be honest with them and guide them in their decisions.

These traits are also critical in dealing with teams, scouts and others.

3. What do you wish you had known going into this profession?

I wish I had known exactly how time intensive and expensive it is. This is not a 9-5 job and no personal time is sacred. There will be phone calls at dinner and text messages while you're at your child's birthday party or e-mails when you're in church. Clients expect you to be on call 24/7 and if you are going to do your job correctly, you must be available. Being an agent is also expensive. Training a player can cost upwards of $30,000, and sometimes more. You, as the agent, are taking 100 percent of the risk by paying these expenses up front. If your player does well, you usually make your money back. If your player gets injured, finds himself in legal trouble, or ends up on a practice squad, you could lose all the money you put into him.

4. Are there many job opportunities in your profession? In what specific areas?

The great thing about being a sports agent is that you can always open your own agency and begin recruiting players. Be prepared to create the proper legal entities such as a corporation or LLC to protect yourself from liability as well as have the money to purchase malpractice insurance and become certified by the NFL Players Association. Athlete agents must go through a specific registration process governed by the secretary of state in the state in which the agent wishes to conduct business.

5. How do you see your profession changing in the next five years? What role will technology play in those changes, and what skills will be required?

In the representation of NFL players, the landscape is changing rapidly. The maximum permissible fee has decreased regularly over the years and now sits at a mere 3 percent of the salary negotiated by the agent in their contract with the NFL team. Technology has made the industry much more convenient. Standard Representation Agreements are executed electronically—which streamlines the process—as are other agreements. Online medical records speed the process of receiving medical opinions and legal assistance regarding injuries. Being proficient with mobile applications is essential.

6. What do you enjoy most about your job? What do you enjoy least about your job?

I most enjoy helping young athletes achieve their goals. I love being able to tell a mom and dad and player how I will protect their son or daughter and maximize their talents and earning potential—and then actually succeed. My clients are my family. There's nothing more satisfying than a player reaching out and telling me how I have improved their life and the lives of their family.

My least favorite part is seeing a player who has reached the end of his career. It's always tough watching them come to grips with that reality. However, with that letdown comes the exciting possibility of life after the game. It's something I work on with clients from the beginning of their careers. We want to have a plan in place for the next step after professional sports.

7. Can you suggest a valuable "try this" for students considering a career in your profession?

Try to do an internship at an agency or do job shadowing to get a firsthand glimpse of the business. And network. The sooner you start, the easier it will be to become successful because establishing relationships with coaches, scouts and general managers is critical.

MORE INFORMATION

Sports Lawyers Association (SLA)
11130 Sunrise Valley Drive
Suite 350
Reston, VA 20191
703-437-4377
www.sportslaw.org

**North American Society for
Sports Management (NASSM)**
135 Winterwood Dr.
Butler, PA 16001
724-428-6277
www.nassm.com

Micah Issitt/Editor

What Are Your Career Interests?

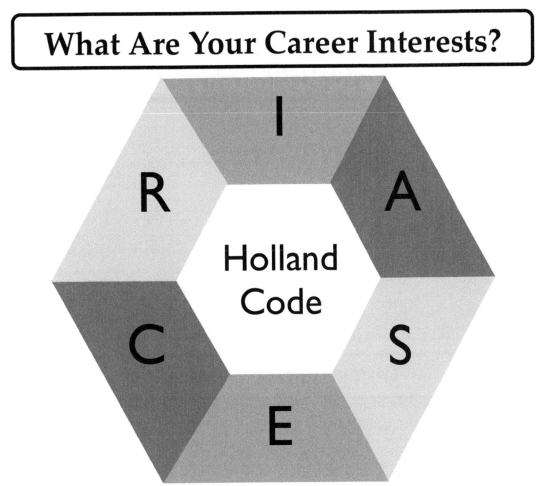

Holland Code

This is based on Dr. John Holland's theory that people and work environments can be loosely classified into six different groups. Each of the letters above corresponds to one of the six groups described in the following pages.

Different people's personalities may find different environments more to their liking. While you may have some interests in and similarities to several of the six groups, you may be attracted primarily to two or three of the areas. These two or three letters are your "Holland Code." For example, with a code of "RES" you would most resemble the Realistic type, somewhat less resemble the Enterprising type, and resemble the Social type even less. The types that are not in your code are the types you resemble least of all.

Most people, and most jobs, are best represented by some combination of two or three of the Holland interest areas. In addition, most people are most satisfied if there is some degree of fit between their personality and their work environment.

The rest of the pages in this booklet further explain each type and provide some examples of career possibilities, areas of study at MU, and co-curricular activities for each code. To take a more in-depth look at your Holland Code, take a self-assessment such as the SDS, Discover, or a card sort at the MU Career Center with a Career Specialist.

This hexagonal model of RIASEC occupations is the copyrighted work of Dr. John Holland, and is used with his permission. The Holland Game is adapted from Richard Bolles' "Quick Job Hunting Map." Copyright 1995, 1998 by the MU Career Center, University of Missouri-Columbia.

Realistic *(Doers)*

People who have athletic ability, prefer to work with objects, machines, tools, plants or animals, or to be outdoors.

Are you?		Can you?	Like to?
practical	independent	fix electrical things	tinker with machines/vehicles
straightforward/frank	ambitious	solve electrical problems	work outdoors
mechanically inclined	systematic	pitch a tent	be physically active
stable		play a sport	use your hands
concrete		read a blueprint	build things
reserved		plant a garden	tend/train animals
self-controlled		operate tools and machine	work on electronic equipment

**Career Possibilities
(Holland Code):**

Air Traffic Controller (SER)	Dental Technician (REI)	Laboratory Technician (RIE)	Property Manager (ESR)
Archaeologist (IRE)	Farm Manager (ESR)	Landscape Architect (AIR)	Recreation Manager (SER)
Athletic Trainer (SRE)	Fish and Game Warden (RES)	Mechanical Engineer (RIS)	Service Manager (ERS)
Cartographer (IRE)	Floral Designer (RAE)	Optician (REI)	Software Technician (RCI)
Commercial Airline Pilot (RIE)	Forester (RIS)	Petroleum Geologist (RIE)	Ultrasound Technologist (RSI)
Commercial Drafter (IRE)	Geodetic Surveyor (IRE)	Police Officer (SER)	Vocational Rehabilitation
Corrections Officer (SER)	Industrial Arts Teacher (IER)	Practical Nurse (SER)	Consultant (ESR)

Investigative *(Thinkers)*

People who like to observe, learn, investigate, analyze, evaluate, or solve problems.

Are you?		Can you?	Like to?
inquisitive	intellectually self-confident	think abstractly	explore a variety of ideas
analytical	Independent	solve math problems	work independently
scientific	logical	understand scientific theories	perform lab experiments
observant/precise	complex	do complex calculations	deal with abstractions
scholarly	Curious	use a microscope or computer	do research
cautious		interpret formulas	be challenged

**Career Possibilities
(Holland Code):**

Actuary (ISE)	Chemical Engineer (IRE)	Geologist (IRE)	Physician, General Practice (ISE)
Agronomist (IRS)	Chemist (IRE)	Horticulturist (IRS)	Psychologist (IES)
Anesthesiologist (IRS)	Computer Systems Analyst (IER)	Mathematician (IER)	Research Analyst (IRC)
Anthropologist (IRE)	Dentist (ISR)	Medical Technologist (ISA)	Statistician (IRE)
Archaeologist (IRE)	Ecologist (IRE)	Meteorologist (IRS)	Surgeon (IRA)
Biochemist (IRS)	Economist (IAS)	Nurse Practitioner (ISA)	Technical Writer (IRS)
Biologist (ISR)	Electrical Engineer (IRE)	Pharmacist (IES)	Veterinarian (IRS)

Artistic *(Creators)*

People who have artistic, innovating, or intuitional abilities and like to work in unstructured situations using their imagination and creativity.

Are you?
creative
imaginative
innovative
unconventional
emotional
independent
Expressive

original
introspective
impulsive
sensitive
courageous
complicated
idealistic
nonconforming

Can you?
sketch, draw, paint
play a musical instrument
write stories, poetry, music
sing, act, dance
design fashions or interiors

Like to?
attend concerts, theatre, art
  exhibits
read fiction, plays, and poetry
work on crafts
take photography
express yourself creatively
deal with ambiguous ideas

Career Possibilities
(Holland Code):

Actor (AES)
Advertising Art Director (AES)
Advertising Manager (ASE)
Architect (AIR)
Art Teacher (ASE)
Artist (ASI)

Copy Writer (ASI)
Dance Instructor (AER)
Drama Coach (ASE)
English Teacher (ASE)
Entertainer/Performer (AES)
Fashion Illustrator (ASR)

Interior Designer (AES)
Intelligence Research Specialist
  (AEI)
Journalist/Reporter (ASE)
Landscape Architect (AIR)
Librarian (SAI)

Medical Illustrator (AIE)
Museum Curator (AES)
Music Teacher (ASI)
Photographer (AES)
Writer (ASI)
Graphic Designer (AES)

Social *(Helpers)*

People who like to work with people to enlighten, inform, help, train, or cure them, or are skilled with words.

Are you?
friendly
helpful
idealistic
insightful
outgoing
understanding

cooperative
generous
responsible
forgiving
patient
kind

Can you?
teach/train others
express yourself clearly
lead a group discussion
mediate disputes
plan and supervise an activity
cooperate well with others

Like to?
work in groups
help people with problems
do volunteer work
work with young people
serve others

Career Possibilities
(Holland Code):

City Manager (SEC)
Clinical Dietitian (SIE)
College/University Faculty (SEI)
Community Org. Director
  (SEA)
Consumer Affairs Director
  (SER)Counselor/Therapist
  (SAE)

Historian (SEI)
Hospital Administrator (SER)
Psychologist (SEI)
Insurance Claims Examiner
  (SIE)
Librarian (SAI)
Medical Assistant (SCR)
Minister/Priest/Rabbi (SAI)
Paralegal (SCE)

Park Naturalist (SEI)
Physical Therapist (SIE)
Police Officer (SER)
Probation and Parole Officer
  (SEC)
Real Estate Appraiser (SCE)
Recreation Director (SER)
Registered Nurse (SIA)

Teacher (SAE)
Social Worker (SEA)
Speech Pathologist (SAI)
Vocational-Rehab. Counselor
  (SEC)
Volunteer Services Director
  (SEC)

Enterprising *(Persuaders)*

People who like to work with people, influencing, persuading, leading or managing for organizational goals or economic gain.

Are you?	ambitious	**Can you?**	**Like to?**
self-confident	agreeable	initiate projects	make decisions
assertive	talkative	convince people to do things	be elected to office
persuasive	extroverted	your way	start your own business
energetic	spontaneous	sell things	campaign politically
adventurous	optimistic	give talks or speeches	meet important people
popular		organize activities	have power or status
		lead a group	
		persuade others	

Career Possibilities
(Holland Code):

Advertising Executive (ESA)
Advertising Sales Rep (ESR)
Banker/Financial Planner (ESR)
Branch Manager (ESA)
Business Manager (ESC)
Buyer (ESA)
Chamber of Commerce Exec
  (ESA)

Credit Analyst (EAS)
Customer Service Manager
  (ESA)
Education & Training Manager
  (EIS)
Emergency Medical Technician
  (ESI)
Entrepreneur (ESA)

Foreign Service Officer (ESA)
Funeral Director (ESR)
Insurance Manager (ESC)
Interpreter (ESA)
Lawyer/Attorney (ESA)
Lobbyist (ESA)
Office Manager (ESR)
Personnel Recruiter (ESR)

Politician (ESA)
Public Relations Rep (EAS)
Retail Store Manager (ESR)
Sales Manager (ESA)
Sales Representative (ERS)
Social Service Director (ESA)
Stockbroker (ESI)
Tax Accountant (ECS)

Conventional *(Organizers)*

People who like to work with data, have clerical or numerical ability, carry out tasks in detail, or follow through on others' instructions.

Are you?	practical	**Can you?**	**Like to?**
well-organized	thrifty	work well within a system	follow clearly defined
accurate	systematic	do a lot of paper work in a short	procedures
numerically inclined	structured	time	use data processing equipment
methodical	polite	keep accurate records	work with numbers
conscientious	ambitious	use a computer terminal	type or take shorthand
efficient	obedient	write effective business letters	be responsible for details
conforming	persistent		collect or organize things

Career Possibilities
(Holland Code):

Abstractor (CSI)
Accountant (CSE)
Administrative Assistant (ESC)
Budget Analyst (CER)
Business Manager (ESC)
Business Programmer (CRI)
Business Teacher (CSE)
Catalog Librarian (CSE)

Claims Adjuster (SEC)
Computer Operator (CSR)
Congressional-District Aide (CES)
Cost Accountant (CES)
Court Reporter (CSE)
Credit Manager (ESC)
Customs Inspector (CEI)
Editorial Assistant (CSI)

Elementary School Teacher
  (SEC)
Financial Analyst (CSI)
Insurance Manager (ESC)
Insurance Underwriter (CSE)
Internal Auditor (ICR)
Kindergarten Teacher (ESC)

Medical Records Technician
  (CSE)
Museum Registrar (CSE)
Paralegal (SCE)
Safety Inspector (RCS)
Tax Accountant (ECS)
Tax Consultant (CES)
Travel Agent (ECS)

BIBLIOGRAPHY

Acsm's Resources for the Personal Trainer. [Place of Publication Not Identified]: Lww, 2010. Print.

Armour, Kathleen M., and Robyn L. Jones. "Physical Education Teachers' Lives and Careers : PE, Sport, and Educational Status." *Physical Education Teachers' Lives and Careers : PE, Sport, and Educational Status*. N.p., n.d. Web.

Cook, Colleen Ryckert. "Dream Jobs in Coaching." *Dream Jobs in Coaching*. N.p., n.d. Web.

Do You Want to Work in Baseball? Advice to Acquire Employment in Mlb and Mentorship in Scouting and Player Development. N.p.: Bookbaby, 2017. Print.

Edelman, Marc, Geoffrey Christopher, Rapp, and American Bar Association. Forum on the Entertainment and Sports Industries,. *Careers in Sports Law*. N.p.: n.p., 2014. Print.

Ferguson Publishing. *Careers in Focus. Coaches and Fitness Professinals*. New York: Ferguson, 2008. Print.

Goodman, Jonathan. *Ignite the Fire: The Secrets to Building a Successful Personal Training Career (Revised, Updated, and Expanded)*. N.p.: Createspace, 2015. Print.

Institute for Career Research. "Career as a Sportswriter, Sports Broadcaster." *Career as a Sportswriter, Sports Broadcaster*. N.p., n.d. Web.

Institute for Career Research. *Careers in Nutrition: Dietitian, Nutritionist*. Chicago: Institute for Career Research, 2011. Print.

La, Bella Laura. "Dream Jobs in Sports Fitness and Medicine." *Dream Jobs in Sports Fitness and Medicine*. N.p., n.d. Web.

Publishing, Infobase. "Career Opportunities in the Sports Industry." *Career Opportunities in the Sports Industry*. N.p., n.d. Web.

Shadix, Kyle W., Milton Stokes, Catherine Cioffi, Kyle W. Shadix, and Academy of Nutrition and Dietetics. *Launching Your Career in Nutrition and Dietetics: How to Thrive in the Classroom, the Internship, and Your First Job*. N.p.: n.p., 2016. Print.

St. Michael, Melyssa, and Linda Formichelli. "Becoming a Personal Trainer For Dummies." *Becoming a Personal Trainer For Dummies*. N.p., n.d. Web.

Wong, Glenn M. *The Comprehensive Guide to Careers in Sports*. Burlington, MA: Jones & Bartlett Learning, 2013. Print.

INDEX